D0040885

# DEBORAH KERR

# DEBORAH KERR

## Eric Braun

ST. MARTIN'S PRESS  NEW YORK

To my sister Pat,
and to the memory of our Parents,
Gertrude and Hugo Braun—
With affection.

First published in the U.S.A. by St. Martin's Press in 1978
Copyright © 1977 by Eric Braun
All rights reserved. For information, write:
St. Martin's Press, Inc.,
175 Fifth Ave., New York, N.Y. 10010.
Manufactured in the United States of America


Library of Congress Cataloging in Publication Data

Braun, Eric.
  Deborah Kerr.

  Bibliography:  p.  236
  Filmography:   p.  237
  Discography:   p.  245
  Includes index.

  1.  Kerr, Deborah, 1921-  2.  Actors—Great
Britain—Biography.  I.  Title.
PN2598.K627B7   1978    791.43′028′0924 [B]    78-3971
ISBN 0-312-18895-1

# CONTENTS

# ACKNOWLEDGMENTS

This biography has come about as a result of following Deborah Kerr's life and career since our first meeting in 1945 at Denham Studios. First and foremost I must thank Miss Kerr herself, and her second husband, Peter Viertel, for making me so welcome at their home in Klosters, Switzerland, and for giving me their time, patience and hospitality. Her family, too, have been infinitely helpful and informative, especially her brother Ted (Edward Kerr Trimmer), head of ATV News in Birmingham, Aunt Jane (Phyllis Smale, now Mrs Harry Forster) and her daughter, Harriet Robinson, and Uncle Arthur and Aunt Gre (Mr and Mrs John Arthur Smale). Miss Kerr's first husband, Anthony Bartley, now re-married and living in Rosscarbery, Co. Cork, Eire, and her second daughter, Francesca (Mrs John Shrapnel), have kindly answered questions and provided information about their families.

I am indebted to the good people of Alfold, Surrey, for their help with memories of the Kerr Trimmers, back to the time when Deborah first moved there as a baby, and especially to the Rev. Derek Parsons, MA, the current vicar of St Nicholas' Church, for invaluable information and dates regarding her kinsfolk. On the subject of Helensburgh, her first home, Mary Bannister, Librarian of Templeton Branch Library, has been most painstakingly thorough.

Especial thanks are due to those who gave me interviews

on their association with Deborah Kerr at various stages of her life, including Jeremy Brett, Jack Clayton, Clifford Evans, Julia Foster, John Gliddon, Mary Johnston, Cathleen Nesbitt, Michael Powell, Joan Sanderson, Esmee Smythe, Ann Todd and Emlyn Williams.

Among the many other people who have kindly given their time in answering questions and in providing reminiscences, and who have helped in countless other ways, are Robert Anderson, Judith Archdale, Frith Banbury, Bill & Marjorie Barrett, Michael Bentine, Michael Bolloten, Gordon Bond, Lesley Clay, John & Ivy Daldy, J. C. Dankwerts, Unity Day, Guy Deghy, Dorothy Dickson, Ken Doeckel, Lyn Fairhurst, John Fernald, Kathleen Fowler, Leslie French, Iain Gordon, Dulcie Gray, Irene Greaves, James Hancock, Frank Harvey, Trevor Howard, John Huston, Anne Hutton, Isabel Jeans, Deryth Jenkins, Sybil Johnson, Elia Kazan, Marjorie Knight, Charles Landstone, Patrick McDonnell, Lief Magnuson, Michael Mara, Barbara Mitchell, Robert Mitchum, Roger Moore, Ruby Murray, Dame Anna Neagle, Christopher Noble, Janet Oakey, Sydney Pegrume, Kerry David Pitts, E. Rhodes, Jack Rossiter, Ceciley Elizabeth Rumble, Frank Sinatra and Michael Thornton.

For invaluable help in lending photographs from their private collections credit is due to Deborah and Peter Viertel, to the Smale and Trimmer families, and to J. C. Gould, Sydney Pegrume and Joyce Evelyn Treloar. Further stills have been generously provided by Robin Bean, editor of *Films and Filming*, Barbara de Lord of Rank–20th Century and Mary Johnston. For permission to reproduce copyright photographs I am grateful to J. Bauer, Sir Cecil Beaton, courtesy of Sotheby's Belgravia, R. W. Brown, René Burri, Comet Agency, Nat Dallinger, Zoë Dominic, Fournol, Mark Gudgeon, London & County Press, Bruce McBroom, Alexander Paal, Sanford H. Roth, Rothschild, Eric Skipsey and Universal Pictorial Press.

I am indebted for permission to make brief quotations from the following publishers: Angus & Robertson for *The Great Movie Stars: The International Years* by David Shipman; Crown Publishers of New York for *The MGM Story* by John Douglas Eames; Hamish Hamilton for *Bring On The Empty Horses* by David Niven; Hart-Davis, MacGibbon for *Jessie Matthews* by Michael Thornton; Kinematograph Year Book Publications for their 1922 Year Book, Stainer & Bell for *I Gate-Crashed* by Charles Landstone, and Independent TV Publications for *The Roger Moore Story*. I thank Frances Hickson for permission on behalf of the Society of Authors to quote Bernard Shaw's description of 'Candida' from his play.

For their inestimable aid during research I thank most sincerely Raymond Mander and Joe Mitchenson, Brenda Davies and the Information Department of the British Film Institute, the management of the Royal Ballet Company at Covent Garden, the Enthoven Collection of the Victoria and Albert Museum Librarians and those of the Westminster Central Reference Library. I am indebted to *Esquire* for permission to print extracts from 'The Days and Nights Of The Iguana—a Journal by Deborah Kerr', and to Richard Krafsur of the American Film Institute in the John F. Kennedy Centre for the Performing Arts, Washington D.C. for postal information.

For providing practical assistance I thank my sister, Pat Cowing, Patrick Kennedy, and my friends in Southsea, Eileen O'Grady and her daughter Maureen Hilborne and family, for making my Alsatian friend Sabre and myself so much at home during the major part of the writing of this book. They did more, in providing Sabre with a companion in Basset Hound Freddie Flubbles and a welcome addition to our household in Twickenham. Thanks too, to the Simpson and Hoodless families, also of Southsea, where the first draft was finished; never were dog and man so well looked after. Back home my thanks are due for their kind help to Tegwyn Cook, Doreen Luke, and, in particular, Bill Rennie, for his invaluable aid and inexhaustible patience in compiling the Index. Last, but not least, I would like to add my gratitude to my editors, the lovely Yvette Goulden and Lisa Marshall.

# PART I

# Crossroads

# CHAPTER ONE

# ALFOLD—DENHAM—PINEWOOD

I

John Daldy, ex-Captain, Indian Army (1914–18), slowed down as his Baby Austin approached the garage at Alfold Crossroads, and pulled in to the side of the road. He was en route for Brighton from his poultry farm at Dunsfold, Surrey, some ten miles away, and his car was loaded with the eggs he delivered on his travels to London or nearby Cranleigh. These trips, involving frequent personal contact with customers, were in restful contrast to the grimmer activities of the recent war: it was 1927. The Surrey country roads, merging into Sussex in the region of Rudgwick, a picturesque village near Horsham on the main Brighton road, were bordered in spring by pale green woodlands; in summer the colours grew bolder, and autumn in Alfold was a painter and poet's dream.

For John Daldy all routes led through Alfold Crossroads and his visits to the filling station usually offered a tiny but cheering bonus in the day's routine. While the owner of the garage, a quiet but affable ex-army captain who had lost a leg in the fighting, filled the petrol tank, his six-year-old daughter would come out to clean the windscreen. The little girl's happy face remained in Daldy's mind, and when she went away as a weekly boarder to a local kindergarten he missed her calm smile and cheerful assistance.

In 1932 he moved to Ewhurst, only a few miles away, but his itinerary no longer took him past the Crossroads Garage. He had a partner in the poultry business, Victor Gray, who stayed in Dunsfold to look after the farm, which was taken over in the Second World War as an aerodrome, the wooden house being moved on rollers to the top of a hill to see service as head-quarters for a commandant. In the meantime Gray and his wife Molly remained in their new home near the Crossroads Garage, receiving occasional visits from their old friend John Daldy and his second wife Ivy, a talented portrait painter.

Once, John Daldy's work as secretary of the Armed Forces Arts Society took the couple to a dinner at which Ivy found herself seated next to Field Marshal Sir Claud Auchinleck and Dame Sybil Thorndike. Their great enthusiasm for living prompted Ivy to confide how much she and her husband regretted having so little contact with people outside their own circle of friends.

Talking of their encounter at a visit to their friends in Alfold one Sunday in July 1960, the Daldys were interrupted by Victor Gray's remark.

'That reminds me: our little girl has married again.'

'Which little girl?' asked John Daldy. His host handed him the *Sunday Express*, opened at the headline 'DEBORAH, THE PONY-CART BRIDE'.

'The one at the Crossroads Garage who used to clean your windscreen: didn't you know she grew up into Deborah Kerr?'


# II


Helensburgh, planned and laid out in the late eighteenth century on the lines of the Georgian new town of Edinburgh, became a favourite retirement place for Glasgow's more prosperous citizens, since it was only twenty-two miles from the city. Mrs Arthur Trimmer travelled that distance from her in-laws' temporary home in West King Street, Helensburgh, to the private nursing home at 7, St James Terrace, Hillhead, Glasgow, where in the early hours of 30 September, 1921, she gave birth to her first-born, a girl to be christened Deborah Jane. 'Deborah' was after her paternal great-aunt; 'Jane' after her mother's sister, who was also the baby's godmother.

Kathleen Rose—Col, short for Colleen to her family—was twenty-eight when her daughter was born; the same age as her husband, Arthur Charles, universally known as Jack, whose work as a civil engineer was the sole reason for the Trimmer family's residence in Helensburgh. They could hardly have wished for a more attractive locality; the town, on a southerly hill slope, overlooking the Firth of Clyde, with its mild climate and wide, straight streets lined with grass and Japanese cherry and red hawthorn trees, had long been nicknamed the 'Garden City of the Clyde'. King Street, where they lived for three years with Jack's father, Arthur Kerr Trimmer, also a civil engineer, and mother, Mary Jane, runs parallel to Clyde Street, which follows the shore of the Firth river, with Loch Lomond only a few miles away.

John Logie Baird, the 'father' of television, was born in Helensburgh in 1888, and at the time of Deborah Kerr Trimmer's birth—the Kerr was adopted by her grandfather from his Scottish maternal grandmother's family name—the late Jack Buchanan, probably the best loved local celebrity of the post-war years, was making his mark in the West End revue *A to Z* at the Prince of Wales, and preparing to go into management on his own behalf. While he was coming up against some of the intricacies of high finance in the theatre baby Deborah was learning about the heartbreak that money, or its lack, can bring.

Her first, and only memory of this period of her life is of being with her grandmother, Mary Jane, in a horse-drawn cab, at the age of two or three, and clutching a bright, shiny penny she had just been given. Suddenly the coin slipped from her grasp and slid down between the seats of the carriage; when Grannie explained that there was no way of getting the lost treasure back the child was inconsolable. Not even the promise of another penny when they arrived home could stem her bitter tears.

15

# III

That Deborah Jane's first recollection of life should be connected with Grandmother Trimmer is only logical: both of her grandmothers were ladies of dominating temperament, and undoubtedly the most potent force of her childhood years. Grandmother Anne Smale, *née* Widdowson, was a born business-woman and manager. She had joined the family grocery and draper's shop in Lydney, Gloucestershire, at the age of twenty-four to work as a milliner, lost little time in marrying the boss, Charles Blackwell Smale, paid off the mortgage inherited from his father, and turned the venture into a financial success.

The males in the family seemed to make up in personality what they lacked in thrift and business acumen. In the first year of the nineteenth century was born the original Charles Blackwell, a colourful Cornish tyrant who settled in Lydney and passed his days fashioning oak picture frames from the beams of an old building which stood on the site of Apsley House, and making the lives of his unmarried daughters a living hell. One morning, during the daily ritual of breakfast with the family, he asked the Lord to make them truly thankful for the gifts He was about to bestow upon them, sat down, and lifted his own special cup to his lips, from whence it slid through his fingers, depositing a copious amount of Chinese pekoe over his immaculate satin and lace waistcoat. His apprehensive daughters rushed to his side to repair the damage, but found it quite beyond their powers of restoration: Charles Blackwell, gentleman carpenter and autocrat, had departed from this life in the grand manner, following a seizure, at the age of eighty-four, in God's bounty.

His married daughter, Harriet Jane, had, in the meantime, borne four children to her husband, John Rowe Smale, founder of the business in Newerne Street, Lydney. Their third-born, Deborah's grandfather, named Charles Blackwell Smale after his notable forebear, was his complete opposite in temperament: outgoing and relatively easygoing, he formed the Lydney temperance choir, was a great sportsman, music lover, conductor of brass bands and a notable tenor in church choirs until shortly before his death at the age of eighty-seven. Despite a permanently stiff leg, broken at an early age by vaulting a five-barred gate, and worsened by his unquenchable participation in football and cricket matches, he was an enthusiastic walker, which is how he met and became friendly with Arthur Kerr Trimmer, a site engineer on the Severn Tunnel construction and another fanatical pedestrian.

Friendship and locomotion were not the only assets to emerge from the mouth of the tunnel, for one end of it comes out at Caldicot in Monmouthshire, where lived young Mary Jane Dodgin, whom Arthur married in 1891. They moved to Newton Abbot, Devon, and two years later their son, Arthur Charles, father of Deborah Kerr Trimmer, was born at Belmont Highweek.

# IV

Early in 1914 Arthur and Mary Jane Trimmer took their family of two sons, Arthur Charles (Jack) and his younger brother, Edmund Howard, graduates in civil engineering from Durham University, to visit the Smales at home in Bath Place, Lydney. The Smale children were of an age to find common interests: Col, the eldest at twenty, became engaged to Jack Trimmer, and Phyllis Jane, eighteen, fell in love with his brother Edmund. John Arthur just had time to take his B.Sc. in electrical engineering at Bristol University before war broke out and he joined the Royal Naval Air Service, eventually being awarded the Air Force Cross for his prowess in gunnery spotting duties.

These three close relatives have remained an integral part of Deborah's life; although her mother died tragically early in an accident after her daughter had made her life in the USA, her influence is strongly felt in every move or decision Deborah makes. Phyllis Jane, always known as Aunt Jane, is certainly

17

the inspiration and guiding force behind the career of Deborah Kerr, actress, and John Arthur—Uncle Arthur—although his work with the Marconi Company kept him moving around the British Isles, so that he saw less than the others of his niece, has become the unofficial recorder of every phase of her career in regard to the family. He married his childhood sweetheart from Lydney, Hilda Marguerita Watts—mercifully shortened to Aunt Gre—the year after his sister Col was wed to Jack Trimmer, and their son John Trevor was born just a month after Deborah Jane.

The war took Jack and brother Ted to Gallipoli with the East Lancashire Regiment, one with the battalion machine-guns, the other with a rifle company, so that Jack often had to cover raiding parties led by his brother. Ted was eventually killed by a sniper and Jack was sent home to convalesce from a wound. Returned to action in France, he was shot through the kneecap at the Battle of the Somme, in the region of Villers Brettoneux. It soon became clear that amputation was necessary, and his condition became so critical that his fiancée, Col, and mother were sent for, as the authorities doubted his chances of survival. The operation was carried out at the British base hospital at Étaples, and slowly and painfully, boosted immeasurably by the presence of Col and Mary Jane, Jack started on the road to recovery.

His mother's qualities of leadership and resourcefulness in emergencies were put to the test during an air raid by Gotha bombers. Ordered out of bed to take cover in the trenches, Colleen was unable to find her steel helmet, whereupon her mother-in-law, ever the organizer, crammed a bed-pan upon her head, as the next best thing.

When he was well enough for repatriation, Jack Trimmer had to endure further surgery on his upper leg to halt the inroads of gangrene: on leaving Roehampton Military Hospital with his Army Discharge he travelled to the Smales' home at Lydney, where his marriage to Col took place at St Mary's Parish Church on 21 August, 1919. He was not through with hospital yet; it was back to Roehampton to proceed with the business of learning to walk with an artificial leg, while his wife stayed in a nearby hotel to lend help and encouragement.

As soon as he was able to manage his limb the newly-weds left for Scotland to join his parents, and he took up his new post with Sir William Arrol's bridge building firm, where Jack's father was already firmly entrenched.

# CHAPTER TWO

# GROWING PAINS

## I

The *Kinematograph Year Book* for 1921 recorded the worst slump to date in American films, with Chaplin's *The Kid* the only remarkable film of the year to come from Hollywood. It went on to say that the average level of British films was infinitely higher than that of the previous year, the national output including more films of an outstanding character than were produced by either American or Continental studios. An encouraging sign for aspirants who might wish to keep this healthy trend flourishing in the future was the *Year Book*'s frontispiece: a full-page photograph of John Gliddon, Director of Productions, International Artists Film Co. Ltd, at 52, Shaftesbury Avenue, London W1.

Deborah Jane, aged two, remained in Helensburgh with her parents when her grandfather decided to retire from civil engineering after some thirty-five years: at fifty-seven he wanted to go into business on his own account and became 'independent'. He negotiated the acquisition of a small timber haulage business in Alfold, and arranged that Jack should follow with Colleen and the baby after working out the remainder of his contract with Sir William Arrol. They moved for the 1923–4 period to a smaller house in Ardencaple Quadrant, on the western outskirts of the town, backing on to the estates and woodlands of Ardencaple Castle. Jack Trimmer and his wife were increasingly impatient to join the rest of the family on

20

the Surrey–Sussex boundaries; apart from the awkwardness of manipulating his new leg Jack was suffering from the after-effects of some gas he had inhaled on the Western Front, which impaired his wholehearted attention to the taxing work of a civil engineer.

Arthur Kerr Trimmer moved his other close relations to be near them at Alfold; his three spinster sisters, Deborah Harriet, Mary Howard and Augusta Margaret ('Great Aunt Gussie') took up residence in a timbered cottage opposite the main local hostelry, the Crown, a stone's throw from the Parish Church of St Nicholas, where many of the Trimmer family have been laid to rest. A local legend has it that when Sir George Trimmer, a cousin, knighted for his services as Chairman of the Singapore Harbour Board, visited Alfold to help put Grannie Jane's financial affairs in order he was approached by the then Rector, the Rev. Howard H. Taylor, as he strolled in the churchyard, and asked if he was looking for anyone.

'Yes,' barked Sir George, 'me aunts.'

'Have they already arrived?' asked the Rector politely.

'Dammit,' said Sir George, 'They've been here for years!'

Deborah's first cogent memory of the family's new life in Alfold centres round the birth of her brother, when she was four. Home to her was a small cosy wooden dwelling—the kind that most children dream of—and it was built with love and optimism and kept immaculately comfortable and bright by her mother, whose taste in all things was impeccable, so that every cushion cover, tablecloth and curtain was handmade and embroidered.

Grandfather's forestry or timber haulage business possessed a number of lorries, and there was an old sawmill at the bottom of the long orchard abutting on to Pound Cottage, the house the senior Trimmers had bought, halfway between the main Horsham–Guildford road, and the village itself. Jack built the family home from three tarred wooden huts of the kind, used to house army personnel in the days before the invention of the Nissen hut. There had recently been a great deal of talk about how there were going to be better homes for heroes to live in, and how every man was going to be able to keep chickens and grow rambler roses and move clear-eyed to a better future. Despite his traumatic experiences in fighting for this ideal existence, Jack set about making dreams into reality. He planted some red roses, his wife's favourite flowers, and transformed one hut into a little filling station, which did well enough for him to be able to make a long chicken run, and to maintain a respectable supply of hens.

## II

Deborah Jane's secure and comfortable cocoon was shattered early on 31 May, 1925, by a loud wail, followed by a series of rather scratchy, spasmodic cries. Brother Edmund Charles had entered the scene, to his sister's intense discomfiture. Jealousy entered her life as she lay crying to herself over all the attention bestowed upon the small creature in its beautiful cot, lined and cushioned so lovingly by Mummy's hands. Although she had been told that this was her new little brother, whom she was to love and care for, she did not really understand who or what the intruder was, and it took her a while to adjust—just as long, in fact, as it took Colleen to make her a real nurse's uniform. Although Deborah Jane's favourite doll was Esmeralda, and no newcomer was likely to supplant her in her affections, she gradually attuned to the fact that Teddy, too, needed dressing, undressing and putting to bed, and that he cried even more realistically and could actually be seen swallowing the food which she had to make believe that Esmeralda was enjoying when she tried to spoon it into her mouth.

In time, she came to enjoy helping with the new baby, and, as he grew a little, he became a satisfactory playmate. As he grew more capable of responding to her direction, she devised little playlets in which she was the main character and Teddy little more than a glorified extra. She was not at all pleased when he focused the attention upon himself, probably unconsciously, by rushing out of the bungalow on several occasions, wearing nothing but a short vest, when his father was supplying customers with their petrol requirements.

As Deborah's productions became more ambitious, with Mother, Father, Grannie Jane and any available friends and neighbours as audience, the young entrepreneuse enlarged the scope of her brother's rôles, mainly to include a number of female subsidiary characters.

'I was always dressing him in Mummy's clothes and making him play women; we have often laughed about how extraordinary it is that he turned out as normal as he is,' she says

He did, however, have some slightly unusual tastes. After a robbery at the garage the family acquired as guard-dog a golden Labrador called Sandy, whom Deborah loved and Teddy did not, mainly because he was as afraid of him as he was of the chickens in his father's run. He used to crawl into Sandy's kennel and steal his biscuits, as he loved the hard square kind that Sandy used to favour; this would set Ted's age at between two and three, as few children would be able to masticate the harder type of dog biscuit until they had their full set of milk teeth. Apart from this obviously patient and tolerant animal, Deborah's great love at this time was a kitten called Phidippides, after the great Greek athlete, as he was able to run so fast. On one occasion he sped with the action of an express train under their wooden bungalow, and there were tears from his young mistress as Phidippides refused to be coaxed out from his new hideaway. She was inconsolable and he intractable.

'But he'll die there, I know he will,' she sobbed. 'He will starve to death and I'll never see him again, and I love him so much.'

Time and nature did the trick that no amount of coaxing or threats had been able to achieve. 'Never get upset; it will all come out for the best' was one of her mother's favourite dicta, and, as usual, she was proved right. A saucer of milk, a small portion of fish-head and mashed potato left over from lunch,

23

and the kitten emerged from hiding, while Deborah restrained her natural impulse to hug him until after he had assuaged his athlete's feline hunger.

Grandfather died at Pound Cottage when Deborah was almost five. He had always been subject to asthma, and the new life in the country to which he had looked forward was short-lived. His worsening health made it difficult for him to take a very active hand in the running of the forestry business, and thus imposed extra strain on his son—a burden Jack could well have done without. The filling station made increasing demands on his time and energies, taking into account the considerable handicap of his artificial right leg, and his own gradually deteriorating health.

Arthur Kerr Trimmer was buried in St Nicholas Churchyard on 2 September, 1926, aged sixty-one, in the shade of an old yew tree of pre-Christian antiquity, by the Rector, Albert J. Treloar. Alfold's community at that time consisted of between eight and nine hundred people and the Trimmer family had already become well known and liked. The village stands on the ground originally covered by the great Wealden Forest which extended from Kent into Hampshire; 'Alfold' being a contraction of Old Fold or clearing for cattle, with St Nicholas Church dating back to AD 1100.

The late Rector's daughter, Joyce Evelyn Treloar, who was present at the funeral, recalls that, even at that early age Deborah 'loved to dance and sing and she loved an audience'. As he grew up, Ted, willing as he was to form the major part of his sister's supporting cast in her original stage presentations, found himself more intrigued by their father's inventions, which took up any spare time left over from running the family businesses. He spent hours watching in the part of the garage set aside as a workshop, while Jack sat with the large red and gold tins of Craven 'A' cigarettes, which he smoked copiously and which nowadays we would recognise almost certainly as a contributory factor to his tuberculosis. In the tins of fifty there were, between the layers of cigarettes, beautiful pieces of blank white paper which were ideal for drawing on; Jack's mysterious diagrams prompted a ceaseless flow of questions, which were always patiently answered.

When Ted was about five his father decided to move down into the village, giving up the filling station and taking his family to live with Grandmother Jane, who had been living on her own in Pound Cottage since the death of her husband.

## III

Sandy had to be found a new home, as Grannie Jane would never countenance a big dog in the house, but she did allow a new canine friend, a half-hound, half-terrier named Bonzo, much-loved even by Ted. Jack Trimmer converted the sawmill at the bottom of the orchard belonging to Pound Cottage, and here he had more space for his inventions in what he had transformed into a miniature engineering factory.

The children, too, found the arrangement far more satisfactory, as they had the run of the orchard, with almost limitless freedom to climb (and fall out of) the apple and plum trees, and there was plenty of space to play pirates, with Deborah as the childish equivalent of Mary Read, and Ted, under increasing protest as he grew older, cast as a number of captive men and maids, whom his sister, making lightning changes from buccaneer to ministering angel, would have to tend to stop them expiring from their wounds.

Jack went into partnership with a Captain Weston, whom he had met during the war, and who brought in two brothers, one to run the works, the other to act as salesman. Jack's most outstanding invention was a product of his great knowledge of hydraulics, and was later summed up by Deborah and Ted's Uncle Arthur as 'an anti-wobble device for motor-car wheels', consisting, in a word, of a cam attached to the car axle. It was, says Ted, 'a model of practical simplicity, and Dad called it the T.T.N. Stabilizer'. It was finally demonstrated at Olympia, and the partners sold enough by early 1936 to be able to move the works to a bigger plant at Wonersh.

'The biggest coup they had was when Malcolm Campbell did 301 miles an hour with Bluebird at Salt Lake that year: he had had two of these stabilizing devices made for the car, an enormous streamlined Rolls-Royce Eagle. This was, naturally, a great publicity and advertising asset to the gadget, but that was where it ended; Dad was not a good businessman, just a fine inventor, and he became involved in great disputes with his partners, besides which his health was beginning finally to give way.'

The church room—'hall' would be too grand a term—near St Nicholas is, according to Deborah's brother, 'almost certainly the first place Deborah performed in public, on the dusty wooden stage where, accompanied by Mother on the piano, we would sing or recite. I often forgot my lines—Deborah never did.'

These performances were not without backstage friction: Marjorie Lewis, a friend of Colleen Trimmer's, who used to accompany her to rehearsals, remembers Grannie Trimmer being very much against the family's participation in these socials.

'She was very stern and put us all in mind of Queen Mary— in fact, she used to model herself on the Queen—and did not approve of young Mrs Trimmer playing the piano for the functions. Still less did she think it right that the villagers should call her daughter-in-law "Colleen", as she insisted we should. On one occasion I remember the old lady saying during rehearsals, "It's not only *infra dig*, but completely unfitting for you to be making a spectacle of yourself in this way" before she swept out of the hall.'

Fortunately for her family, Colleen had a mind of her own, for all her gentle manner, and the show went on: she was an extremely good pianist and really enjoyed the few chances of social life afforded by the concerts.

# IV

Deborah was just seven when she started to attend St Martha's Kindergarten at Bramley in September 1928. The village lies between Alfold and Guildford, and was reached by the 49 bus. The headmistress was Miss Ceciley Nash, who had started the school three years previously in a private house in Station Road, with the number of pupils limited to twenty-two, with room for a maximum of ten weekly boarders. After a few weeks of making the journey twice daily by bus, it was decided that with winter approaching it would be advisable for Deborah to become a weekly boarder, especially as she seemed so happy to be a pupil of Miss Nash's, who says:

'She was the sweetest child one could ever wish to meet and a great asset to the school. She was very good in all subjects, and exceptionally so at piano, elocution and dancing, which was taught her by Miss Marjorie White. Miss Bond Nash taught her French, and I myself all the other subjects.

'Deborah *never* wavered from her desire to become an actress, and her greatest wish was to see her name in bright lights in London: whenever essays were written on "What I want to be" one always knew what she would write about. At the end of the autumn term we would put on a concert for the parents, and Deborah always shone as the star (there is no other way to put it) at every show. For two consecutive years she chose a story, turned it into a play, chose her performers, trained them during play time and lunch breaks, and on each occasion it was a great success. Particularly noticeable was her thoughtfulness for the other children.'

These words are not only an indication of what so many people who worked with Deborah Kerr in later years were to echo, but a record of the only period of time she enjoyed being at school. Her later educational experience was all too frequently traumatic: she was, in her own words, an 'overly sensitive child', and Ceciley Nash such a sympathetic person that they formed a friendship which has lasted through the years.

The headmistress became friendly with the family and spent many weekends at their home. She confirms that 'Grannie Trimmer liked to rule', often causing distress to her daughter-in-law, who already had more than her share from the knowledge of the suffering that was seldom absent from her husband's life. As young Ted grew more capable of assuming household duties he was assigned the important responsibility of making early morning tea. There was no gas or electricity, and he had to light the oil stove and boil the kettle, then take the tea round: when he came to his parents' room he would try to avoid looking at the incredible structural leg with a flannel pad at the top, but it exercised an almost mesmeric fascination over him.

Deborah left St Martha's in July 1932, and Ted took her place there as a pupil. He stayed until the headmistress's marriage in 1935, when she became Mrs Ceciley Elizabeth Rumble, sold the school and went to settle in South America.


# V


Summer holidays were almost invariably spent with Mother's family in the West Country. Deborah's first recollection is of Sunday lunch with Great Grandfather (John Rowe Smale) in his solid mansion in Chepstow. There was, of course, roast beef, which he carved with traditional ceremony: when all were served he would say, 'There will now be complete silence, while our good repast is enjoyed!'

When the senior Smales moved to Weston-super-Mare Deborah and Ted had the dubious advantage of ready-made, free seaside holidays. Indelibly imprinted in their memories, and on snapshots taken by the family Box Brownie are the interminable days they spent shivering on the beach, under the watchful eye of Grannie Anne, who was securely coated against the wind and shaded from any chance rays of the watery sun by her rigidly positioned cloche hat. Usually their cousins, John

Trevor, the same age as Deborah, and Shelagh Mafanwy, born the same year as Ted, were there to share the joys of Weston with their parents, Uncle Arthur and Auntie Gre, and for a short period Deborah lived with her grandparents and was a pupil at Rossholme School in Weston.

At this time Jack Trimmer's health had deteriorated to an alarming degree and Colleen found the additional strain of coping with two children more than she could stand for long periods at a time. Ted was still attending Ceciley Nash's school at Bramley as a boarder, and, for the time being, Deborah's upbringing was in the authoritative hands of Grandmother Anne. Escaping from Grandmother Jane's 'ruling' ways to those of her West Country prototype was from the frying pan into the fire, with a vengeance.

'Grandmother Smale', remembers Deborah, 'was incredibly strict and authentically Victorian in her attitude towards discipline. She was a real martinet, even more than my paternal grandmother, who was just terribly demanding and rather egotistical. Grannie Anne made me lie on the floor after lunch, flat on my back, for an hour and a half, or even two hours, in order to "straighten my spine" and give me a "beautiful posture". I wasn't even allowed to read, and to a young child it was absolute torture.'

Nor did her enrolment at Northumberland House Private School, Bristol, in 1933, more than a hundred miles from home in Alfold, do anything to make her adolescent life more enjoyable, except for the presence at the school of her much-loved Aunt Jane, who was to achieve distinction under her stage name of Phyllis Smale, and who taught drama and elocution at Northumberland House. The school, at Durdham Down, was set in beautiful grounds, being one of the country seats of the Percy family: the spinster sisters Percy were still alive when Deborah went there as a boarder. In summer the pupils would help with haymaking and milking the cows. The gardens were always immaculately kept, while some of the fields had been made into hockey and lacrosse pitches.

Aunt Jane was not only a positive help in many practical ways when her niece's family fortunes were in a parlous condition, but also a positive source of encouragement and moral support. If Deborah's redoubtable grandmothers helped to form the resilience which is one of her most marked characteristics, it was Aunt Jane who nurtured the natural aptitude for acting her niece had already shown in early childhood. But Deborah's relationship with the other pupils was something over which her aunt had no jurisdiction.

Deborah was 'different' in a subtle way the girls could not define but instinctively resented. The 'overly sensitive' nature which Ceciley Nash had found endearing was intolerable to the more extrovert and hearty pupils who devised a score of ways to make her life unbearable.

'She was,' says one of the companions of her days at Northumberland House, 'rather a whiney child at times.' No wonder: among the torments devised by the 'rather snobby', but definitely also rather St Trinian young ladies, was the treatment of the handsome new paintbox Deborah was given as a present. Her love of painting was already marked and occupied much of her leisure time at school. One day she went to her desk to get the box out during a break, and found that all the paint had been squeezed empty and the box filled with mud and leaves. She could hear barely suppressed titters and whispers of 'Bet she cries'. Not to do so required a very painful application of Grandmother Anne's disciplinary precepts; what with her strictness and the sadistic tendencies of Deborah's school companions this period unquestionably represented her youthful nadir.

The compensations for hellish schooldays and uncomfortable holidays were Aunt Jane's reassuring presence and the thirteen-year-old's staunchest and most effective champion, the German language mistress, Mademoiselle Wompach, who was actually Belgian-Flemish, and who defended her when the bullying of the school toughs became too apparent. Apart from this valuable and highly regarded ally, Deborah's method of outfacing her enemies was to work harder at everything and to cultivate an impression of extreme sophistication, so that she ended by being better at games, able to outrun most of her rivals and to maintain an aura of superiority which became an effective form of self-protection.

She had a few good friends, notably Janet Philp, who later joined Deborah at the Drama School in Bristol run by Mrs Cuthbert Hicks and Phyllis Smale after Aunt Jane left Northumberland House to concentrate on her own career as an independent drama teacher and actress. Another friend, Barbara Mitchell, recalls Deborah as being 'nice, fairly dark, and vivacious', presumably after she had established herself within the school hierarchy. She was also one form higher, and therefore normally unapproachable, but a mutual interest in the current film stars weakened protocol to the extent of allowing the two girls to swap film photographs from magazines and cigarette cards. Barbara collected Gary Cooper; her friend concentrated on Merle Oberon, who represented to Deborah everything she would like to be and was not. Oberon really looked a 'star'— exotic, oriental, and with a perfect oval face, which Miss Kerr Trimmer contrasted disconsolately with her own features—in her own words, 'mousy and dumpy'.

At fourteen love entered her life, in the shape of the curate who took confirmation classes. He was handsome and Welsh, with a beautiful voice, and when Confirmation Day came she felt like a bride in her white dress and veil. For his part he had no idea of the passion his presence evoked. She felt at that moment that she might have become a nun, but the purity of the whole episode was slightly shattered when, after the Confirmation, her mother had friends and relatives into the house and Deborah was given her first glass of sherry, which rendered her completely drunk within minutes.

## VI

Jack Trimmer was only forty-three when he died on 26 August, 1937, and was buried in the same grave as his father at St

Nicholas Church. Deborah had loved him deeply, but was always closer to her mother; at fifteen death seems an unreal and unfathomable thing and Father had always been a lovable but slightly remote figure. 'I knew him and yet I didn't know him,' she says. Ted is sure that had penicillin been invented just a few years earlier Jack need not have died so young. His prime inventions were all adopted in varying forms in later years. Apart from the T.T.N. Stabilizer, there was a landing gear for aeroplanes with a descending strut to cushion the impact, and a hydraulic mustard pot which ejected the mustard through gaily coloured bakelite cones, and with which the Trimmer household was inundated at the time. Had he been able to keep on the larger factory premises in Wonersh it would have been an ideal place for handling contracts for small arms.

Jack had been a machine-gun expert when he was with the East Lancashire Regiment, and his knowledge of hydraulics in the use of machine-guns from aircraft might well have made his fortune. 'Had he been able to carry this out, I suppose Dad would have been dubbed a wartime profiteer,' says Ted. 'Instead, he left the business in a terrible mess, with poor Mama at her wits' end to know what to do about it all. She had very little money and was tired out from the constant struggle to make ends meet and to put a bright face on things.'

Help arrived in the person of Sir George Trimmer, Grandmother's cousin by marriage, who returned from his work for the government in Malaya, moved in with an accountant, wound up the business, paid off the various partners and sold out. He also purchased Pound Cottage for Grannie Jane to live in for as long as she wanted to—a long tenancy, in view of the fact that she lived to the age of ninety-six, outliving her counterpart, Grannie Anne by twenty-two years. Mrs Smale Senior's health had always been indifferent, but, apart from giving her children a good start in life by her keen business acumen, she had the vision to encourage the musical ability they all possessed, although she herself did not share it. She died aged seventy, in a nursing home near her house in Weston-super-Mare, just two months before her son-in-law. When Colleen

Trimmer, with the family affairs restored to some kind of order by Sir George, could no longer stand the strain of living under the same roof as her demanding mother-in-law, she moved to her widowed father's home to be near her children in the part of the world from which her family had originated.

Grandmother Jane continued her rule in Alfold, looking after herself as long as she was able, with the help of a young lady called Marjorie Hubbard. The latter remembers the old lady's life revolving around her kitchen of which she was inordinately proud, with its array of black iron pans hanging in ordered precision. She had a passion for herrings and mackerel, which were hung on the taps for a few days to drip into the sink until she judged them ready for sousing. She sat in her rocking chair and had her meals in the room where she spent most of her life; if she issued a summons it had to be obeyed.

One night she called out to Marjorie Hubbard: 'I've got a rat in my cupboard; I shut the door on its tail, and will you please dispose of it.'

By the time Marjorie got there, and opened the cupboard door there was a tail, but no rat. He'd fled, leaving his tail behind him; Grannie Trimmer had added her own individual twist to the tale of Three Blind Mice. Marjorie's fiancé, Bill Barrett, was one of the chosen few to enter Pound Cottage socially: as part-time gardener for the old lady he was regularly chosen to do the 'first footing' for her at New Year, when, as a dark young man, he had to wait until midnight, knock at her door and be invited in for a whisky and a piece of cake, taking with him the traditional piece of coal. Mrs Trimmer would then entertain him in her parlour, a custom to which she adhered long after Bill and Marjorie were married.

33

# CHAPTER THREE

# OPEN AIR ROAD TO FAME

## I

Deborah's budding confidence was boosted by the news that when Aunt Jane moved to join her friend and partner Mrs Cuthbert Hicks at her Drama School at nearby Durdham Park she could accompany them. Mrs Hicks was an examiner at the Guildhall School of Speech and Drama, a leading light of the Bristol Playgoers Club, and had taken the young Phyllis Smale under her wing from the moment she had seen her, as a promising violinist at the age of eighteen. Deborah dimly remembers her aunt being talked about at home as being 'in the theatre' and then as working on the wireless when Bristol's Broadcasting Service started up during the twenties. So by the time her niece went to Northumberland House Aunt Jane was not only the leading light of her schooldays as teacher of her two favourite subjects, drama and elocution, but a 'star' in the world outside as well.

The actress Joan Sanderson, who was Head Prefect at Northumberland House, remembers Deborah as a junior, 'small and rather startled-looking, but in no way giving the appearance of self-pity or overt unhappiness'. Being by training and by nature an acute observer of people—her comedy characterizations are so accurately true—she also recalls the rather private smile which gave Deborah an air, not only of serenity, but of having her own inner judgments on everything. In this Joan Sanderson may have caught something of Deborah's character,

34

without ever knowing her well, that would have escaped less intuitive students.

At the Hicks–Smale Drama School, a spacious and handsome old house on the edge of the Downs, Deborah was happy to help out by giving a few lessons herself, as well as being a full-time student there. She lived at home with her mother, grandfather and Ted at Weston, some twenty miles away, and added to an already full schedule by enrolling as a ballet student at the School of Dance run by Miss Katherine Blott, another of whose pupils to achieve fame was Michael Somes.

Acting was only one aspect of Deborah's ambition. One of her earliest successes had been at the age of thirteen in Phyllis Smale's production of *Robin Hood* at Northumberland House. Now she wanted to excel as dancer and singer as well. Her singing teacher at that time was Kathleen Fowler, who still lives at Farrington in the Bristol area and feels that, had her pupil kept up her lessons, she would have had no difficulty in handling the entire score of the film *The King and I* unaided.

Deborah's friends at the Drama School were Janet Philp, from Northumberland House, and Unity Day, with whom she worked at Eisteddfods, and who says: 'She was very versatile and a marvellous mimic. All this talent was lost in the film world—at least, that is my own personal feeling about it.'

Ted Trimmer also attended the Drama School, and even had a shot at ballet training. 'I pointed my toes—and hated it' he says, 'but very much enjoyed elocution lessons from Mrs Hicks—Aunt Jane always called her "Lally"—herself. She was a marvellous *grande dame* with a rich elocutive voice, who got me into one of the early Bristol television Eisteddfods, reading a poem. She must have had a soft spot for me, because she also gave me my first Meccano set, but I died there on the stage, blushed and stammered my way through to the end, while Mrs Hicks' unforgettable voice boomed out. I never had the courage to go back for elocution lessons again.' Later, however, he became a keen amateur actor, after joining the *Bristol Evening World* as a reporter; the paper's drama critic and future editor,

John Coe, used to organize shows and take them to the Welsh
Eisteddfods, where they got into some of the Drama Festivals.


## II


Phyllis Smale had played her own one-woman shows at the
Little Theatre and the Haymarket in the West End, and between
acting, producing and teaching drama, did not find time to
marry until the age of thirty-nine, after coming to terms with
the tragedy of the death of her fiancé, Edmond Trimmer, in
the First World War. Her husband, Harry Forster, was West
Country manager for Burrough's Machines, and a man of
understanding and generous spirit, who encouraged his wife to
carry on with her profession. He also used to host lavish parties
to mark the end of the radio and television productions in which
she appeared. Having no memory for names he called all the
men 'George' and on one occasion, when Derek McCulloch,
a pioneer of early broadcasting and as 'Uncle Mac' of *Children's
Hour* the self-appointed king of the air, was a guest, Harry asked
him, with his customary bonhomie: 'Tell me, are you mixed
up in this broadcasting racket, too?'

Two of the BBC's most celebrated actresses, Mary O'Farrell
and Gladys Young said later: 'For that remark, Harry, we'll
treat you to drinks for the rest of our lives!'

Phyllis Smale introduced Deborah to radio work from
Bristol's studios, and she proved particularly popular at reading
children's stories. Far more influential on her career was Aunt
Jane's mime production of *Harlequin and Columbine*, a curtain-
raiser to a play about Dr Barnardo by Christopher Fry, given
at Bristol's Assembly Hall in aid of Barnardo's Homes. In the
audience was Roger Eland, who was sufficiently impressed by
the young Harlequin's performance to recommend her for an
interview with Ninette de Valois, who included her among the
next term's list of ballet students at Sadler's Wells.

Roger, the unwitting 'deus ex machina' who first set Deborah

Kerr on the road to London and stardom in films within the space of two years, took her out to a couple of concerts after she had been accepted as a student at the Wells, and then disappeared completely from her life. She thinks she still owes him ten pounds, but has never had the opportunity to repay a debt which, in terms of compound interest, would by now be immeasurable.

## III

'Are you mad, my dear?' friends asked Mrs Kerr Trimmer, 'allowing Deborah to go to London alone?'

'We shan't worry about her,' replied Colleen. 'She's got her head screwed on right.'

Between them Lally Hicks and Aunt Jane made arrangements for the new Sadler's Wells student to stay in theatrical lodgings in Muswell Hill, run by a Mrs Bamford, whose daughter Freda was making a name for herself in the theatre, and was sufficiently near Deborah's own age for them to become friends.

Admittance to the Ballet School entailed complete dedication to dancing studies, and students were encouraged to attend rehearsals of the ballets in course of production. Ninette de Valois was in command, and Margot Fonteyn the new star whose progress Deborah watched with envy and admiration. She also studied with interest the work of Weston's prize pupil, Michael Somes, and was fascinated to observe the creation of Frederick Ashton's ballet *Horoscope*.

During that season of 1938 Deborah Kerr made her first professional stage appearance on 29 March as a member of the corps de ballet in *Prometheus*. By this time, a conviction was beginning to take firm root in her mind that she was never going to make it as a dancer. This *idée fixe* first occurred to her when she watched the ten-year-old Beryl Grey execute an intricate *enchaînement* and reflected that she herself, at sixteen, was unlikely ever to be able to master such a complicated movement.

37

Besides, at five feet six and three-quarter inches, she was taller than usual for a ballet dancer.

To Freda Bamford she confided that, while she could probably continue as a member of the corps de ballet, she stood little chance of progressing to solo work: at the time the ideal height for a ballerina would be five feet three or four inches at most. Freda suggested she change course and try acting—a plan which Deborah did not contest. She had, after all, been performing since the days when she had her own cardboard theatre in Alfold and directed her small brother in playlets, made up with her dolls and animals as supporting players. In the theatre height could be an asset: the sky, comparatively speaking, was the limit.

As it happened, in the place where Deborah Kerr made her professional acting début, the sky was all too often the limit. Freda Bamford was married to the son of actor-impresario Robert Atkins, director of the Open Air Theatre at Regent's Park. She arranged for her friend to attend an audition, which she passed. Deborah made her first appearance, under the direction of Atkins Senior in the initial production of the 1939 season, *Much Ado About Nothing* which opened on 3 June. Cathleen Nesbitt played Beatrice and D. A. Clarke-Smith, Benedick. The dances were by Wendy Toye, and, listed in small print, among the 'Ladies' was Deborah Kerr.

The second production of the season was *Pericles*, with Robert Eddison in the title rôle and Cathleen Nesbitt as Dionyza. Deborah, with a slight sex change, was elevated to play, all in yellow, the Page to Pericles, Prince of Tyre.

One fine evening, in late June, John Gliddon, the London agent whose Shaftesbury Avenue office address was listed underneath his photograph in the 1921 *Kinematograph Year Book*, settled in his deckchair to watch the play. He says:

'If it had been raining, the story of Deborah Kerr might have been a very different one. The discovery of a star is so often a matter of chance, and the excitement of finding a new personality can come along when you least expect it. In the second act, in the Prince's Palace, I found myself watching a young girl dressed as a page-boy. She had no lines to say—merely to pour out wine for her mistress—and I noticed how expressive her eyes were, and how graceful her movements. Although she was there simply as background to the scene, she became a part of it; she was obviously very young and her hair appeared dark and straight. The delicate way she used her hands suggested the training of a ballet dancer.

'After the play I went "backstage", under canvas at the Open Air Theatre, and asked Robert Atkins, whom I knew well, to introduce me to the girl playing page-boy to the Prince. He took me along to the tent used as dressing-room and called out: "Deborah—you're wanted!"

'She looked more like a young art student than an actress: close to, her hair, which looked black from a distance, disclosed hints of amber, and her figure, although good, was inclined to plumpness. Her voice was quiet and a little tremulous.

'I asked her what experience she had had of acting other than at Regent's Park, and she admitted that she had none, but mentioned her training at her aunt's academy in Bristol and her work in ballet at Sadler's Wells. She told me she was then seventeen and would be eighteen in September. I said I thought she was star material, and would like to sign her under contract.'

Deborah's reaction was that of many girls of her age, not long out of school, in those days, just prior to the war: she giggled.

'I was totally unaware of what was going on, really, and certainly wasn't lured by the idea of being famous. I knew I wanted to go on working, but the thought of stardom was far from my mind. That belonged with the half-a-crowns I spent to see Dietrich and Garbo at the movies, with all these magical names, like Crawford and Colbert, Cooper and Gable. To be in films was something I just couldn't imagine for myself.

'In any case, when I bounced back to Muswell Hill, after having time for the enthusiasm to sink in during the journey home, and said to Mrs Bamford: "A *film* agent has been to see me and says I can be in films," she replied darkly: "You watch it; film agents can be nasty old men, notorious for promising little girls the earth and using them for their own ends once they get

39

them in their power." That rather dampened my spirits for the time being.'

She went back to being a mere attendant—this time to Patricia Tucker's Hippolyta—in *A Midsummer Night's Dream*, with Leslie French as Puck, Robert Eddison as Oberon and Romney Brent as Bottom. *Twelfth Night* followed, at the end of July, and a curious coda to this fourth production of the season is provided by Charles Landstone, licensee and manager of the Open Air Theatre:

'Once more I am coming to the end of an epoch, but there is still a tale to tell about Regent's Park in that doom-ridden summer of 1939. It was Bob Atkins' custom each year to take half-a-dozen of the leading students into the company. Towards the end of the season he always put on *Twelfth Night*, giving the part of Viola to one of the RADA graduates. That year he tried out two of the girls in the part; the one he selected gave quite a nice performance but made no great mark (*sic*). The unsuccessful candidate came and sat in the bell-tent which was my office, and I had the unhappy duty of telling her she had failed. She was a woebegone figure as she sat there in dejection and asked, "How does one become a star?" I felt very sorry for her, but I thought she had given such a poor showing at the audition that I said (I hope, in as fatherly a fashion as I could): "My dear, the best thing you can do is to get married, have a lot of children, and forget that you ever wanted to go on the stage!"

'How wrong I was. Her name was Deborah Kerr.'

Apart from the fact that she never attended RADA, the rôle of Viola that season was played by Jessica Tandy, a former Ben Greet student, who had been a popular West End star for ten years. D. A. Clarke-Smith was Malvolio, and Deborah Kerr one of the attendants to Iris Baker's Olivia.

Kerr's comment on the episode is: 'Completely untrue. A good pay-off for Charles Landstone. But no truth to it.'

She switched from Shakespeare to Bridie as a Girl in attendance on Sara, who was played by Edana Romney, in *Tobias and the Angel*. Robert Eddison was the Archangel Gabriel and the season's other leading man, Leslie French played Tobias, husband to Sara, in the final production on 7 August.

Edana Romney was another who played a key part in this crucial period of the Kerr career, by suggesting that Sonia Carol, talent scout for John Gliddon, take a look at Deborah during rehearsals. Miss Carol was impressed by what she saw, tipped off her boss, and another skein was woven in the rung of the ladder by which Deborah Kerr was to climb, so swiftly and gracefully, though not, as Mae West said of some bad guy, 'wrong by wrong', to stardom.


# IV


*3 September, 1939* 'Come home immediately; the bombing's bound to begin at once,' said Colleen Kerr Trimmer, in common with parents all over the British Isles. So her daughter returned to Weston-super-Mare and family life, until it became apparent that there were to be no immediate raids on the capital.

She convinced her mother that now was the time to follow up her first professional engagements; with Sadler's Wells and Regent's Park behind her there was a chance that managements might be, if not enthusiastic, at least inclined to bend a sympathetic ear. Aunt Jane, now, as Mrs Harry Forster, even more up to her ears in acting, teaching and a gay social life, agreed wholeheartedly. Thus Deborah returned to London with her mother's slightly apprehensive blessings, and an allowance which enabled her to take up residence at the YWCA for thirty shillings a week. She existed on bars of chocolate, egg and chips—when funds allowed, and an occasional 'square meal' in the evenings from such youthful swains as the Armed Forces had as yet left untouched. In her 'entirely chaste' existence she was still far too young, at eighteen, to have to lament with Bette Davis that *They're Either Too Young Or Too Old.*

41

The theatres which had closed down on the declaration of war had opened again, and the casting agents' offices were a hive of activity.

'Where've you bin all this time?' boomed the voice that had on innumerable occasions added an extra dimension of rich rotundity to Sir Toby Belch and Falstaff, as Robert Atkins Senior's mountainous form loomed up before his recent employee in Shaftesbury Avenue. 'There's a gentleman bin looking for you for six months: you're to come with me immediately.' Then and there he dragged her to John Gliddon's office in Regent Street, burst open the door, announced: 'Here she is!' and withdrew, leaving her staring at a huge signed picture of Vivien Leigh which dominated the room.

Allowing for slight theatrical exaggeration—this was October, and John Gliddon had first set eyes on Deborah Kerr in June—there had been an appreciable time lapse, during which she had done nothing to take up his initial offer, and had convinced herself that all that talk about potential stardom was so much pie in the sky. With great beauties like Vivien Leigh and Sally Gray on his books, how could he really be interested in a small-part actress with so little experience?

This time, however, Gliddon was taking no chances, and his prospective client had decided that a shove in the right direction from Robert Atkins himself was not to be ignored. Within days Deborah's mother made the journey to the office at 106, Regent Street, and the contract was signed and sealed, on 1 November, 1939, appointing John Gliddon her 'Manager and Business Representative throughout the World during the term of this Agreement'. Deborah Trimmer signed over a sixpenny stamp bearing the head of King George VI; Kathleen Trimmer, as 'Guardian of the above named Artiste' did likewise, and Sonia Tregaskis, 'Married Woman, *née* Carol, talent scout for the above named Agent', signed as Witness.

Gliddon lost no time in putting her up for a small part in Michael Powell's *Spy in Black*. Powell, always ready to give new talent a chance, recalls her as a 'plump dumpling of a girl', but there was nothing suitable for her to play in the film, which was a big commercial success. *Contraband* was designed as a quick follow-up for the team of Conrad Veidt and Valerie Hobson, and Powell mentioned to John Gliddon that there was a tiny part as a cigarette girl in a nightclub scene which his client should be able to fill. At their first meeting, in her agent's office, Michael Powell subjected her to a quick-fire and penetrating conversation on a variety of subjects, then said: 'Now tell me about your background'—a gambit that had been known to reduce newcomers to a state of acute nervous tension.

She answered his questions calmly, and he explained that, although *Contraband* was actually fully cast, there was just an opening for an attendant in an early scene. 'You can play it any way you like. We'll pay you five guineas a day and will want you at Denham Studios for two days.' Before leaving the office, Powell turned to his outwardly self-possessed new actress and predicted that she would be a star within two years.

'Rank always allowed you to make films using whatever artists you wanted,' he says. 'Deborah looked very cute in a mini-skirt and spoke her few lines well, but when it came to the editing the film needed tightening, and her scene was one of the things to go. She was shy then, and is probably so today, but her air of quiet confidence has always completely hidden the fact. At some point she must have learned to hide her inner doubts, and to consider the feelings of other people before her own.'

She was philosophical about the fact that her first scene in motion pictures had ended up on the cutting-room floor. 'After all—ten guineas for only two days' work,' was her reaction. She has never seen the completed film. 'I believe all that is left in of the scene is Maggie Vyner's hand opening the grill in the nightclub door to see who was seeking admission, and her voice over the action.'

Margaret Vyner, a great beauty from Australia who made a name for herself in several British films during the thirties and early forties, retired from acting after marrying the late Hugh Williams, and they later formed the highly successful play-writing team which was to provide an excellent part for Deborah

43

Kerr in the film version of *The Grass is Greener* in the early sixties.

Incidentally, more important rôles have been cut from films than the two cigarette girls played by Kerr and Vyner in *Contraband*: four years previously Joan Gardner, one of Alexander Korda's contract leading ladies, married to his brother Zoltan, spent several weeks filming the rôle of the heroine in his Edgar Wallace jungle epic *Sanders of the River* with Paul Robeson, only to find at the London première that the part had been considered superfluous and completely edited out.

Deborah Kerr's contract with her agent was for five years, during which period his agreement was to secure for her 'from a responsible employer or employers a bona fide offer or offers at a remuneration (exclusive of percentages or royalties) of at least £400 in the aggregate, whether wholly payable during the first two years or not', which was a start, but if results were to be kept to the bare minimum there was not likely to be much left to celebrate with after paying her way at the YWCA out of a salary of less than four pounds a week.

Fortunately, Michael Powell turned out to be as striking a prophet as he was a film-maker.

# V

Sonia Carol was deputed by John Gliddon to undertake the important business of grooming their new client for films. It was Sonia who persuaded her, reluctantly at first, to lighten her hair. The idea did not appeal at all, until it was explained that casting agents were more likely to turn an interested eye in the direction of a blonde. Sonia then accompanied her to a hairdresser who transformed her, presumably to everyone's satisfaction, into a strawberry blonde. Together they had then chosen a dress and coat; total cost twelve guineas, deductible from future earnings. The all-important arranging of new and saleable stills made further inroads into the Kerr finances, which Deborah eked out by a few photographic and modelling sessions. A family friend, Basil Shackleton, was among those who came up with useful suggestions and took some film which helped to give her confidence in how to move before the cameras; Sonia Carol, in whose judgment Deborah had considerable faith, was usually on hand with advice and encouragement.

She played a key part in the meeting which was to change Deborah Kerr from an unknown quantity into a name to be reckoned with in British films. The Hon. Richard Norton, later Lord Grantley, was at that time deeply involved in various aspects of film production, and from the early days had helped many artists and production companies both financially and technically. Being well into the social scene in addition, his influence was considerable, and John Gliddon arranged for Sonia to take their most promising new client to meet him over lunch at the Mayfair Hotel.

It just *happened* that, sitting at a nearby table was Gabriel Pascal, the Hungarian producer–director, who had swiftly become a force in the British Film Industry by not only persuading the intractable and anti-film George Bernard Shaw to sign over to him the exclusive rights to bring his works to the screen, but also by making an enormous financial and critical success of the first *Pygmalion* in 1938. Now, Pascal was preparing to produce and also direct the second of what he hoped would be a series of films based on Shaw plays, *Major Barbara*. Early in 1940 he had his stars, Wendy Hiller and Rex Harrison, and most of the supporting cast lined up, but there was a small key rôle yet to be filled—that of Jenny Hill, the Salvation Army lass who is the embodiment of moral strength behind a gentle exterior.

Deborah Kerr, in her new outfit and wearing her blonde hair piled high, was well equipped, even at the age of eighteen, to suggest sophisticated poise, and there was nothing about her that lunchtime to indicate that she was a resident of the YWCA, or that one of her main preoccupations was when she might be able to look forward again to as lavish a meal as the Mayfair were providing. Richard Norton, of course, knew Pascal, who came over to the table to join them for coffee. He looked directly at Deborah and said: 'Sweet virgin, are you an actress?'

She tells the rest of the story, which has had so many conflicting versions.

'I gasped out that I *was*, and he said abruptly: "Take down your hair—you look like a tart." With alacrity I complied, while Sonia fidgeted, and attempted to make a formal introduction. He then solemnly pronounced, "You have a very spiritual face," and turned to Sonia to repeat my name and where he could get in touch with me.

'It wasn't until a week later—I in the meantime having thought it all just another lot of movie talk—that Sonia called me and told me to go that evening to the Dorchester Hotel and ask for Mr Pascal's suite. It was pelting rain and I had only *just* enough for the taxi fare: I remember thinking, Well, at least I will arrive dry; it won't matter if I have to walk home to the YWCA afterwards and get soaked!'

She was ushered into a room full of what seemed to her very imposing gentlemen. Later she recalled they included David Lean, Vincent Korda and Nicholas Davenport, Pascal's financial adviser.

'Recite to me the Lord's Prayer!' commanded Pascal, and she obeyed without hesitation. She had got no further than 'Our Father, Which art in...' when he said: 'STOP! Take off your shoes: you are too tall.' She meekly complied and started again.

The next interruption was a phone call; all she could hear was his end of the conversation: 'Not tonight, sweet Princess...' and he hung up.

The result, a few days later, was that he gave her a film test in the form of a short scene from *Major Barbara* in the character of Jenny Hill. Meanwhile, Pascal had taken an option on her services for a one-film contract, but everything would depend on the outcome of the test, which had been photographed by Harry Stradling. She was already unhappy over the way she had been made up to face the camera, and when Stradling actually said, in her hearing, 'I can't photograph this girl' she felt like a prize cow at an agricultural show, with everyone staring.

It was no surprise to her that when the rushes were shown at Denham Studios there was general disappointment over the way she photographed. She phoned John Gliddon to say how deeply depressed she was and that she wondered if she would be given another chance. Pascal decided to make further tests and invited her agent down to the studios to see the results. He had to agree, that for some unfathomable reason, his client had not photographed well. One feature of her, he maintained, stood out—her eyes, which no amount of bad make-up or unsuitable lighting were able to spoil. When Gliddon pointed this out Pascal agreed, and decided to make one more test, with a different cameraman.

The reason for the unfavourable reaction was quite simple, and it was one which had in the past threatened to jeopardize the film careers of many great stars, including Dietrich, Colbert, Stanwyck, and in England, Jessie Matthews and Greer Garson: a lack of rapport between the lighting cameraman and his subject. When these and other stars whose initial screen appearances had been dimmed by unimaginative lighting met cinematographers who could define and interpret their best features in terms of cinema the result became a love affair with the camera which could transform the star into a being the public were happy to pay to view whenever a suitable opportunity offered.

The requisite combination between cameraman and subject came about when Ronald Neame, who was to photograph *Major Barbara*, was chosen to film Deborah Kerr's final and decisive test. Under his sympathetic lighting know-how and personal gentleness she blossomed; just ten years older than Pascal's new discovery, Neame already had considerable experience of cinema, having worked for Hitchcock in the 1929 *Blackmail*, and reacted instinctively to her eagerness to learn and intuitive sense of the needs of the camera. After a few anxious days Pascal called her to the studios to confirm that she was to play Jenny.

# VI

In the meantime it was Gabriel Pascal's idea that his protégée should join the Oxford Playhouse for their spring season in 1940 to gain some more acting experience. His business adviser, Nicholas Davenport, who was influential at the Playhouse, was partly instrumental in getting her into the company, where the producer was Leslie French, with whom she had worked throughout the season at Regent's Park. He says:

'The opening production, James Barrie's *Dear Brutus* had a marvellous part in it for Deborah as Margaret, the "dream child", and she performed with a sureness of touch and instinctive sense of characterization astonishing in one so young and inexperienced. She made a big personal success in her first appearance at the Playhouse, was well liked by everybody, and worked extremely well at everything she was given to do.'

In her next play, Eleanor and Herbert Farjeon's musical *The Two Bouquets* Leslie French played Edward Gill, to whom Deborah Kerr as Patty Moss, an actress, is secretly married; in this part she sang and danced in musical comedy for the first time on a professional stage, in settings and costumes designed by Anthony Holland, soon to establish a lasting success in the West End theatre.

*The Playhouse Revue*, devised by and featuring producer French, and originally put on for a week, was such a success that it ran through May and June, and was only taken off when its continued run upset the Playhouse's scheduled programme. André Van Gyseghem, Elizabeth French, and the late Pamela Brown were also in the show; there were two pianos, played by Winifred Bury and Berkeley Fase, who wrote the words and music for Deborah Kerr's romantic duet with Michael Felgate, 'Forgot the Moon'.

J. C. Dankwerts, who was up at Oxford at the time, just before joining the services, was a regular Playhouse-goer, and recalls the resident company as extremely talented. Apart from performing and coping as assistant stage manager in productions like French's *The School for Scandal*, Deborah had time to enjoy life a little with the company and the young friends they made in Oxford, where she had lodgings in Wellington Square.

One would have had to be very stolid and unimpressionable not to relish the freedom of life in a University town in wartime, and Deborah was neither: she enjoyed the attentions of undergraduates who were ready and able to demonstrate their skill at manœuvring a punt on the Isis, but romance was a pastime to be parried with as much charm and humour as the circumstances warranted.

What she cherished was time to reflect: this for her was a kind of cocooned period in which she was enjoying a measure of success in the work she loved doing, for a stipulated length of time, and there was little point in brooding over contracts and future parts on stage or screen, when she had her own personal philosophy to formulate. Aunt Jane's outlook, summed up in her phrase to cover all eventualities, 'Mustn't make heavy weather,' was already a good working guide for reactions to life's little ironies.

To help her prepare for the part of Jenny Hill, Deborah had asked Pascal to arrange for her to join the Salvation Army as a helper, with only the Captain of the particular group she joined being aware that she was an actress. The others accepted her as a volunteer; although she did not wear the uniform as they did they did not question the Captain's introduction— 'This is a nice young girl who's come to help us'—and took her along with them. She was enormously impressed.

'The work they did, and, of course, still do, among the poor and destitute is something you can't imagine until you've actually experienced it: the utter *selflessness* of their lives is unbelievable until you've lived with them. There were the great cauldrons, one with soup and one with porridge, from which all who asked would be served; people would come up with old jam-jars, old tin cans—anything they could put the food into . . . Old ladies, old men, living in the most derelict of brokendown ruins—"shelter" would be too grand a word—to which we would take bread, coal, anything that could alleviate in any way their suffering. "Gabby" Pascal commended me for my "devotion to my art", but it had nothing to do with that: it was just something I had to do, before I could presume even to begin to portray a character like Jenny, who, young as she was, and at an age when most girls would be dedicated to boy-friends, had chosen to give her time to the friendless.'

Her experience with the Salvation Army touched her deeply; their work, which was being carried out quietly and efficiently day after day and night after night, was love in its purest sense, of one's neighbour as oneself, implying consideration for others at all times, as a counterbalance to what was going on in a world at war again. The example of Jenny Hill was, clearly, not the one for her, but she had at eighteen to find for herself an answer to her seeking, a way of life.

Nicholas Davenport, who was a London stockbroker and financial correspondent for the *Economist*, as well as Pascal's business adviser, had a great influence on her early life, and his house at Hinton Waldrist, near Faringdon, was less than twenty miles from Oxford. 'It was', she says, 'one of the loveliest houses I have ever known, and he still lives there. He and his wife, the actress Olga Edwardes, made this my spiritual home in those days, and a very large amount of my *real* education came from Nicholas—his taste, his marvellous collection of paintings and exquisite antique furniture, his vast library; many of the volumes of great antiquity and value. All of this I soaked up like a sponge. A boarding-school doesn't teach you much about inlaid walnut Queen Anne chairs, or Lutyens' paintings!'

Davenport was a Christian Scientist, and it was under the tutelage of his personal practitioner, the Swedish Mrs Claire Rauther, that Deborah studied the philosophy of the religion which contained, for her, the answers to so many of the questions with which her mind was filled. The Spartan discipline of her two grandmothers, and, in particular, the rigid physical obedience of Grandmother Smale in Weston, began to assume a new significance in her mind.

'Of course one grumbled about it at the time, and for years reflected on what a monstrous thing it was to have had to endure such an ordeal, but gradually one grew to realize the tremendous importance of discipline, whatever one intends to do in life, which can deal such blows that if you don't have some form of personal code of behaviour you're liable to go to pieces with nervous breakdowns, or worse. That's my theory, at any rate, though I probably wasn't very strict with my own children, because of the vivid memories of my childhood. Everyone reacts differently, of course, but there has to be a set of rules, before you can start modifying or adapting according to circumstances.'

That she found the basis of her personal philosophy at an unusually early age has struck many who were close to her at the beginning of her professional career. According to Michael Powell, 'She had an inner strength and assurance quite remarkable in one so young. There was nothing goody-goody about it; she has a tremendous and sometimes wicked sense of humour, and even then, her remarks could startle people who didn't know her well.'

## VII

At Denham, filming for Deborah went smoothly until the scene where Robert Newton, as the brutal and drunken Bill Walker, has to slap Jenny and knock her to the ground for refusing to reveal the whereabouts of his girl, Mog, who has sought refuge with the Salvation Army. Pascal and Deborah Kerr herself were insistent that the blow be for real, but the gentle Newton, consistently, and with brilliant success, cast against type, kept pulling his punches. Despite exhortations from the director, himself in no way a puller of any kind of punches, the scene was shot seven or eight times, until the victim assured her assailant that one good blow would not only be more effective, but also far less painful than an endless series of half-hearted ones. Take Nine—and Bill Walker dealt Jenny such a whack she went down with a bleeding mouth. The shot was in the can—but almost ruined by Robert Newton rushing forward to pick her up and apologize.

'He was a very dear man,' she says, 'and it was a great tragedy that in the end he destroyed himself through his increasing dependence on alcohol. He and everyone else on the film did everything possible to help me with this first part, although most of my scenes were with Bob and Wendy Hiller, who did all she could to make things easy. Sybil Thorndike, although we did not come into contact much in the action, was a positive hurricane of enthusiasm, carrying all along with her. I just used to sit and gape at her and marvel how it was that I had come to be acting in the company of such a great performer.'

If talent abounded in the cast of *Major Barbara*, there was no lack of it on the studio floor: apart from Ronald Neame behind the camera, David Lean was editor, Michael Anderson and Jack Clayton second and third assistants and Arthur Ibbetson the clapper boy. The first four named wasted little time in becoming leading directors, first in Britain and then internationally, while Ibbetson became a brilliant cinematographer. Deborah Kerr was to work with them all again on many occasions, with the exception of David Lean, who told her, 'You're going to be a star' during the party to celebrate the completion of filming. To date they have not worked together again, despite various plans to do so.

She took the prophecy, once again, in her stride. All that concerned her at the time was whether Gabriel Pascal would take up the option on her contract and she would be given the opportunity to go on working in films. Notices for the film, premièred at the Odeon, Leicester Square, were excellent, with praise for the stars and strong supporting cast, including Robert Morley, Marie Lohr and Emlyn Williams. *Picturegoer*'s Lionel Collier saw 'Robert Newton's magnificent performance as the keystone of Pascal's faithful adaptation of Shaw's play, dealing more or less philosophically with the Salvation Army, armaments manufacturers, love and life generally. Deborah Kerr is excellent as the Army lass who is assaulted by Newton...It is a very good picture and should rival the success of *Pygmalion*.'

That it did not quite do so was because, at the time of its general release, delayed in Britain until August 1941, the war had struck the country in earnest, and films about armaments, however star-studded and finely presented, were not what the British public were willing to spend their shillings on.

Deborah Kerr's Jenny was a signpost to the kind of part in which she would excel—moral fortitude concealed by a frail appearance—and which contained the seeds of the threat to her growth as an actress and her potential as a world star in later years, when lesser writers than Shaw tried their hand at reproducing for her the same kind of character.

# CHAPTER FOUR

# *'STARDOM WITHIN TWO YEARS'*

## I

Pascal did take up the option on the services of his new 'discovery', but her rise to stardom would have been slow indeed had she been obliged to rely on his own productions to keep her in employment. But 'Gabby' was quite ready to hire out her services to other companies, as soon as word got around that she was leading lady material: besides being within the reach of producers planning worthwhile films on a modest budget. Deborah's employer, who did nothing that was not on a grand scale, from time to time announced grandiose plans for his new contract artist, so her name was kept before the public, and unlike so many other beginners in films, she was able to produce work to substantiate the publicity circulated around her personality. Pascal made the decisions: she did as she was told, working quietly and efficiently to gain stature and experience in the profession.

Under the heading 'Search for Talent', the magazine *Picturegoer*, Incorporating *Film Weekly*, an early war casualty, and the best popular film paper ever to be produced in Britain, wondered if British National Films would unearth 'another Wendy Hiller in their search for a leading lady in the film version of the long frowned-upon but now approved *Love on the Dole*. Miss Hiller, then an unknown, made her name in the play.

'We have long advocated that British starmakers should get out of the West End theatres and dramatic schools that have filled our studios in the past with denatured young females with superior accents and inferior talents and look over the provincial repertory companies. In the case of *Love on the Dole*, Walter Greenwood, the author, and David MacDonald, who is to direct the picture, will do just that. They are leaving shortly in quest of the two leads for their film.'

With a little encouragement from Sonia Carol, on behalf of John Gliddon, they took in the Oxford Playhouse on their travels, and Deborah Kerr found herself testing again, this time for the part of Sally Hardcastle, Greenwood's vulnerable but resourceful Northern heroine. She was in good company; before setting out to explore the theatrical talent around Britain, the makers of the film—it was John Baxter who eventually directed *Love on the Dole*—had actually tested a number of well-known stars, including Jessie Matthews, whose career as Britain's Number One box-office star of musicals had come to a full stop with the termination of her contract with Gaumont British two years previously.

John Baxter told writer Michael Thornton that Jessie Matthews, attracted by the idea of playing the Lancashire girl who becomes a bookie's mistress to help her workless family—a rôle which contrasted so completely with her starry song–and–dance image—tested excellently, 'with only the faintest suggestion of a Lancashire accent. There was no doubt whatever of her acting ability, and I think she would have played it beautifully. But her casting was really a promotional idea foisted on us by Wardour Street. It was always my intention to play an unknown in the lead, because *Love on the Dole* was the sort of subject that would have been artistically unbalanced by big names. A star of her magnitude, billed over the title, would have created the wrong sort of interest, I feel.'

Deborah Kerr, on reflection, thinks that 'Jessie should have been a "natural" for the part.'

In any case, British National finally picked an established young leading man, Clifford Evans, who had made such a good impression as a miner with Paul Robeson the previous year in Pen Tennyson's *The Proud Valley*. Tennyson died tragically early the same year of 1940, at the age of twenty-nine; he had been married to Nova Pilbeam, Britain's most popular teenage star, who made her first success in *Little Friend* for German director Berthold Viertel, whose son Peter was to play a major part in Deborah Kerr's life years later.

Clifford Evans, cast as Larry, the love of Sally's life, an engineer with strong political views, tested opposite the newcomer. 'I can still hear her utterly distinctive cadences, with just the right amount of a Lancashire accent to be acceptable to audiences of the time. I had to adjust my natural Welsh intonation, but in those days the complete realism of today would have been unthinkable. Audiences get used to different degrees of what is realistic and permissible, but I don't think they change in their instinctive subconscious reaction to the "rightness" of a performance. Deborah Kerr was "right" for Sally Hardcastle, and they knew it. I sensed this quality early in the test.

'Having some experience of films—right back, in fact, to an extraordinary British film in which Erich von Stroheim appeared, called *Mademoiselle Docteur* with Dita Parlo, three years before—I felt the onus to carry the scene might be on me. Deborah and I had just met for the first time, and she had a lovely out-door quality, as though she were straight out of school, and yet as we did the scene I began to find myself reacting to her, just listening to her, and, as it were, being drawn into the acting with her. It was all over quickly, with the minimum of fuss and Walter Greenwood, whom I knew very well, agreed that it had been satisfactory, but both he and John Baxter were somewhat noncommittal, and I couldn't help wondering how this kid had come across. Had the inter-reaction between us that had felt so right while we were working together transmitted itself to film?

'When we went into the viewing theatre I wasn't all that sure, but as soon as Deborah's face came up on that screen, it just knocked you for six. The camera loved her and picked up all the genuineness and sincerity that were in her as a person. Greenwood and Baxter reacted before the test was even over: "That's it," they said, "Great—just can't go wrong."'

In this connection, Clifford Evans had a good friend who had made something of a name for herself in the theatre, but who confided to him, after making umpteen tests for films, 'It's no good—they just can't photograph me. My face is all wrong for the screen.' By the time Deborah Kerr made her two successful 1940 tests Evans' friend had proved 'them' all wrong. Her name was Greer Garson.

*Love on the Dole* was shot at Borehamwood Studios, Elstree, with John Baxter going all out for realism: even the early forties kind could make life something removed from the bed of roses the public assumed film acting to be

Deborah Kerr's first love scene with Clifford Evans took place outside her slum home, when they exchanged their first kiss among the dustbins. 'Those bins stank to high heaven, and it didn't seem such a far cry from the realism of Jenny Hill's experiences in *Major Barbara*.

'What a blessing it was to have as strong an actor as Clifford as one's leading man. I saw him acting again, for the first time in decades, when I was back in England a few years ago. He was in a television play, and, quite simply, magnificent. Yet in those early days in films I think he was rather taken for granted, as were so many first-class actors.'

Deborah's first real publicity build-up came in Britain's *Picture Post*, on 7 December, 1940. Under a front-page picture ran the caption: 'Deborah Kerr—Is this a New Star?' She was photographed in tweed, slightly plump-faced but sexy in an un-self-conscious way, and hugging an equally beautiful King Charles spaniel. It was an eye-catching picture, and the fact that *Picture Post*, a mainly serious publication, should accord a front cover and two-page spread to a film actress—and British at that—in wartime, was something of an accolade to the status of playwright Greenwood, the subject of *Love on the Dole* and to the 'New Star' herself. The editorial was euphoric:

'Though the British film industry is pretty far down in the dumps...luckily films are still being made...and luckily for her, a pretty girl is still noticed by the men who make these films...she is what they call a Botticelli blonde—reddish-gold

57

hair, light blue eyes, and face capable of expressing "spiritual wistfulness".

'The Financial Director of Capitol Film Productions, Nicholas Davenport, who first noticed her possibilities maintains her face is a new type for the screen. "It impressed me," he says, "because of its profile resemblance to the woman in Botticelli's 'Purification of the Leper'."'

Just to show she was not too remote from reality, and the working-class heroine, she was pictured boiling a kettle for her morning cup of tea: 'She makes her own breakfast in her tiny room near Elstree Studios.'

## II

*Love on the Dole* had its première at the Odeon, Leicester Square, in April 1941, with Deborah Kerr top-billed; it proved as popular in terms of the cinema as it had in the theatre, showing that British audiences could accept, even in time of war, a well-made film about grim realities. *The Cinema* found it 'powerfully appealing entertainment of unique British pattern' and the *Monthly Film Bulletin* went further, asserting that the film 'ranks with the best we have ever produced'.

The part of Sally had made a star of Wendy Hiller on the stage six years before when her husband Ronald Gow turned Greenwood's novel into a big box-office success, despite the uncompromising view it offered of the under-privileged in the days when the public wanted to overlook unemployment, and drawing-room comedy was king. The plot dealt with the problems of an unemployed miner, Larry Meath, victimized because of his attempt to improve the lot of his fellow workers, and his affair with a courageous girl, Sally, who proposes they try to make a life together on the wage she makes at work, plus his dole money. When he is tragically the victim of an accident, Sally borrows the money for his funeral expenses from Sam, a wealthy bookmaker (Frank Cellier), with the inevitable result.

The critics voted Deborah Kerr a star of the cinema, with the *Evening News* voting her Sally 'One of the most gripping performances I have ever seen.' Ernest Betts in the *Sunday Express* congratulated 'Miss Kerr, whom you certainly must see', John Baxter, Frank Cellier and Maire O'Neill, leader of the 'quartet of gin-drinking harridans who boil up a filthy brew of gossip, slander, table-rapping and money-grubbing'. He also praised Clifford Evans and George Carney, Mary Merrall and Geoffrey Hibbert as Sally's father, mother and young brother.

British National, who already had Clifford Evans under contract to play William Penn, founder of the Quakers, decided to re-team him with Deborah Kerr in Anatole de Grunwald's original screenplay of *Penn of Pennsylvania*. The film was well into production under the direction of Lance Comfort at Elstree when *Love on the Dole* had its West End première; Pascal and his advisers were anxious to keep the Kerr name and face before the public and reap the benefit of the excellent publicity her first two films had attracted.

The rôle of Gulielma Springelt, Penn's gentle bride, did not give her a great deal to do, as most of the action centred round his taking his fellow-Quakers in a boat to America to escape persecution at home for their religious beliefs and founding the colony which was to become Pennsylvania. The main honours of the film belonged, naturally, to Evans, who brought an impressively spiritual feeling to his portrayal of the young man who tires of the emptiness of life at the court of Charles II, played with just the right touch of world-weariness by Dennis Arundell. Penn survives a smallpox epidemic on the voyage, builds his colony and returns to England to find his wife dying in childbirth. At first grief and disillusionment cause him to refuse to go on with his work, but finally he returns to complete Pennsylvania, where 'all can live and worship without let or hindrance'.

In a sincere and dignified, if episodic, motion picture Kerr, in the words of her co-star, 'illumined the part of the wife in a way that no other young actress at that time could have done. She looked so lovely in the period costumes, and her beauty can suggest goodness at the same time as sex appeal and humour.' She played her death scene touchingly and the film lost much of its holding power after her demise.

Like *Love on the Dole* the modest *Penn of Pennsylvania* did well in the art houses of America, where it has cropped up from time to time under the title *The Courageous Mr Penn*. Its initial production had been promulgated with an eye to helping bind together Anglo-American relations—although the film was hardly strong enough to make a very positive contribution.

## III

With three films on the run completed Deborah planned a holiday with her mother on the Continent. They had not had time to decide on the exact location when John Gliddon left a message at the YWCA to say that she was needed immediately to replace the pregnant Margaret Lockwood (in her pre-*Wicked Lady* days) as Mary, the pure and sorely put-upon heroine of A. J. Cronin's *Hatter's Castle*. Lance Comfort was again the director, the third time Kerr had worked under his aegis, as he had been associate director on *Love on the Dole*, and as such had directed her in many of the sequences of that film.

The summer of 1941 saw her back at Denham and, for the second time, in a film with Emlyn Williams. They had worked together only peripherally in *Major Barbara*, but in *Hatter's Castle* their relationship was basic, as he was her seducer. The loss of her virginity resulted in her being turned out into the cold, cold snow by her sadistic hatter father, James Brodie, played by Robert Newton. Williams reminded her of a remark he had made the year before when work at Denham was halted by an air-raid alarm, and the cast were treated to a preview in the little studio cinema of Hitchcock's *Rebecca*, which had turned out to be the hit of the film year and made an instant star of Joan Fontaine, who until then had been very much in the shadow of her more famous sister, Olivia de Havilland.

'I remember saying to Deborah when the film ended: "If this hadn't yet been made and you were in Hollywood at this moment and made a test for the part of the wife—even though you'd be quite unknown—I bet you'd get it: it's so right for you!"'

Emlyn Williams was probably the first person to draw a parallel between the work of Joan Fontaine and Deborah Kerr, but he was certainly not the last.

Colleen Trimmer paid her first visit to a film set to watch her daughter at work during the making of *Hatter's Castle*; Lance Comfort entertained her to lunch in the studio restaurant, and she was photographed with the incredibly handsome James Mason and thrilled to meet all the other stars. She was, however, adamant on one point: the rôle of the heroine's young brother, Angus, driven to suicide by his father's callous treatment, was one which Deborah had suggested to Lance Comfort that her brother Edmond, then fifteen, could have played, but Mother decided it would interfere with his studies for his School Certificate—and that was that.

*Hatter's Castle*, like *Love on the Dole*, had its première at the Plaza, Paramount's showcase in the West End, in November 1941, and went on general release in January of the following year, the same week as *Penn of Pennsylvania*. The Cronin was high-class melodrama ('prime ham' in the words of Dilys Powell), and played for the maximum effect by a superior cast against the backcloth of Lance Comfort's father-dominated Victorian household. Robert Newton's mad Hatter, an autocratic Scottish shopkeeper who builds a domestic monument to his own authority and destroys it and himself when his megalomania brings about the loss of everything and everyone he holds dear, carried all before him in an all-stops-out characterization, but Deborah Kerr more than held her own by playing with just the correct balance of trembling innocence and gallant fortitude.

James Mason could do little with the character of the decent doctor, Renwick, whom she loves, but looked as broodingly sexy as only he could in those days, while Emlyn Williams, also

61

true to his film image of the early forties, was superbly reptilian as the heartless seducer, Dennis. The late Beatrice Varley, as Brodie's sad wife, neglected, bullied, and dying of cancer, was the classical downtrodden mother, and the bright spot of the film was another actress no longer with us, Enid Stamp-Taylor, stage star of the thirties and forties. In one of her rare good film parts as Nancy, Brodie's barmaid mistress, she gave a Rabelaisian twinkle which suggested an anglicized Mae West, and which might, had she not been up against such stiff competition, have made the film her own. Young Angus was poignantly played by Anthony Bateman, who grew up into an excellent actor, leaving Ted Trimmer to prove himself later in journalism and the world of television.

## IV

At the beginning of 1941 Deborah Kerr had left her room at the YWCA and moved into the English-Speaking Union in Charles Street, where she had her own room. This caused some surprise to Mrs Sybil Johnson, the accountant there, who used to make out her bills and watched her leave for work every day. Her name was now known well enough for the staff to take a keen interest in her comings and goings; she was well liked and admired for her equable manner and complete lack of 'side' but everyone was mystified by her continued presence as 'permanent residency was not the object of the club'. In fact, Nicholas Davenport had been able to use his considerable powers of persuasion with the authorities of the English-Speaking Union.

Mrs Johnson says that Deborah still seemed very close to her Aunt Jane and that Mrs Kerr Trimmer visited her daughter frequently. She did not really care for Deborah living in London with the war on, but her attitude was: 'If I'm going to buy it I'll buy it wherever I am.' It was at the Union that she took lessons from a Norwegian lady who was happy to coach her to attain a 'reasonably proficient' Norwegian accent for her part of Karin, the daughter of a Norwegian skipper in her next film, *The Day Will Dawn*. The object of the club was to provide a meeting-ground for people of various nationalities; meals were provided and students passing through London were given accommodation. It was a good background for the new star, with her keen ear for accents; her reaction to her friend Unity Day's complaint that Hollywood has not made use of her great gift for mimicry is characteristic:

'Well, what is acting but mimicry? You listen to people, and subconsciously you're storing their way of speech for future use. Every actress has to have her own card index system, or she's going to be lost when it comes to using an accent other than the one she's used to.'

Two incidents stand out in her mind during the filming of *The Day Will Dawn*, for which producer Paul Soskin had had a convincing Norwegian background constructed on the back lot at Denham. There had been a first meeting with Britain's top star, Anna Neagle: only four years previously Deborah had insisted that her mother accompany her into the front row of the local cinema in Weston-super-Mare to get a good view of the star, who was making a personal appearance with her film *Victoria the Great*.

Dame Anna recalls Deborah Kerr as 'incredibly young and unspoiled, and so ingenuous and unaware of her own blossoming stardom that she spent her lunchbreak collecting autographs'. Anna Neagle and her director husband Herbert Wilcox were making the Amy Johnson film *They Flew Alone* at the time; co-starring was Deborah's old sparring partner Robert Newton, playing Amy Johnson's flier husband, Jim Mollison.

The second incident of that period of filming *The Day Will Dawn* could have put a sudden stop to Deborah's promising career, and has already been recalled by one of the protagonists, Lilli Palmer. The Kerr version of the story is as follows:

'Rex Harrison and Lilli then had a cottage at Denham: he was at that time in the RAF, stationed at Uxbridge, a couple of miles away. They invited myself and Harold French, a mutual friend, who was directing *The Day Will Dawn*, over for drinks after work one evening. We were all standing round with our drinks; an air-raid alert had sounded, but they were such a commonplace that everyone had got used to taking very little notice. Anyway, we suddenly heard the unmistakable sound of a German aircraft: we had all got very well attuned to which were "ours" and which were "theirs". We heard this sound and all stopped and stared at each other, because it was quite low.

'There was a pause, and as we heard the whine of the approaching bomb, we all flung ourselves on the floor, then—Boom! I remember hearing the tinkle of glass and a clatter, and looking up: everything was black. There was smoke everywhere, and I thought the house was on fire. All it was, in fact, was earth: with incredible good luck the bomb had dropped in the vegetable garden, in the softest possible earth. It was only a small bomb, and had covered the house in black earth. I don't know how it had happened, but I found myself at the other side of the room—in those days one wore one's hair held up by two combs, both of which had been blown out of my head and were in smithereens. Rex, in his RAF blue, was cut across the forehead by flying glass. All my Girl Guide training came to the fore, and I said: "Everybody up—all out of the house—the house is on fire—quick!"

'They had a Hungarian refugee cook, who was screaming and having hysterics, and I remember saying again: "Everybody out—let's get out of the house at once; let's get out!" and when we did, and found the cottage was not on fire at all, only smothered in earth, Rex whiffled and said: "I think I need a little drink." My training well in control, I said: "Alcohol is very bad when you've had a shock: we must have some tea." So he had to settle, like all of us, for hot tea. That was all there was to it, but for nights and nights after I used to have terrible dreams that all my teeth were being blown out, and crumbling in pieces.'

History and Lilli Palmer are silent on the subject of whether Rex Harrison actually appreciated the fact that their guest had

Deborah's parents: Kathleen (Colleen), *née* Smale, and Jack Trimmer.(*A.Smale Collection*)

Deborah's grandparents: left to right, Arthur Kerr Trimmer, Mrs Mary Jane Trimmer, Mrs Anne Smale, Charles Blackwell Smale. (*A. Smale Collection*)

Deborah aged four, with her doll Esmeralda. (*P. Smale Collection*)

Deborah in nurse's uniform outside the front porch in Alfold. (*J. E. Treloar*)

Deborah aged six in her grandmother's garden in Weston-super-Mare. (*P. Smale Collection*)

Deborah aged ten, with brother Ted, four years younger. (*J. C. Gould*)

Aged sixteen—first 'theatrical portrait' by R. W. Brown.

As Harlequin (third from left) in Phyllis Smale's production of *Harlequin and Columbine* at Bristol's Assembly Hall, 1937. (*P. Smale Collection*)

Open Air Theatre, Regent's Park: first rôle as a 'Lady' in Robert Atkins' production of *Much Ado About Nothing*, June 1939. (*Kerr Collection*)

As Patty Moss in *The Two Bouquets*—Oxford Play-house, 1940. (*P. Smale Collection*)

As Mary Brodie in *Hatter's Castle*. Paramount, 1941. (*Kerr Collection*)

On the set of *Hatter's Castle*: left to right, Lance Comfort, Emlyn Williams, Mrs Kerr Trimmer (standing) and Deborah. (*Kerr Collection*)

Twenty-first birthday party on the set of *The Life and Death of Colonel Blimp*; the key of the door from director Michael Powell. (*Kerr Collection*)

Left to right: Mary Merrall, Geoffrey Hibbert and Deborah Kerr in *Love on the Dole*. British National, 1940. (*Kerr Collection*)

As Ellie Dunn in *Heartbreak House*, 1943. (*Cecil Beaton*)

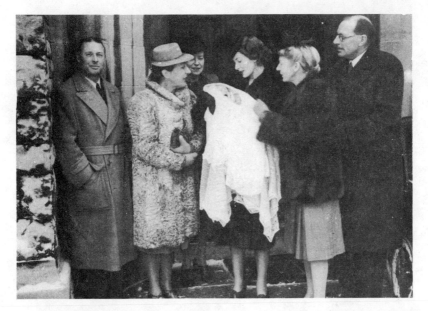

Christening of Harriet Robinson, *née* Forster, Deborah's cousin, 28 January, 1945. Left to right: P. V. Roberts (director of Imperial Tobacco—godfather), Miss K. Gotch Robinson (godmother), Mrs Kerr Trimmer, Deborah (godmother, holding baby), Phyllis Jane Forster (*née* Smale) and husband Harry Forster. (*P. Smale Collection*)

Official Order to entertain forces overseas in *Gaslight*, 1945.

Two sides of the coin: Deborah Kerr as young Bridie Quilty in *I See a Dark Stranger*.
Above: the teenager in Ireland. Below: matured and involved in espionage with Trevor
Howard in the Second World War. Individual, 1945.

St George's, Hanover Square, 28 November, 1945, with brother Edmund (Ted) who gave the bride away. (*London & County Press*)

The groom, Squadron-Leader Anthony Bartley, cuts the cake at Claridge's reception. The best man, Group Captain 'Sailor' Malan, is on the right. (*Kerr Collection*)

Arrival in New York, 28 November,
1946. (*Kerr Collection*)

Daughter Melanie aged eighteen months with her
parents at their Pacific Palisades home. (*Nat Dallinger*)

With Clark Gable in *The Hucksters*. MGM, 1947.

With Spencer Tracy in *Edward, My Son*. First Oscar nomination. MGM, 1948.

On board 'Lugard', Murchison Falls,
Uganda, while on location for *King Solomon's
Mines*, 1949. (*S. Pegrume*)

With Alan Ladd in *Thunder in the East*. Paramount, 1951.

With Robert Taylor in *Quo Vadis?* MGM, 1951.

Left to right: Greer Garson, Louis Calhern, Richard Hale, John Gielgud,
James Mason, Deborah Kerr in *Julius Caesar*. MGM, 1953.

With Stewart Granger in *The Prisoner of Zenda*. MGM, 1952.

With Cary Grant in *Dream Wife*. MGM, 1952.

had the full training at Northumberland House School, from Brownie to Elk to fully fledged Guide and leader of the Skylark Patrol; in any case they must have recognized that they were dealing with an authority in such matters.

# V

*The Day Will Dawn*, the first film to deal with Commando raids on occupied Europe, was technically well made and popular; 'first-class entertainment' said *Picturegoer* at the time of its general release in June 1942. Finlay Currie, as Scots as the kilt, but always acceptable in grizzled authoritarian rôles, played Alstad, the father of Deborah Kerr's Karin; he offers to show Colin Metcalfe (Hugh Williams), irresponsible racing journalist turned foreign correspondent, where U-boats are operating. Karin's father's death, at the time when she and Colin are captured and about to be shot, called for some effective emotional acting, although the part did not really give her a great deal of scope. It did, however, show Deborah's ability to *look* as well as sound in character; she could well have passed for a Scandinavian.

The cast was first rate, with Ralph Richardson top-starred as Lockwood, ace foreign correspondent: Kerr was second-billed, before Williams and Griffith Jones, who played the quisling police inspector and Nazi stooge. After *Major Barbara* Deborah's contract stipulated top or co-star billing. Francis L. Sullivan, Roland Culver, Bernard Miles, Niall McGinnis and Patricia Medina were featured under Harold French's firm direction and the film released in the USA as *The Avengers*.

Although producer Paul Soskin's prediction that his film about Norway would make a world star of Deborah Kerr was somewhat over-optimistic, her day was indeed about to dawn. Her career was still being guided by John Gliddon as her agent, but Nicholas Davenport had taken over as her personal manager, following a rearrangement of her original contract.

The Davenports had become a guiding force in her life, and she spent most weekends at their country home. However, it was outside John Gliddon's office that she ran into Michael Powell again, and was greeted by: 'Hello, Deborah, I want you to star in my next film, *The Life and Death of Colonel Blimp*.'

Powell had been watching her career with more than fatherly interest. His company, the Archers, in partnership with Emeric Pressburger, held a record of versatility in range of subjects, artistic integrity combined with business acumen and imaginative treatment over a twenty-year period, which represents the cream of those creative days of the British film industry. *Colonel Blimp* was to be their most ambitious to date, and the first in colour. The story combined three wars—the South African, the 1914–18 war, and the conflict which began in 1939—illustrating as its theme the eternal clash of ideas between generations.

Written, produced and directed by Powell and Pressburger, the film was to encapsulate the history of the first forty years of the twentieth century. There were three star parts of magnitude: the two male leads going from youth to old age, and the female split into three aspects of the ideal woman in three generations. Laurence Olivier, announced to play Blimp, withdrew, for reasons not unconnected with his wife, Vivien Leigh, then playing Jennifer Dubedat in Shaw's *The Doctor's Dilemma* in the West End, and Roger Livesey, for whom Powell had unbounded admiration, took over the title rôle. Wendy Hiller had actually signed for the female starring leads, but found herself pregnant before the film went into production, and also bowed out. Pregnancy seemed to be an occupational hazard for female stars in those times—in Britain, if not in Hollywood. Esther Williams told Deborah Kerr a few years later: 'I only have babies *between* films.' 'Typical,' says Deborah, 'of her peculiarly salty sense of humour!'

The number of times the careers of Kerr and Hiller have crossed, succeeded each other and run parallel is remarkable: on this occasion Deborah stepped into Wendy's shoes and the biggest opportunity of her career to date. It not only fulfilled Michael Powell's prophecy about her imminent stardom, but led directly to world-wide recognition. The next two occasions Powell was anxious for Kerr to film for the Archers failed to materialize: the first was to have been for *A Canterbury Tale*, the year after *Colonel Blimp*.

'I think she didn't do that one because she didn't like the script. A couple of other actors didn't either, and they were right: the film was a flop. Emeric's premise was too far-fetched—it was the one where Eric Portman was unearthed as the village menace, who ran about pouring glue on girls' heads—and this was one of the few occasions when I didn't tell my partner bluntly what I felt, but thought "Well, we're so clever we'll probably get away with it!" I was wrong. Sheila Sim, (now Lady Attenborough) played the part Deborah had turned down.

'Then she was going to play with James Mason in *I Know Where I'm Going*, and James, who was very young and snorty in those days—very arrogant—started to dictate and say he didn't want to go too much on location, and more shooting should be done in the studio, so I said "All right, James, we'll drop the idea", then I had to look around for another leading man, which wasn't too easy with the war on. Then Roger Livesey said: "Give it to me, Mickey; I'll take ten pounds off, blond my hair, make myself fifteen years younger—and I can play it." Of course, I knew he could—Roger could play anything if he set his mind to it, so he played it absolutely marvellously. And, on the rebound, because I couldn't have Deborah on account of her contract with "Gabby", Wendy acted opposite him, and splendid she was, too. So what she lost on the Blimp she gained on the Livesey.

'We would have liked to have made many more films with Deborah: we disagreed over her contract with Gabby after he sold half of it to MGM. I maintained that, because of the war, she was in a position to break her contract; I imagine that Gabby neatly side-stepped that by stipulating that she should not leave the country to film until after the war was over. We had a bust-up; I said I didn't think people should go to Hollywood at a time when the British film industry had really established itself, because all the people who got in our way had run away, which was splendid. I hoped they'd stay away, and we would prove we could make better films without them. But I imagine she hadn't got much choice, and that the contract with Pascal was a tough one.'

However tough the terms of the contract—by the time of which Michael Powell speaks Nicholas Davenport had, by agreement with John Gliddon, taken over the running of all Deborah Kerr's business affairs—she did not leave it at that. At the period when she had established herself as one of the top box-office stars in the British Isles she went to see the late Lord Rank, then plain Mr J. Arthur, undisputed benevolent despot of the flourishing British film scene, and explained her dilemma: she told him that she would infinitely prefer to stay in England, which was where her friends and relatives and all her interests were. Could he suggest any way out of her having to go to Hollywood, now that the war was over?

The Great Man was most paternal and understanding. 'You must do what you think right, my dear,' an effective cue for song, but ineffectual in pointing a way for Deborah Kerr to stay in England without breaking her contractual obligations. 'I had a feeling they just weren't very interested, one way or the other' was her conclusion.

## VI

Indifference formed no part of Michael Powell's attitude to-wards Kerr or her career in 1942 and it was he who played the major part in entrusting her with rôles which demonstrated her star potential to the public, as well as to other film-makers.

'She was so young—actually we gave her a twenty-first birth-day party during the shooting of the film—and yet she had, even then, the quality of complete malleability: playing three parts, a governess in 1902, a nurse in 1918 and an ATS driver in 1942, she had the ability to *feel* herself into the changes of rôle, without relying on make-up. There was a scene, in the First World War section, where Deborah as a nurse, whom the Colonel, played by Livesey, marries because she bears a striking resemblance to his first love, has to disagree gently but firmly with her husband, putting him right with assurance.

'She played this scene so well and so truly that Emeric who, being Hungarian, had set ideas about woman's place in the scheme of things, said "The scene's all wrong! I wouldn't let any woman talk to me like that." "Thanks to Deborah," I replied, "that is why the scene's all right."

'Alexander Korda came on the set to watch the filming— he was in England, setting up the deal to merge London Films and MGM-British—and brought with him William Wyler, who was shooting a documentary in Britain. They both agreed about the quality of Deborah's performance, then Korda took me on one side and said, "I know what you're doing—this is a very important film, but why an 'unknown' girl for the lead?" I answered, "If you think she's unknown now, I promise you won't by the time the picture is released!"

'Because of her performance in *Blimp* Ben Goetz, the head of MGM in Britain, bought half of Deborah's contract from Gabby Pascal, with the result that Korda, after his merger with Metro, had to star Deborah, as one of their roster of contract players, with Robert Donat in *Perfect Strangers*. "Unknown" or not! Everyone at Denham was mad about her—head over heels—and I was no exception.'

Powell was echoing what Clifford Evans had said about the cast and crews of their two films together, and particularly about the camera, and its love affair with the Kerr features. As Georges Perinal, the absolute master of lighting cameramen, was in charge, and as her beauty is enhanced a thousandfold by colour, she not only acted, but looked like a dream. The film opened in June 1943 at the Odeon, Leicester Square, with a general release the following month. In the meantime she had returned to the stage and made an enormous critical success in Shaw's *Heartbreak House* in the West End.

The critics, too, were enthusiastic about her acting in *The Life and Death of Colonel Blimp*, although most of them pointed out that Powell and Pressburger's script did not, in actual fact, hand many plums to the Kerr characterizations, and it was mainly due to her sense of differentiation between the personalities involved that the ladies not only avoided being stock figures, but gave the film the fairly high degree of emotional appeal it possessed, with Dilys Powell in *The Sunday Times* referring to her 'vivacity and discretion'. American film writer Jim Meyer wrote: 'Miss Kerr was among the foremost actresses to emerge during the war years'. He also pointed out that when the picture was cut by about an hour for showing in the USA, the FTC called United Artists on the carpet for showing the mutilated *Blimp* as a complete film. The hearings, which did not begin until 1949, could have had little practical benefit on the movie, which relied as much on its leisurely pace as on its story, acting and photography for its overall effect.

VC Winner Clive Candy, the Blimp figure of the title, starts his career in the Boer War and fights a duel with a German Lieutenant, Theo Kretschmar-Schneldorff (the late Anton Walbrook, in one of his always incisive performances), who survives to marry the woman Candy secretly loves. In the 1914–18 war he becomes a brigadier and marries a VAD, finally joining the Home Guard in the last war. It is when he is taken prisoner in a Home Guard attack while enjoying a Turkish Bath that he finally realizes how ridiculous and antiquated he has become, with his intolerance and resistance to change.

Eternal woman as represented by Deborah Kerr is Edith Hunter, an English governess in Berlin (1902–12); VAD Barbara Wynne (1914–18); and 'Johnny' Cannon (1939–43), an MTC driver. To Blimp, personifying the idea that men always fall for the same type of girl, Barbara and Johnny look exactly like Edith. For Livesey it was the part of a lifetime, and his true-life wife, the beautiful Ursula Jeans, was also in the film. The supporting cast included Roland Culver, Albert Lieven and A. E. Matthews, who continued playing vague, endearing and crotchety old English buffers until his death in 1960 at the age of ninety-one.

CHAPTER FIVE

# TUG OF WAR

I

In December 1941, Hugh ('Binkie') Beaumont, managing director of H. M. Tennent, one of London's leading theatrical impresarios, wrote to John Gliddon:

'I am very interested in your letter about Deborah Kerr. I have seen her in several pictures and I agree with you she is a very exciting idea for the theatre. As soon as I have an idea for a vehicle I will get in touch with you.'

The vehicle materialized when shooting on *Colonel Blimp* was completed. What Deborah referred to at the time as her 'refresher course in acting' was in the most distinguished company possible: George Bernard Shaw's *Heartbreak House*, co-starring Robert Donat, Edith Evans and Isabel Jeans and directed by the BBC's John Burrell, which opened, after a short tour including her birthplace, Glasgow, at the Cambridge Theatre on Friday, 19 March, 1943, with Deborah Kerr in the rôle of Ellie Dunn.

Shaw's 'Chekhovian comedy' concerning a group of oddly assorted characters gathered together in the same house and facing the destruction of the world, has been said to be his favourite play, and the work in which one sees most clearly the struggle between Shaw the moralist and Shaw the sensualist.

Ellie Dunn is a young romantic who has been invited to spend her annual holidays at Heartbreak House, the home of the eccentric ancient mariner, Captain Shotover (Robert Donat). She is seeking romance, forms an attachment with Hector

71

Hushaby (Vernon Kelso) and is desolated to find him not only worthless and a liar, but married to Shotover's daughter Hesione (Edith Evans). Shotover's other daughter, played by Isabel Jeans, earned her father's undying condemnation twenty-three years earlier for running away from home, returning a wealthy woman of the world, thoroughly spoilt after her travels round the globe as Lady Utterwood, wife of the governor of a far-flung outpost of Empire. Ellie refuses the offer of marriage of another guest at the house, Boss Mangan (George Merritt), the embodiment of capitalism, whose object in life is making money and acquiring possessions. She and Shotover have a mutual respect and understanding and she finds consolation in his wisdom.

'Life with a blessing: that is what I want,' she tells him. 'Now I know why I couldn't marry Mr Mangan. There would be no blessing on our marriage.'

Beverley Baxter in the *Evening Standard* praised the acting unstintingly: 'Robert Donat was superb as the ancient, perambulating Captain Shotover. He has all the best lines as well as a beard, for while each character is an expression of Shaw, the author gives the plums to the character with the beard. Edith Evans' acting was a joy: Isabel Jeans, as a passionless enslaver of men, was disturbingly good...Twenty-one year-old Miss Deborah Kerr won the feminine award. She has the rare gift of thinking her lines, not merely remembering them. The process of growing from a romantic, silly girl to a hard disillusioned woman in three hours was remarkably moving and convincing.'

Ivor Brown in *The Observer* voted her 'far the best Ellie of my acquaintance', and *The Guardian* wrote: 'Already well known on the screen, Miss Deborah Kerr is proving herself an equally accomplished actress on the stage, and her portrayal of the penniless, heartbroken Ellie Dunn is firm and convincing.' *The Tatler* averred her to be 'excellent. She acts with both head and heart, and can share a duologue with Miss Evans without being eclipsed.'

Shortly before her death in October 1976 Dame Edith wrote,

regretting that she would not be able to see me to talk about her impressions of *Heartbreak House*, as 'my advisers have very much restricted my activities'—she was then eighty-eight, and had just officially announced her retirement—and 'the time Deborah Kerr was with me was very short and a very long time ago'. The impression Dame Edith had made on her young co-star was, however, unforgettable:

'I learned more from watching Edith Evans than from any subsequent experience. She was a superb master of control over her own presence—of a repose, or seeming repose that is difficult for young people to achieve. She made me sit on my hands for one scene (shades of Grandmother Smale), because I was using them too busily, and to teach me how much more effective it is to use one gesture economically and rightly than to fidget and gesticulate all over the place.'

Isabel Jeans, who had the next dressing-room to Deborah at the Cambridge Theatre, recalls that none of the cast had any opportunity to socialize. 'With air raids imminent, we just used to do our work and clear out of the theatre as soon as possible. But Deborah had a natural charm, at a time when people often did not have leisure to cultivate such graces any more. We didn't have any individual scenes together, but I enjoyed the brief talks we had in the theatre. I used to watch her from the wings, while waiting to go on stage, and think how exquisite she looked in the turquoise gown Cecil Beaton had designed for her. I admired her calm and total lack of pretension: she had style and elegance, and when we met again at a party recently she hadn't changed at all.'

There were occasional evenings out, to vary the routine of 'theatre, then "home" to bed'—still at the English-Speaking Union—and among the friends Deborah made were designer Kitty Foster and her then husband, actor Guy Deghy. He recalls their first meeting:

'My wife had asked her to dinner, and as I too was playing in the West End, it was arranged that I should pick Deb up after our respective shows and take her to our flat in Shepherd Market. I duly presented myself at her dressing-room and took her home. An American doctor friend of ours, back in London in a colonel's uniform, made up the dinner party. Deb looked so young and innocent—honey-blonde with great big magical blue eyes, very much her Jenny Hill image—that at first I feared she would be shocked by the rather sophisticated small-talk we affected in those days. Far from it: she broke any ice before it might have started forming. She had a fund of not only funny but genuinely witty stories and I have never heard anyone tell them better. The evening was a huge success and my doctor friend was still raving about the young Deborah when I saw him a few years ago in New York. After that my former wife and I saw her a few more times: she came to us, or we went out to restaurants in blacked-out London, until she went, a few years later, to Hollywood to become a star of the first order.'

## II

The year 1943 was Deborah Kerr's year of recognition, amply bearing out her inclusion in the American *Motion Picture Herald*'s 1942 polls as a 'Star of Tomorrow'. It was also a year of contrasts: on 15 May she joined the all-star concert at the London Coliseum by the National Council of Labour in aid of the Help for Russia fund, giving an oration, accompanied by Geraldo and his Concert Orchestra. Among her co-stars, for the one and only time in her life were two of the surviving legends of the golden days of music hall, Nellie Wallace and Max Miller.

Contractual obligations caused Deborah to leave the cast of *Heartbreak House* in August, and Joan Greenwood took over as Ellie Dunn. Robert Donat was to star in the first film of MGM's merger with Alexander Korda, and switched from the aged character part he had played so brilliantly on the stage to a clerk turned naval officer about his own age in *Perfect Strangers*. Despite having made only one film in Hollywood, *The Count of Monte Cristo* in 1934, Donat was still able to command whatever he wanted in terms of billing, production and co-stars. He had been absent from the screen for three years, due to the chronic asthma which blighted his life and career.

Deborah Kerr, cast as his wife in the new film, had worked with him most happily on the stage, although his illness had given him a reputation for being difficult. She says of their partnership: 'What a lovely actor he was, and how little, really, the public saw of him because of his intense shyness, and his nervousness of strangers. He was wonderfully helpful to me, both on the stage and in the movie, because I was indeed pretty "green", and worked mostly out of instinct rather than technique. He was very co-operative towards his fellow-actors and technicians, even if a little distant. One must remember he was a big star at that time and people *were* in awe of him.'

The trade papers announced the amalgamation of 'Lion and "Big Ben"' at the beginning of 1944, providing for the production of four pictures during the year at a total cost of about one million two hundred thousand pounds. Side by side with this news was a full-page advertisement of 'New Year Greetings from Deborah Kerr', and under her most ethereal portrait, the legend, 'A Gabriel Pascal Star'.

In fact, the first production of the newly formed company was also the last. The second was to have starred Vivien Leigh in 'an original dramatic story by Enid Bagnold'; the third to be adapted from John Buchan's novel *Greenmantle*; and the fourth to co-star Robert Donat and Merle Oberon in the life story of Robert Louis Stevenson by G. B. Stern called *Velvet Coat*. This was to come up some years later in Hollywood, as a mooted subject for Deborah Kerr and Stewart Granger.

*Perfect Strangers* (released in the USA as *Vacation from Marriage*) went into production at Denham with American Wesley Ruggles directing—a strange choice for a very British subject, since his most notable successes had been films starring Bing Crosby, Mae West and Claudette Colbert. It soon became apparent that neither Ruggles nor anyone else concerned was happy with the way things were going. Alexander Korda took over the direction himself, and the result was highly entertaining and popular, at least in Great Britain, once the superficial premise of the story had been accepted.

Donat was cast as a clerk, Robert Wilson, and Kerr as his frumpish wife Catherine, an unenterprising couple whose marriage is dying of sheer anaemia. War service shows Catherine becoming glamorous and desirable during her term in the WRNS and an affair with Richard, a naval architect (Roland Culver), while Robert achieves the same result through a naval career and a romantic encounter with Nurse Elena (Ann Todd). The stars of the film, separated during much of the story, were handicapped by sharing the least interesting scenes, before they both 'found their true identities' in the Armed Forces, but played with such skill and charm that audiences were relieved that they eventually found happiness with each other.

In the nature of things and because of the story line, it was in the company of others that they really blossomed, and the supporting cast were of star quality. Glynis Johns, as Dizzy Clayton, Catherine's frank and amoral Wren friend, was outstanding: she is an actress for whom Deborah Kerr has the highest regard, and they have been friends ever since this first celluloid encounter. Roland Culver's dry British wit also drew sparks from the Kerr character in their scenes together, particularly when Catherine gently but firmly rebuffs his advances after he has sketched her during a picnic together.

The combination of Korda, a director especially adept at handling women stars, and Perinal, so inspired in photographing them to best advantage, worked extremely effectively here for Kerr, Johns and Todd. Perinal's effects in highlighting Deborah's beauty in the subtle Technicolor employed in *The Life and Death of Colonel Blimp* were matched by his achievements in black and white, showing the development of Catherine from dowd to alive and alert maturity, while Korda's direction allowed her to display a natural aptitude for comedy which had for the most part lain dormant in her previous rôles.

Both Glynis Johns and Ann Todd had worked for Korda as producer before, in Victor Saville's *South Riding*, but *Perfect Strangers* brought out in them new potential as film actresses.

Todd as Elena was a revelation, after a number of films which had failed to do her justice, and she had never been so well photographed: her quiet scene where she explains to Donat how she could never be unfaithful to her dead husband, stays in the mind as an example of perfect screen acting, and paved the way among cinema audiences for her emergence, so soon after, as a world star in *The Seventh Veil*.

Delays in filming brought Deborah Kerr back for retakes on *Perfect Strangers* after she had toured the war zones in Europe for ENSA: her hair had grown quite unsuitably long in the interim, and had to be trimmed back to Wren requirements. The film was premièred in London at the Empire, Leicester Square in August 1945, a full year after its initial 'saturation' publicity was released. In America it did not do well, but Louis B. Mayer, after his first private viewing at Metro, decreed at once of his company's part-contractee: 'That girl is a star!'

III

During breaks in her film and stage work Deborah spent as much of her free time as possible in visits to the family. Grannie Jane Trimmer, still queening it in Alfold, was inordinately proud of Deborah's progress and informed her friends in the village of each new development in her career. In Weston brother Ted lived at home with his mother and grandfather during his early days as a journalist on the Weston and Bristol papers, and was called into the RAF in October 1943. After basic training in Birmingham he was placed on deferred service and returned home. During the Christmas holidays he discovered for the first time that he had a detached retina in his right eye: the Medical Officer prescribed treatment in the RAF hospital. Colleen told Deborah who, says Ted, 'marched in with all guns blazing. She said "Right—we're going to get the best person,"' and before he really knew what was happening he found himself whisked into hospital for an operation, which at that time was a very tricky one, and performed by one of the leading men in ophthalmic surgery.

'Deb set all that up and paid for it and it's just one example of how forceful she can be when the occasion warrants. I've always made a point of not trading on the fact of having a famous sister: the one occasion I was happy to have her pull a string on my behalf was when she asked Arthur Christiansen to give me an interview to see whether I was worth hiring by the *Daily Express*. He saw me and I got the job—I like to think because he found me suitable, rather than as a favour to Deb.'

The war had already claimed one of the family circle: their cousin John, the son of Uncle Arthur and Aunt Greta Smale, with whom Ted and Deborah had spent so many holidays by the sea at Weston, was killed in action with the RAF in 1941, at the age of twenty. His family had by this time moved with the Marconi Company to Shenfield, Essex, and had very little opportunity to see their niece and nephew, who were by now fully engaged wherever their respective occupations sent them.

All artistes who went abroad from Great Britain to entertain the Forces did so under the official aegis of Basil Dean, who had been appointed Director of ENSA in 1939. One of the brightest shows to go overseas, in May 1943, starred Vivien Leigh, Dorothy Dickson, Beatrice Lillie and Leslie Henson: they went to Gibraltar and toured extensively in Africa, with Beatrice Lillie and Leslie Henson in charge of the comedy side of things, Dorothy Dickson dancing as effortlessly on make-shift stages and fit-ups as though she had the whole of Drury Lane at her feet, and Vivien Leigh giving her Scarlett O'Hara monologues from *Gone with the Wind*. Gracie Fields sang to the Armed Forces and to munitions workers in all the Allied Theatres of war, and, from Hollywood such stars as Bob Hope, Bing Crosby, Frances Langford, Martha Raye, Kay Francis and, particularly, Marlene Dietrich channelled their main activities into entertaining the troops.

Drury Lane, serving as HQ for the Entertainments National Service Association, provided both rehearsal rooms and launch-ing-pad for Deborah Kerr's National Service. At the Theatre

Royal, under the direction of John Fernald she spent March 1945 rehearsing the rôle of Bella Manningham in Patrick Hamilton's *Gaslight*, opposite Stewart Granger. Fernald recalls his gratitude for her good humour and professionalism, the chief factor in smoothing over some of the more intolerant patches of the leading man's behaviour.

Granger, then at the peak of his box-office success in such films as *The Man in Grey* with Margaret Lockwood and Phyllis Calvert and *Madonna of the Seven Moons* with Calvert, was quick-tempered and volatile: he was also inspired casting for the part of Massingham, in that his image was sufficiently romantic for there to be a doubt during the opening of the play as to his real attitude towards his wife, a silly woman, if ever there was one, epitomizing the ideal masochistic object for Victorian chauvinist domination. This beginning of his partnership with Deborah Kerr is notable in that, during their subsequent teaming in films it was always Granger as Action Man, and Kerr the object of his protective affections: his sadistic streak was only in view in their one play together, and for the exclusive delectation of His Majesty's Armed Forces.

Under the 2nd Tactical Air Force Movement Order No. 68686, D. J. Kerr Trimmer (Rank, Miss: Religion, C. of E.: Nationality, British), flew with the company of the play *Gaslight* to Europe 'on Duty, for a period of — days, from 1 April 1945.' The play had already been filmed twice, in Britain with Diana Wynyard and Anton Walbrook, and in Hollywood with Ingrid Bergman and Charles Boyer; the new stars played to ecstatic audiences in Belgium, Holland and France, sometimes in large and well-equipped theatres, at other times on make-shift stages under canvas. Often the sound of gunfire was too close for comfort, but happily Deborah's experience of the bomb in the Harrisons' vegetable patch was never equalled for shock value during her tours overseas. The tour lasted for eight weeks.

In Brussels *Gaslight* played the comfortable and luxurious Opera House, and after the show the cast were invited to the neighbouring Officers' Clubs, where, says Deborah, 'all the companies sent out by ENSA would be entertained. They were a great meeting-place as all the available personnel would go to the shows—they all needed entertainment, whether it was in Eindhoven, or Brussels or Lille or Paris—and very often we would have a drink afterwards.'

On one of these occasions Stewart Granger introduced his co-star to a friend, Squadron-Leader Anthony Bartley, stationed in Brussels with the RAF. They talked of the war and of mutual friends, and parted politely after the party. The next evening 'Jimmy' Granger mentioned casually that Tony Bartley was in to see the show again and would be joining them for a drink afterwards. From then on he saw *Gaslight* every night during the run at the Opera House, and just before the company left Brussels Deborah and he dined together, and he confided that he did not know what he would do when she left. Their meetings had been very polite, very reticent: they had danced together and Deborah found him attractive and charming, but she was cautious. 'We had been warned that RAF types were great ones for a bit of casual hanky-panky, but Tony made no passes and I thought him terribly nice. He was so sweet that when he asked "May I kiss you?" I held up my face, then, as he careered off in his jeep I thought I'd never hear from him again.'

Just three weeks later he telephoned her from Croydon Airport to say he had managed a spot of leave and would like her to dine with him. She put off the engagement she already had 'by telling a lot of terrible lies' and kept the appointment with Tony Bartley. At the time she was immersed in re-takes for *Perfect Strangers*.

The Bartleys are an Irish family: his father was a barrister of the Irish High Court and subsequently a High Court Judge in India, for which service he was given a knighthood. Although Squadron-Leader Bartley had friends in the acting profession, he was uncertain as to how Sir Charles and Lady Bartley would regard his determination to marry Deborah. He expressed his doubts to Laurence Olivier, who uttered words of reassurance: 'Don't worry what your family will think. She is a good actress. She is also unreasonably chaste!' When this dictum eventually got back to her, Deborah's wry reflection was: 'Word of such a dreary reputation has a way of getting around.'

## IV

Gabriel Pascal's customary two-page announcement in the 1945 trade press stated, in bold red letters: '1945–46: Bernard Shaw's *Doctor's Dilemma* starring Deborah Kerr (under exclusive contract to MGM and Gabriel Pascal).' Underneath, in slightly smaller letters *Androcles And The Lion*, and, on the second page, again in bold lettering: '1946–47: Bernard Shaw's *Saint Joan.*'

Of these, only *Androcles* was actually to reach the screen several years later, in Hollywood. *The Doctor's Dilemma* was finally made, many years after Pascal's death, in Britain in 1958, with Leslie Caron and Dirk Bogarde. For *Saint Joan* Pascal announced Garbo on several occasions, oblivious of the fact that she had resisted all inducements to return to the screen after her final, highly entertaining and unfairly criticized appearance in George Cukor's *Two-Faced Woman* in 1941. Another Pascal dream as intriguing as the Garbo project was his announcement that Gracie Fields would star for him in the film of Shaw's *Mrs Warren's Profession*, although he never seemed to have gone as far as to ask Gracie her opinion of the idea. He also declared himself planning to film Deborah Kerr as *Candida*, another scheme which could have been inspirational, as were so many of his ideas. The complications of his wheeling and dealing were such, however, that the majority of them were doomed to cancel themselves out.

The Kerr contract is a case in point. By the time *Perfect Strangers/Vacation from Marriage* awakened so much additional interest in her star potential, her sole manager was Nicholas Davenport and John Gliddon had resigned his financial interest in her career. The parting of the ways came when Michael

Powell was interested in starring her in a film of Mary Webb's *Gone to Earth*—an extremely tricky subject for the screen, as the heroine had a hare-lip. Davenport did not see this as a viable rôle for his client, and at this point he and Gliddon agreed to differ over the future path her career was to take. Powell eventually made the film, starring Jennifer Jones. It was not a success.

Sam Goldwyn was among the moguls eager to sign Deborah Kerr to an exclusive contract, along with Hal Wallis and Loew-Lewin, but, apart from Pascal's having sold half her contract to Ben Goetz for MGM-British, there was an added complication in the fact that he had also guaranteed her a certain sum after British taxes had been met which made her price very high indeed. Negotiations carried out by Davenport on his client's behalf were complicated and protracted in the extreme; in the meantime the object of all the hassle carried on quietly with her work and wondered secretly where it would all end.

Her financial position had become stable enough in early February 1944 for her to buy herself a home of her own, after so many years in family and institutional backgrounds. It was at Tunbridge Wells, on the Kent–Sussex border, and consisted of two old farmhouses knocked together, with a beautiful garden—a 'must' in her scheme of things ever since the orchard at Pound Cottage in Alfold. As things turned out she was to enjoy less than two years there: the house was auctioned off in 1946, by which time her contractual difficulties had been resolved.

Metro already had the advantage over the other contenders for the Kerr signature, in that her career was already half in their keeping: Mayer's interest, already awakened by her appearance in *The Life and Death of Colonel Blimp*, was finally crystallized by *Vacation from Marriage*, although the film itself did not impress him or his henchmen. Its financial success in the UK, however, helped them to take a tolerant view, and finally the new contract was signed and sealed: seven years at a total of two hundred and fifty thousand dollars, fifty-two weeks a year, with no options, at a guaranteed three thousand dollars a week. In the meantime, before this eminently satisfactory—not to say staggering—conclusion to the negotiations was announced, she had two final films to make in Britain as Gabriel Pascal's protégée.

V

In the summer of 1945 Deborah Kerr was loaned to Individual Films, working at Denham Studios as a unit under the Rank combine in the persons of Frank Launder and Sidney Gilliat, to co-star with Trevor Howard in their comedy-thriller *I See a Dark Stranger*. As scenarists the team had been responsible for two of Margaret Lockwood's most entertaining pre-war successes, Hitchcock's *The Lady Vanishes* and *Night Train to Munich*, and when they had extended their activities to producing and directing their own screenplays the results had been both popular and profitable. Their excellent *The Rake's Progress* gave first-rate opportunities to Rex Harrison and Lilli Palmer, with Jean Kent smouldering most effectively on the sidelines, and *Dark Stranger*, with Launder directing and Gilliat producing, was its successor. The opening called for several weeks' location work in Ireland and the Isle of Man.

Simultaneously, I myself, waiting in the wings at an extremely tender age to receive a call to the studios, as a no-talent, but boundlessly enthusiastic cinema fan with a yen for writing, was summoned by Rank's Studio Manager, Tom White, to Pinewood, to discuss a possible opening as a trainee scriptwriter. My father, whose world was centred in the City, and who thoroughly disapproved of all aspects of the entertainment scene, had been persuaded, against his better judgment, by my mother and my headmaster, Fr Tom Sherlock, to drop a tiny word into the ear of J. Arthur Rank: one year later I was called.

Tom White told me that as I was not in the Union, the Association of Cine Technicians, and under-age anyway, the best they could do for me was to take me on unofficially as a

83

Fourth Assistant Director—there being no such grade in the Union—at a nominal wage of fifty shillings a week. To gain experience, I would be sent to Denham to help out on the final weeks' location work on Pascal's *Caesar and Cleopatra*, which had been in production for over a year—since June 1944—and was well over budget, time, and patience limits.

As an introduction to film-making in the hey-day of the Rank Organization, working for Pascal was an experience never to be forgotten, especially as we were allowed to see the previous day's 'rushes'—the feet of film actually printed from what had been shot by cameraman Jack Hildyard. As we went into or emerged from the small preview theatre there were always artists or technicians from other productions awaiting their turn.

Pascal would pause in the entrance with the demeanour of an emperor, take in the assembly at a glance, and hail such luminaries of the day as Valerie Hobson, Sally Gray, Ann Todd and Kathleen Harrison with magnificent impartiality as 'My sweet virgins and demi-virgins'. When Deborah Kerr was present (on return from location work on *I See a Dark Stranger*) he always bowed gallantly and especially low over the hand of his protégée, as a sign of special proprietary favour.

After a few fascinating weeks' work on David Lean's *Great Expectations*, which entailed attendance as tea-boy and general dog's-body on tests for an unknown actor to play the young 'Pip' opposite Jean Simmons, already cast as the teenage Estella, I was told I had been accepted into the ACT, which involved a pay-rise of three pounds, promotion into the grade of Third Assistant Director, and a transfer across the lot to Individual Films' *I See a Dark Stranger*, now back from location and well under way, in September 1945, at its Denham Headquarters. It also meant that I would get to work with Deborah Kerr, a star whose friendliness was already a byword among studio technicians, and whose every film appearance I had attended until that time.

My few weeks on the Dickens film had taught me two important lessons: how to respect star status, and to be ready for

84

every contingency that might arise. In the first case, I had called Valerie Hobson on to the set: her co-star John Mills had been alerted, but had not yet arrived. Apart from director David Lean and the relevant technicians I was alone. With Miss Hobson. 'Where is Mr Mills?' she enquired. 'On his way; he should be here by now,' I replied. 'Indeed, he should. And where are my people?' 'Your people, Miss Hobson?' 'My make-up; my hairdresser; my stand-in. Never call me on the set again until my people are already here!' So saying, she swept off, a lovely crinolined vision of outraged stardom.

The second lesson also involved Miss Hobson, although less directly. Actually, she and the director were not seeing entirely eye to eye over her difficult scene with Pip, in which, as the grown-up Estella, she rejects his declaration of love. Rehearsals had been a little fraught and John Mills asked that his co-star should not be called until he was satisfied that his side of the scene was working as it should. The camera was to move in for a close-up in which Valerie Hobson was not required, but he needed someone for reaction. Her stand-in was not on the set, as she was not likely to be needed for at least an hour.

'This boy will do,' said Mr Mills, so I obediently took up my position next to him on the couch while he looked into my eyes and repeated, time and again, 'I love you, Estella, I love you.' This was progress, of a kind, after being in personal charge of Gabriel Pascal's supply of the raw carrots which helped provide his inspiration, but I began to hope that my future in films would hold even more exciting prospects!

# VI

*I See a Dark Stranger* was the first time Deborah Kerr had been top-starred in a film written specifically around her as a personality, and it was exciting to be in on such a project, no matter how minor one's contribution to the film. For her rôle of Bridie

85

Quilty, a young Irish girl in wartime whose hatred of the British leads her to undertake some spying for the Germans against England, her hair had reverted to her original dark with gold overtones, which photographed almost black. Make-up expert Norman Arnold devised a Hollywood-type gloss, which not only contrasted effectively with the freckles and no make-up look of her early Irish scenes as a teenage colleen, but set the tone of youthful sophistication, highlighting her cheekbones and exquisitely moulded nose: a style that was to persist through her early years in American films.

Georges Perinal had brought out the best in her features, first in the three period settings of *Colonel Blimp*'s colour photography, then in the dowdy housewife-into-radiantly-glowing woman of the world in *Perfect Strangers*. Wilkie Cooper, whose work on *The Rake's Progress* had contributed so largely to the film's critical success, was another cameraman to highlight the best in the female stars who came under his technical expertise. He had particular admiration for Greer Garson's face, and must be the only cameraman who ever persuaded Marlene Dietrich that, for all her formidable knowledge of lighting, she was not displaying herself to her best advantage. The film was Hitchcock's *Stage Fright*, several years after *Dark Stranger*, and in the early scenes she fixed the lights the way she wanted them. Then she came to him and said: 'I don't like the way I look.' From then on she let Wilkie Cooper light the rest of the movie, with results that Von Sternberg himself could hardly have bettered, twenty years earlier.

Cooper had instant rapport with Deborah Kerr, plus an instinctive knowledge of how to light her so that she would photograph to epitomize the ideal star image of the day. Through his fine black and white camerawork the two sides of the coin that represent the Kerr persona emerged definitively for the first time: on the one hand there was the fresh and unspoiled young girl of the early sequences, and on the other the entirely acceptable Hollywood-type beauty ideal of the forties and fifties. It was what Joan Crawford referred to, in her own case, as a 'built' face, and by that she was referring to 'photo-

86

genic'. Though in no way similar in looks, temperament or personality to Kerr's, the Crawford face of those days represented a model of the Hollywood star, and Deborah fitted into the lighting composition in a way that no other British actress was equipped to achieve.

As time passed and the American movie star image began to change she was to revert to the other side of the coin and the naturalness of her own beauty, freckles and all, to reach its apotheosis from the mid-fifties onwards. In herself the two complementary sides of the coin were already apparent at the time I had the unexpected pleasure of working with her. On the one hand there was the film beauty, quiet, apparently completely confident—a model of behaviour to all aspirants to the acting profession, yet recognizably a star; and on the other 'the proper person', treating everyone as a human being, ready to check inefficiency or bad manners with the most salutary brand of pointed sarcasm that deflated without leaving permanent scars. She was the first to see the point of even the most Rabelaisian jokes, which people always hesitated to repeat, in view of the extreme innocence of her blue eyes.

*I* was the one to blush when Deborah once joined a group of studio technicians, who had just exploded into raucous mirth over a crude but hilarious story told by one of the stagehands. 'What's the joke?' she asked. 'Come on, let's hear it.' 'I couldn't possibly,' said Joe. 'But I insist,' replied the star. After more argument, the embarrassed raconteur agreed to repeat the story, 'but I'll have to clean it up just a bit, Deborah, if you see what I mean.' 'Well, if you insist, but get on with the story.' At this point the First Assistant called me away, so I never heard the end of the story, and when I returned to the group Joe said, 'Deborah says we're not to repeat it to you—it's not at all suitable for your ears.'

It was Beryl Reid, who has a neat line in repartee herself, who coined the 'proper person' description of Deborah Kerr, whom she had never met. 'That's why she's such a true actress,' she concluded. 'You can tell she's never got silly with it.'

CHAPTER SIX

# *TWO SIDES OF THE COIN*

## I

The Launder–Gilliat unit, which I joined in October 1945, worked like clockwork, as far as the technical staff were concerned, because everyone was expert at his job. Except for myself, that is: having been elevated to the rank of Third Assistant Director, my secret fear was that the First and Second would both be away together, and I would be called upon to take over. I was very happy calling the artistes on the set, watching the filming and doing as I was told, but actual control over the unit—never.

Happily everyone was not only highly competent, but equable with it. Frank Launder, dark, quiet and serious, was a comfortable man to be around; outbursts of temper were utterly foreign to his nature. Producer Sidney Gilliat was rounder, slightly more forthcoming and friendly, but we saw less of him than his partner, who, as director of *I See a Dark Stranger*, was on hand all the time.

His team of assistants could hardly have formed a greater contrast. Percy Hermes, First Assistant, had worked his way up from odd job man to the property department and thence to assistant director at Irving Asher's British Warner studios, whose output of cheaply made and often diverting quota quickies were shot at such a rate that those involved had to learn everything about the business from A to Z—and quickly. He had worked with everyone from Warner-British's top star, Chili Bouchier, who later married one of Pascal's assistants on

*Caesar and Cleopatra*, 'Bluey' Hill, to Errol Flynn, whom Percy had piloted through his first film part in *Murder at Monte Carlo* in 1934. He had no great opinion of him, but Percy's opinion of actors and actresses in general was nil: a great Cockney character, quick, wily, cheeky and alert, with a face like a wombat with Dumbo ears, which he would shake about and flap to emphasize points, his favourite terms for the artistes with whom he came into contact were 'Peruvian ponces', 'ecclesiastical cockroaches' and 'pregnant linnets'. These epithets he applied to all and sundry, although the extras he mainly described as 'old boilers'. His rule regarding all artistes was to call them on the set at the earliest possible opportunity, so that they would be there when wanted—training which stemmed from his Warner days, when speed was the essence of filming, and every second counted. This applied to stars as well as small-part players, and was not at all popular with Trevor Howard, whose still recent training in the Armed Forces made him impatient over delays, and who did not appreciate Hermes' attitude.

'Get Trevor,' came the command, 'and we'll have him here ready for the next shot—then there won't be no delays.' 'But I'm not in the next shot,' Trevor Howard would protest. 'Percy says "you never know", and he wants you there!' 'They're all mad, you know; they won't get to me today—you'll see.' 'Do me a favour—Percy will carry on alarmingly if I come back without you.' 'All right, old boy, but they won't use me. They're all completely off their heads.'

I would report back that Howard was making his way (in his own good time) to the set. 'I want him here *now*!' roared Hermes, ears akimbo: 'I'll show the ecclesiastical cockroach who's in charge. They're a lot of Peruvian ponces. I'll have them *all* on the set. Not Deb, though; good as gold, she is. We never call her 'til she's actually needed for the shot: the stand-in will do in her case.'

I worked with the unit on three films, and Deborah Kerr seemed to be the only star for whom Percy had any real respect and affection. Without any special effort to win over the wily oldtimer, whose first loyalty was to his director, her general demeanour convinced him that she was completely genuine. He was lucky in his Second Assistant, at seventeen the youngest in the business: Christopher Noble was efficient, unflappable, good-mannered and had a tremendous sense of humour. Without his help and support I doubt if I'd have lasted a week with Percy Hermes, who, for all his apparent affability, could be a hard man, and was subject to grand rages. Chris Noble's attitude towards everyone on the set was a model of correctness and we used to discuss modes of behaviour towards the star of the film.

'I always call her "Miss Kerr"', said Chris. 'She doesn't really like everyone calling her "Deborah"—still less, "Deb"—you know. Anyway, I show respect.' 'What makes you think she doesn't like it? In any case, she told me to call her by her first name.' She had, in fact, the first time I went to her dressing-room to call her on to the set. 'Nevertheless,' asserted Chris, 'I shall continue to call her "Miss Kerr".'

This became a running gag between us. Chris Noble, unlike myself, was not remotely star-struck, although deeply interested in the technical side of the business: our arguments over the respective talents involved would go on long after shooting time in the local pub, or wherever else we happened to be. Probably because I was so aware of my own inefficiency, I used to impersonate the expert way he took over when Percy Hermes was absent from the set. The title Youngest Second Assistant in the Business delighted Chris and he would command in cultured tones, so very different from our master's.

'Quiet, now: settle down ... Quiet at the back there, *please*. OK. Now—Roll 'em!' as Wilkie Cooper got his cameras into action, and not a pin could be heard to drop, although occasionally a spanner's clatter might mar the blissful hush, or an electrician knock over a teacup from the heights of the gantry.

Like so many British technicians Chris felt that the British lead players were not 'stars' in the sense that Gable, Lombard or Dietrich were stars: ours were just actors doing a job. I argued: 'Anna Neagle and Jessie Matthews are stars, and so is Deborah—or will be very soon.' 'Hmmm ... we'll see. Do

90

you know her real name's "Trimmer"?' 'What has that got to do with it: in any case, it's Kerr Trimmer.' And so the weighty problems were threshed out, until we reached a truce on the joint agreement that, whatever else, she certainly was one of the favoured few with 'A sense of the fitness of things'. Looking back, the only kind of excuse I can find for such pomposity was that we *were* very young.

Deborah's popularity on the set was general: from the make-up and hairdressing departments, who had seen too much to be inclined to enthuse over anyone, to the 'chippies', 'sparks' and prop men; from the continuity girl, Pat Arnold, to the witty and friendly Thelma Myers (now Connolly), editor for all Individual's films; and from the two Abbey Theatre actresses, Eithne Dunne and Maureen Pook (later Pryor, of West End stage and television fame) who had come over from Ireland to coach the star with her Irish accent. These ladies would sit at the side of the set, on call during most of Deborah's scenes.

'She doesn't need our help—she's accent-perfect: it's really money under false pretences,' said Maureen, who sadly died during the writing of this book. Also present was Pat Ronald, the star's stand-in, who had been in the film business for years and was fifteen years older than Kerr, but was right where colouring and size were concerned. She had taken over the position from Sheila Scott, Deborah's original stand-in during the location work, who was to become rather better known as a flier some years later. Placidly knitting most of the time, Pat Ronald had a matter-of-fact philosophy about the business:

'I've stood in for most of them, including Anna Neagle and Phyllis Calvert . . . this kid's got what it takes . . . no nonsense—just gets on with the job. Nice, too . . no airs and graces.' Pat herself had been an actress in films: her high spot was when she played second female lead to Chili Bouchier in a thirties romance called *To Be a Lady*. I met Pat during the sixties again, immaculately coiffed and made-up as though ready to step before the cameras, but by then she was manageress of a restaurant near the London Palladium.

'Can't beat this job, dear,' she said. 'Filming got me down in the end. Besides, where did all the films go? No time to knit now.' Matter-of-fact to the end: I was told she died soon after that encounter, but her life would make a fascinating story.

Occasionally my general enthusiasm for the cinema overrode my devotion to duty, and once I rushed off the set without first giving Deborah her call for the next day. In the morning Chris Noble told me: 'Miss Kerr wants to see you. She's in make-up.' 'Good morning,' said her reflection in the mirror. 'What happened last night?' 'I had to leave early to see a film. So sorry about your call, but I hear you got it from Chris in time.' 'Only because he happened to be in when I phoned him. Supposing he hadn't been. What then? As you know, I'm in the first shot and I shudder to think *what* Percy would have said if I hadn't been there. What was the excitement about? What did you see, or should I say, whom did you see?' 'Kay Francis in *Divorce*. Did you know she's gone into production on her own account for Monogram after some of the rotten pictures she's been given lately?'

Deborah lifted her eyes from the magazine she had been studying and met my anxious gaze in the mirror. 'I had read something to that effect,' she said, 'and your enthusiasm for your favourites does you credit. However, you're soon going to have to make up your mind in which direction it's taking you. Versatility is all very well, but do you think the world is *quite* ready for your interpretation of Bridie—and shouldn't Trevor be prepared, as gently as possible, for the change?' Obviously the story of my unofficial sit-in for Valerie Hobson had travelled beyond the four walls of the sound stage where *Great Expectations* was nearing completion.

'Miss Kerr's right, you know,' was all the sympathy I received from Chris Noble. 'I don't think your heart's in getting to be another Percy Hermes. Why not try doing a few interviews and send them to *Picturegoer*: you spend enough time on the other sets to be gathering material for a hundred articles.' He was loyal to a fault, with a stock answer to Percy when he shouted 'Where's that other pregnant linnet?' 'Oh, Eric's just trying to get Trevor on to the set,' which, while generally the truth, also covered the occasions when I was watching David Niven filming *A Matter of Life and Death*, or Sally Gray doing re-takes with Michael Wilding on *Carnival*, or *nearly* standing in for Richard Greene while I was lurking on the set of Ann Todd's musical, *Gaiety George*. 'We've been looking for you everywhere, Mr Greene,' said a fledgling assistant director. 'Would you please take your place opposite Miss Todd?' I decided that she, like Trevor Howard, was not quite ready for me yet, and fled back to my rightful place beside Frank Launder and his other assistants.

## II

My misplaced enthusiasms were never entirely quelled while I remained as assistant director for Individual Films, and also took the form of tactless butting into other people's conversations. After the première of *Caesar and Cleopatra*, at which most of the senior personnel of *Dark Stranger* had been present I asked Deborah: 'Do you see much of Michael Rennie?' He had been one of my favourite artists during the final days' shooting on Denham's City Square location, which had transformed the vast expanses of field near the studios into an impressive replica of ancient Egypt. My meaning, of course, was how large a rôle had the late Mr Rennie played in the final production—but I could have phrased my question more exactly.

Deborah's eyes seemed a deeper blue than usual as she looked at me musingly for an appreciable period of time. Then she replied: 'Would you be so kind as to ask "Ormie" to fetch my cardigan from the dressing-room: I feel a distinct chill in the air—don't you?' I did, especially as Mrs Orme, her devoted dresser, who had the air of a well-groomed Nellie Wallace about her, used to give me the impression she had not too high a regard for anyone in the film business, with the exception of her well-loved employer.

93

After another film opening Frank Launder was discussing the evening's entertainment with Trevor Howard, Wilkie Cooper and Deborah Kerr, who mentioned that the star of the movie, who had been a favourite since silent days, and was still playing ingénues, was beginning to look a little less so off-screen. 'She's a sweet woman, but I'm afraid anno domini is soon going to become a problem.' Lurking, as usual, within earshot, I interjected indignantly: 'But she still plays young girls and looks marvellous. How could she do that if what you say is true?' Wilkie Cooper replied, with his quiet, slow-burn grin: 'Didn't you know they photograph her through the thick end of a beer bottle?'

Deborah's escort at several of these premières, the quiet young man who used occasionally to wait at the side of the set until the day's filming was through, and who Chris and I decided bore a distinct resemblance to William Holden in RAF blue, was identified for us towards the end of production on *I See a Dark Stranger*: the national press carried photographs of Squadron-Leader Anthony Bartley, DFC, above the headlines 'Deborah Kerr To Marry One Of "The Few"'. Twice decorated, he had shot down fifteen German planes and was 'one of the handful' of surviving Battle of Britain pilots honoured in Churchill's epoch-making tribute.

It transpired that while the film unit were in Ireland Bartley had sent a telegram: 'Have been posted to the South Pacific Stop Will you marry me.' The reply was: 'Yes Stop Where and When.'

Squadron-Leader Bartley waited, as unobtrusively as usual, for shooting at Denham Studios to finish on the evening of Friday, 27 November, 1945. There was nothing in his demeanour to suggest that the compassionate leave for which he had applied from the South Pacific had been delayed until only forty-eight hours before the date set for the wedding. Deborah had travelled to Sir Charles and Lady Bartley's home in Swanbourne to meet her prospective in-laws soon after Tony had made clear his serious intentions: he had hoped to be present to effect the introductions, but the RAF had matters of more immediate urgency to keep him occupied in the war zone. As time went by even his application for urgent compassionate leave seemed to be in jeopardy, but in the nick of time permission was granted. The entire film unit gave their blessings to the happy couple and Deborah Kerr withdrew to her dressing-room, with Mrs Orme in attendance, to remove the make-up and character of Bridie Quilty, Irish rebel, and avowed enemy of the British.

The next morning, at St George's, Hanover Square, her brother Ted gave her away, and she became Mrs Anthony Bartley, with top air ace Group-Captain 'Sailor' Malan as best man. Sir Charles and Lady Bartley mingled at the Claridge's reception with a number of Tony's other good friends, including another kingpin of the air, Peter Tollemache, scion of the famous brewery, Lord Beaverbrook and his son Max Aitken. Among the bride's family and friends were her mother, step-father to-be Tom Purvis, the artist (a distant cousin of Grannie Jane Trimmer's), and Aunt Jane and Uncle Harry. The press, well and truly represented, reported that it turned out to be 'an extremely convivial affair' and almost 'as much an RAF reunion as a wedding'.

An American friend of mine composed a telegram for me to send to Claridge's. He said it 'couldn't miss' and it ran: 'The time of your life today and a merry-go-round for ever after.' Deborah thanked me the next time we met and said: 'But what on earth did it mean?' Since that day I've always composed my own wedding greetings.

## III

By the time Squadron-Leader Bartley had been demobbed and taken a job with Vickers as test pilot and foreign representative, his wife had virtually completed furnishing 'Bassetts', the seventeenth-century house in Mayfield, near Tunbridge Wells, which she had bought early the previous year. Inspired by the

Davenports, she had combed the country for additions to her house.

'The weekends I spent with Nicholas and Olga were somehow like going home for the school holidays, with Mother so far away in Weston, though it was lovely when she could come and stay at Mayfield. By this time she had become very close to Tom Purvis, who did some paintings of me which the family still have, and whom she later married. Aunt Jane, so happily married to Harry Forster, and carrying on with her acting, astonished the family by producing her daughter, Harriet, when she was pushing forty-seven. I was filled with awe and admiration and asked Jane what the experience had been like. Her reply was just what I should have been prepared for: "Oh, well; mustn't make heavy weather of things"!'

Deborah was ready, willing and able to be godmother at cousin Harriet's christening in January 1945. Aunt Jane was another visitor at Mayfield, with the new addition to her family, as often as her own and Harry's busy activities in the Bristol area would allow.

The Bartleys also had a flat in town in Claridge House: with so much activity in both their lives it formed an indispensable second home during a working week, as well as an attractive clearing-house for the new acquisitions Deborah continued to collect in antique shops all over Britain in her search for perfection. The furniture van was a familiar feature outside the flat, swopping perfect Sheraton for doubtful Hepplewhite to be transported to Mayfield, but one discovery remained a fixture while they had tenancy of Claridge House—a divan bedhead made from a Louis Quinze mirror found in a little shop around the corner. Most of the original glass was broken, so it was replaced by striped upholstery to match the other soft furnishings in the flat: the silver-gilt cherubs remained intact.

The house in Mayfield was regarded as their real home, and was run by Eva, the housekeeper who had been with Deborah since she was first able to afford a real home of her own. Jason, the pedigree sealyham lived there with Eva during the week: the other permanent resident was the black cat, Peter Geekee, named after the cat in Tommy Handley's classic radio series *ITMA*. Peter became the family's unofficial air-raid warden when the dreaded V1s (buzz-bombs or doodlebugs) were in the vicinity. His cat antennae warned him of their imminence long before mere humans got the signal, and he would come tearing into the house, his tail as rigid as a submarine's periscope. Jason and Peter were the latest in a line of dogs and cats over whom Deborah has always been 'ridiculously sensitive and soft-hearted.' In 1942 she had a miniature sealyham called Dumpling, after the nickname 'Dumps' which Michael Powell had bestowed on her during her own 'puppy-fat' days. Dumpling died suddenly when very young and Deborah was inconsolable for weeks.

The first pet she could call her own was Simon, the white Fox Terrier, given to her at the beginning of the war by her mother and Tom Purvis. Simon stayed on with them in Weston when Deborah went to work in London: he became Colleen's inseparable companion, dividing his time between accompanying her everywhere and his daily runs in the park with the still extremely agile and athletic Grandfather 'Charlie' Smale, for whom golf had succeeded football as his main recreation.

Life for Deborah and Tony, in the early months of their marriage, was very much that of any well-to-do young couple with independent careers. Tony would usually leave for work in the morning a couple of hours after his wife's early call for the studios, then they would meet in the flat in the evenings, either for a snack at home, or to dine out at a quiet restaurant nearby. They visited nightclubs seldom—and never when she was working.

When the complications of the Pascal–Metro contract were nearing final solution and the question arose of Louis Mayer wanting his new star to make her career in Hollywood, Tony Bartley agreed that it was too good an offer to turn down. Before their marriage they had discussed all foreseeable eventualities, and she had told him that she would give up acting if that were his wish. Because she had been part of the profession since the age of sixteen she knew the extreme demands it could make, and they weighed the pros and cons very thoroughly. They had settled for keeping on with their jobs: films for her and testing and selling planes for him. However, Hollywood, as he said, was a challenge to her own self-respect, and, for her part, she was eager to go for the experience.

## IV

Deborah was well into her third film for Michael Powell by the time *I See a Dark Stranger* had its London première at the Odeon, Leicester Square in August 1946. Hedda Hopper, high priestess of Hollywood gossip columnists and not renowned for her charitable attitude towards any stars who incurred her displeasure, seemed to have formed a genuine liking for Deborah Kerr, and attended the occasion, spectacularly hatted, as was her wont. The notices were generally good, and the credit for making palatable such a potentially distasteful idea as a light-hearted romantic thriller based on an Irish girl's lethal hatred of the British in wartime went to the star, 'playing with such skill and charm that deeper criticism is disarmed . . . it seems that she is not only the most beautiful British actress but also the best.' Elspeth Grant pointed out that there were 'holes in the story you could drive a pantechnicon through', but that the heroine, 'with dark hair and a delicious brogue, gives an enchanting performance'.

Trevor Howard made a genuinely likeable character out of the conventional British officer hero, David Baynes was understandably perplexed at the antics of the girl he has fallen for, while Raymond Huntley's villain had just the right touch of the sinister to be completely convincing. The supporting cast, all excellent, included Liam Redmond, Olga Lindo, Brenda Bruce and Garry Marsh, in a neat cameo as an Intelligence Officer. *Picturegoer* commented disapprovingly: 'We are used to Americans making Englishmen look perfect fools, but even they could not have improved on the two Intelligence Officers looking for the Irish spy in the Isle of Man.'

Kerr's second Irish characterization, in *Black Narcissus*, from Rumer Godden's best-selling novel, could hardly have been a greater contrast: she was cast as Clodagh, the Sister Superior of an order of Anglo-Catholic nuns, based in an old palace in the Himalayas. Michael Powell says that arranging to get her signature for the starring rôle was no simple matter.

'Ben Goetz was asking an enormous amount of money for her. I was very fond of him; the epitome of the top Hollywood executive—kind, experienced, awful, and rather splendid. I understood them well—Ben and his wife "Goldie" Goetz: the money they wanted for Deborah's services was crippling, from our point of view, and I was struggling to get them to lower their price a little. I remember Ben saying, in a tone of great commiseration: "Is it budget trouble, Mickey?" as though I had a duodenal ulcer or a grumbling appendix.

'I said: "Yes, Ben, it is"—and I managed to get her a little bit cheaper. She had a bit of a struggle in that picture: I said to her from the very beginning: "You're too young." Emeric was keen that she should do the film; I said "It's a part for somebody like Garbo—if I could get her to return to the screen I would play her in the rôle." Deborah, Emeric and I had lunch at the Étoile; she had read the script and was determined she would play the part . . . so had most of the other young leading ladies in London, and they all wanted it. Two or three years previously, when the subject was first discussed the choice was Mary Morris, when she was still under contract to Korda. She had read the book, and was eager to do it. When the idea next came up and the war was over, it was Emeric or his wife who suggested it as a film to make, and very fascinating it was to do, especially as we never went to India and made it all over here, on the set at Pinewood, and on location in Surrey. The Himalayas were simulated all around that magnificent expanse of country between Hindhead and Guildford and no one would believe we'd never left England to do it.'

It was, in fact, an achievement on the part of Alfred Junge and his art department that has never been excelled in Great Britain. Powell's ambition ever since *Black Narcissus* has been to film again with Deborah Kerr. Despite his earlier misgivings about her youthfulness he thought she played with fine humility and conveyed complete spirituality. Of the rest of the cast he says: 'David Farrar was born to play Mr Dean, the local, rude, but fascinating English agent, who awakens in Sister Clodagh feelings she hoped she had put behind her. They were all well suited to their parts, and worked as a team, but perhaps Kathleen Byron was more prickly than most, because she was playing that sort of a part. She was quick, enormously intelligent and quite a scene-stealer. Whereas Flora Robson was suffering in her inimitable Robson way, and Judith Furse sweeping through like a great galleon and Jenny Laird like the sweet person that she was, the character played by Kathleen Byron was always in the middle of trouble and always up against the Sister Superior. Although Kathleen did very well and got some excellent notices, it was still Deborah's picture.'

## V

I was at Pinewood Studios, working on the Launder–Gilliat thriller *Green for Danger* at the time *Black Narcissus* was being made, and was able to watch as much of the filming as possible, whenever I could get away from Percy Hermes' watchful eye and ask Chris Noble to cover up for me. I still had the valid excuse that I was absent trying to get Trevor Howard on to the set: he was starring with Sally Gray, Alastair Sim and Rosamund John in *Green for Danger*, which Gilliat was directing.

My loyalties were as divided at Pinewood as they had been at Denham: apart from Sally Gray in our film there were Judy Campbell and Megs Jenkins, and on the next sound stage Greta Gynt was playing a temperamental opera singer under Ronald Neame's direction in *Take My Life*, opposite Hugh Williams. 'Chris, get that Peruvian cockroach off Miss Kerr's set, or out of Sally's dressing-room and tell him he's being paid to work for Individual Films, not to go star-gazing,' said an exasperated

Percy whenever I was absent for more than a quarter of an hour from the set.

*Black Narcissus* did, in fact, draw me like a magnet. Deborah Kerr in her creamy nun's habit had a grave, contemplative beauty that seemed to radiate from within. She had just one sequence out of 'uniform'—a flashback to Clodagh's native Ireland in which she had a brief and touching love scene with her boyhood sweetheart, played by the handsomest of the young contract players officially and, in many cases highly unsuitably, dubbed the Charm School. His name was Shaun Noble, he was Chris' elder brother and never had the opportunity to fulfil the early promise held out by his good looks and ability: his health was not good and he was one of several Charm School students whose contracts were not renewed. His rôle was small but pivotal; the unhappy conclusion of his affair with Clodagh is what causes her to dedicate her life to God. Another young actor who had a brief experience of playing small parts under the Rank regime was Roger Moore, who wrote: 'While waiting for admission into RADA I did several jobs in crowd scenes: the best entailed sitting opposite Deborah Kerr—whom I loved madly—in a studio railway coach for two days.' On the phone from location scenes on his latest James Bond movie he confirmed that the film in question was *Perfect Strangers*.

Michael Powell's ambition to film Guy de Maupassant's *Boule de Suif* with Deborah Kerr was eventually abandoned, although it was a project they both agreed to attempt to set up one day. He owns that it was, undoubtedly, the Metro star building system that made her an international name, even though she did initially have some pretty thankless parts to play.

'They carried out their plans for her, but never really realized her potentiality. In Hollywood they haven't got time for the quality I described to you, which I saw in that girl in the restaurant—this extraordinary imagination and way of almost changing her physical shape as she listens or imagines the different parts. They could have done wonderful things with her.'

By the time *Black Narcissus* opened at the Odeon, Leicester

101

Square, in April 1947, Deborah was in Hollywood, but she could hardly have left a more eloquent testimony to the use made of her talents in her own country. The story, in cold print, seems melodramatic in the extreme. It concerns five nuns who open a school and hospital in a remote Himalayan village, whose atmosphere they find disrupting their work. Sister Ruth (Kathleen Byron) goes mad from sexual frustration and tries to murder the Sister Superior (Kerr) who has also found herself dreaming of old lives and old loves when she should be praying in chapel; it is the rugged English agent (Farrar) who plays havoc with their serenity. Sister Philippa (Robson) plants flowers when she should plant vegetables, and one of the local girl pupils (Jean Simmons) seduces the young Indian prince (Sabu) who has enrolled at the school.

However, the film was so imaginatively made it drew a good deal of praise from the critics. Stephen Watts in the *Sunday Express* went so far as to call it 'One of the most beautiful films ever made. Miss Kerr is quite flawless.' The colour photography of Jack Cardiff was also voted the 'best ever', and the *Sunday Pictorial* accorded it an Award for the Best Film of the Month. C. A. Lejeune in *The Observer*, after praising the colour 'used with the vision of a painter,' wrote of Deborah Kerr's 'quietly magnificent authority, within the few square inches revealed by her coif', while Fred Majdalany in the *Daily Mail* said, 'She achieves spiritual beauty in performance as well as appearance. Her wimple seems to belong to her, where with some other cinematic nuns it has been merely a cute item of fancy dress.' Jean Simmons in her dusky make-up as the youthful seductress was praised, as were Esmond Knight and that fine old character May Hallatt as her ancient native Ayah.

The Trade Press announced, for the last time: 'J. Arthur Rank presents DEBORAH KERR (By arrangement with Metro Goldwyn Mayer)', then, still above the title, but in much smaller letters, 'Sabu, David Farrar, Flora Robson' and, under the title, in the smallest letters of all, 'with Esmond Knight, Jean Simmons, Kathleen Byron'—in the case of the latter, a strange positioning, in view of the importance of her rôle.

The New York critics gave Deborah Kerr their Award as the Actress of the Year for 1947, for *Black Narcissus*, jointly with *The Adventuress*, the title given to *I See a Dark Stranger* in the USA.

# PART II

# World Stardom

CHAPTER SEVEN

# THE FRIENDLY LION

I

The Bartleys sailed for New York aboard the *Queen Elizabeth*, arriving on their first wedding anniversary, 28 November, 1946. They remained four days in the capital before leaving for Hollywood. To Deborah everything seemed out of this world.

'I had thought the food aboard ship was really something, after our wartime fare in England, but it was nothing to the divine food in New York. I remember what a pig I made of myself the first day I was taken to lunch at "21": I just ate and ate—soft shell crabs for the first time in my life—we don't have them in England. It all tasted so jolly good, but best of all were the silly things like real butter and real white bread, which I hadn't tasted since before the war. We also had turkey, because it was around American Thanksgiving time. That seemed almost criminal to me: we were used to only having turkey at Christmas in England.'

The photograph of her arrival shows her in mink, looking only tentatively happy: she had just been interviewed in the ship's stateroom by hordes of reporters, press agents and film studio representatives, most of them calling her 'Miss Cur' and asking what she thought of America—not an easy question when so far she and Tony had not yet set foot on dry land. The lunch party at the 21 Club was laid on by Metro's publicity team, who were slightly shattered at the way the new arrival, whom they had been busy presenting to the press as a 'rare piece of fragile porcelain', ordered all the dishes in sight. In their hotel room that night her husband said, 'You certainly shook them at lunch, darling.'

'I don't care,' was the reply. 'I was hungry.' Thus sustained, the first real ordeal was her screen test for *The Hucksters*, Frederick Wakeman's hard-hitting best seller about radio, for which the studio had paid two hundred thousand dollars, budgeting the prospective film at two and a half million dollars after their most valuable property, Clark Gable, had agreed to play the lead, providing the more lecherous side of the hero's character was toned down. L. B. Mayer and his advisers thought that their new star from England would be ideal casting for the heroine, but producer Arthur Hornblow Jnr. hesitated over risking 'a new girl' to co-star with Gable. Her US contract also stipulated starring or co-star billing in all films. The screen test was their compromise. The Bartleys arrived at the Culver City studios shortly before midday and were ushered into the offices of Benny Thau, one of MGM's top executives, then one by one other members of the hierarchy filed in and were presented. Deborah says:

'It was like being anaesthetized. I was cross-eyed looking at everybody,' which included photographs on the walls of the legendary stars she had paid her pocket money to see during her formative years at home: Joan Crawford, Lana Turner, Greer Garson, Myrna Loy. 'Those superhumanly beautiful faces,' she said later. 'By contrast I was just a strapping wench with a good workaday face.'

Her first meeting with Gable was not at all what she had imagined. He held out his hand and strode towards her, saying: 'You old son-of-a-gun. What are you doing here?' He then walked past her and shook her husband's hand: it transpired that Gable and Bartley had been friends when Tony was lecturing to American airmen during the war. The big moment came when they were ushered into the presence of Louis B. Mayer and introduced formally with the explanation: 'Miss Deborah Kerr—it rhymes with car.' L.B. knew a good publicity slogan when he thought of one: his reply 'it rhymes with star' was quickly noted for future reference.

After lunch, during which Mayer showed considerable interest in Tony Bartley's war record, they were taken down from the fourth floor executive dining-room to the publicity office and introduced to Malvina Pumphrey, Deborah's immediate contact with press and public. She told them: 'We want you to think of yourselves as part of our team. The important gossip columnists to remember are Louella Parsons and Hedda Hopper. Sheilah Graham is also important.' Malvina Pumphrey also made it clear that she would be present at all interviews, and it took some time for the studio to catch on to the idea that the Bartleys were reasonably intelligent people who could be trusted to comport themselves without undue indiscretions.

The test was set for a week ahead: coutourière Irene discussed the prospective wardrobe and Jack Dawn, Metro's ace make-up man, experimented on the Kerr features. When he and producer Hornblow studied the hairdressing tests they decided that simplicity was the keynote and that she was admirably equipped to face the cameras with the minimum of embellishment. Gable made the test with her—a sequence which called for him to make a pass which she firmly but kindly rebuffs. After the producer had cut the test and declared it first-rate, the rest of the studio were allowed to see it, and the columnists duly notified according to protocol. Louella Parsons informed her public that the viewers 'all but cheered'.

When shooting started on *The Hucksters* Gable sent six dozen red roses to her dressing-room with a note 'Good luck on your opening night from your leading man Clark Gable'. Her husband also presented flowers, and the first scene, with director Jack Conway in charge, and Hal Rosson (who had been Jean Harlow's favourite cameraman, and, briefly, her husband) in control of the lighting, went without a hitch.

## II

Everything possible was laid on to make the newcomers feel at home: screenwriter Casey Robinson's Pacific Palisades ranch house, set in the middle of an orange grove, was provided for their temporary quarters. Mayer's daughter, Edith, married to Ben Goetz's younger brother William, befriended them and did everything she could to smooth their first months in this strange but exciting country. In fact they adapted happily to the novel surroundings, and far from missing the things for which the Americans expected them to pine, like London fog, they loved the hot, dry sunshine, with oranges growing outside their windows, so close they could indulge in the supreme luxury of leaning out to pick one whenever they had a mind to.

Like most expatriates in those immediately post-war days they thought it 'great fun to eat in drive-ins. We consumed enough hamburgers and hot-dogs in the first few weeks to last us a lifetime. Restaurants seemed very tame and staid, compared to the wonderful informality of eating a hot-dog in your own car.

'Edith was a great friend then, and has remained so ever since. She was a great "fixer": "You don't have a dentist—right, I'll get you one. No doctor? I'll fix it." She introduced us to Dr Krohn, who has become an indispensable part of my life. He brought both of my daughters into the world. The whole of life was so different that this kind of practical help from Edith and from the studio was a great comfort. Their motto was: "If you have a problem, call us." Anything you wanted, from a car to a house, was immediately organized, following Mr Mayer's dictum: "A happy star is a successful star."

'It was like moving into a giant close-up of the dream factory. One house we looked at was dominated by a gorgeous painting of Tamara Toumanova, one of my favourite ballerinas, painted by Theyre Lee Elliott, whose work I had always admired enormously. Of course, it turned out to be Toumanova's house, and was the one we decided, there and then, to rent.

'Size was what impressed us about everything: we were like a couple of Gullivers in Brobdingnag. Everything was on such a vast scale, and the studios so enormous. After endless rounds of introductions to people in key positions, it took me weeks to see one face I recognized. At first it was somewhat scary—

110

those huge make-up departments, with hundreds of rooms—such a contrast to the scale of everything at home, but then everyone was so friendly, and put themselves out on such a grand scale to put one at one's ease, that in the end they all became my dear friends.'

Socially, too, there were surprises. A neighbour was David Niven, an old acquaintance of Tony's and later one of Deborah's most regular co-stars. He has written of taking the Bartleys to their first Hollywood party. They made the Britishers' gaffe of arriving on time, which, in Hollywood was equivalent to 'early', at one of producer Nunnally Johnson's no-holds-barred receptions to celebrate the completion of a new film.

'We found lying outside his front door half-a-dozen sour-faced, topless blondes, with everything below their hip bones squeezed into shiny green fish tails. "We're waiting to be carried in and propped up at the bar," they told us. Nunnally was launching his picture *Mr Peabody And The Mermaid*.'

## III

Deborah has considerable respect for the serious side of the world's film capital. She says:

'Right after the war it became fashionable to knock Hollywood, but I could never find it in my heart to do that. They made me, to a certain extent: I was in there at the end of the big studio star-building publicity machine. Let's face it, I was on the front cover of every magazine from Tokyo to the Fiji Islands.' *Time* magazine covered every aspect of the start of filming of *The Hucksters* as it concerned the new star from Britain, with a cover portrait by Boris Chaliapin, which was interesting rather than flattering, making her look, frankly, exhausted, and from then on (February 1947) she received systematic coverage which made her a world name.

'It was certainly tiring, because one was constantly being

111

photographed against different backgrounds for each rival publication: different photos, poses, dresses—a green background for this one, a red for that—an incredible business, and I did everything I was told. How could I complain? It was to my advantage as much as the studio's. They don't do that kind of thing any more: if you make it, it's by luck, or by being in a great big hit, and then if that's followed up it's luck again.'

As far as luck was concerned her own had held out from the moment of signing her first contract with Gabriel Pascal. Although the British studios' publicity methods made them babes in arms compared with the American exploitation machine, Deborah Kerr's name had been systematically built and kept before the public, so that by the time her first MGM film was released the movie-going world was familiar with her face, her opinions and her personality to a degree that guaranteed sufficient interest to keep people going to see her films, even when the finished product did not always live up to the pre-publicity.

In *The Hucksters* she appeared for the first time with an actress, who played Gable's ex-girlfriend, and as such did not have many scenes with Metro's new star, but all the same, Deborah was deeply impressed by her beauty and potential. In a letter to Michael Powell, Deborah wrote: 'This will make you laugh, but we have in the film a girl who's capable of being as great a "menace" as "Sister Ruth" in *Black Narcissus*. Her name is Ava Gardner.' Like Kathleen Byron Ava may have had comparatively small billing, but she saw to it that she was going to get her share of the notices. In fact, Deborah Kerr later referred to the character she herself played as being 'about as exciting as an oyster'.

*The Hucksters*, built around American commercial broadcasting, proved more popular in the States than on its arrival at the Empire, Leicester Square, in July 1947, where the record-breaking Anna Neagle–Michael Wilding family saga *The Courtneys of Curzon Street*, which had moved next door to Metro's much smaller sister cinema, the Ritz, was more to the liking of the general British public. The advertising slogan was 'Gable's New Star is Deborah Kerr' and the film did well enough for queues to form outside the cinema, despite the hot summer weather. With a cast including Gardner, Adolphe Menjou, Sydney Greenstreet and Gable as Victor Albee Norman, a go-getting advertising man whose mission is to persuade a society beauty to endorse a certain brand of soap, the film was entertaining without being outstanding. Jack Conway's slick direction was a considerable asset, and Kerr's rôle as Kay Dorrance, the society widow in question, did nothing to tax her acting abilities. F. Maurice Speed wrote in *What's On In London*: 'Miss Kerr is as lovely as ever and acts just as much as she is called upon to do.'

Olivia Lester of Craven Park, in a letter to *Picturegoer*, was less complimentary: 'Can this be the radiant beauty who became a nun, or the recurrent charmer of *Colonel Blimp*? Not only is she badly photographed, but Deborah is written up dumb; she has to be slow on the uptake, fumbling in behaviour, falling into mush on surrender.'

Working with Gable proved a happy experience for his co-star, who says: 'He did everything possible to put me at my ease, and was a man utterly without regard for himself as a film technician, or for his status in movies.'

IV

'The name Hollywood is, to this day, a misnomer—one very small section of an enormous area where many people work in the movie business, but hardly any people who worked in that business actually lived in Hollywood, as such. It is, and always has been, an area in which you can lead any kind of life you like: if you want to be with the English group, you can be with them; if it's the Bohemians you prefer, you can join them—or the cultural group, of any of a number of diverse life-styles. It was natural when we first went out there that I rather clung to Douglas and Mary Lee Fairbanks as representing some sort of section of society that I understood. Mary Lee and

I became very close friends, and when we bought our own house, it was the Fairbankses, and a small circle of film friends we used to entertain. Never big parties—we never cared for that scene, but occasional meals with the David Nivens, the Bill Holdens, Evie and Van Johnson, and Dinah Shore and her then husband, George Montgomery.

'The house at 15040 Corona del Mar, Pacific Palisades, was Riviera-style and very comfortable, built on a cliff, about three hundred feet above the sea. It had a nice garden—something that has always been very important to me, and we planted masses of the kind of flowers we were used to having around us at home. There were trees all round us, and giant honeysuckle climbing all over the front porch; the living-room opened on to a terrace beside a lawn which stretched right to the cliff's edge, overhanging the Pacific.

'Although it looked very Californian from the outside, inside it was English. We felt settled at last, with somewhere comfortable to relax in, among things we knew and cared for. There was a swimming pool, which came with the furnishings in Hollywood, and the shed near it contained plaques representing the various air squadrons with which my husband had fought when he was in the RAF. Things personal to me in my career—books autographed by their authors and bound scripts of plays and movies in which I'd appeared—were kept in the library.'

A book published the year of her birth formed the subject of Deborah's second picture for Metro—*If Winter Comes* by A. S. M. Hutchinson. Already filmed as a silent, the remake was first proposed as a vehicle for Robert Donat and Greer Garson, under the Korda–Metro tie-up at Denham. It was to have been made in England, and when Donat proved unavailable for the lead, Walter Pidgeon was announced as his replacement. It was then decided that the subject, updated from the First World War to the Second, would co-star Deborah Kerr, under the direction of England's Victor Saville, with an almost all-British cast.

The story presented Kerr as Nona Tybar, first love of Mark Sabre (Pidgeon), who returns with her husband Tony (Hugh

114

French) to the English village where Mark, a writer, lives with his shrewish wife Mabel (Angela Lansbury). She leaves him when she learns that Effie (Janet Leigh), a village girl whom he had befriended, is pregnant. Effie commits suicide after Mabel has cited her as co-respondent. Mark is pilloried, but eventually finds a letter naming the father as Freddie Park (none other than Hughie Green in his acting days, long before *Opportunity Knocks* was to make him a top TV celebrity in Britain). As Freddie has given his life for his country in the RAF, Nona and Mark decide to burn the letter and face life together. To do everyone justice they all acted as though they believed every word of this fustian, and Dame May Whitty gave her usual kindly twinkling performance as Freddie's invalid mother, whose feelings the lovers spare by burning the incriminating letter. The plum parts—if that is the apposite term—went to Pidgeon, Lansbury as his cold and bitchy wife, and Janet Leigh in one of her first film rôles as the unfortunate Effie. The part of Nona Tybar called for noble suffering from the sidelines, and Deborah Kerr did this beautifully. Neither she nor her co-star were exactly agog to do the film, but as she says:

'If you're paid an enormous sum of money every week under a seven-year contract, you do as you're told—that's the way I was brought up. I have suffered all my life from too much respect for the boss—for authority, just because it is authority. I took it for granted that the heads of studios, with all their experience, knew instinctively what was best for me. It took me six years to find out that perhaps they didn't know, but, in the meantime, there was a marvellous offer just around the corner— my best break, acting-wise, to date—to co-star with Spencer Tracy in the film version of the London hit play *Edward, My Son* to be directed by the great George Cukor.'

There was a slight snag, in the fact that there had to be a delay, due to her having carried on filming until her fifth month of pregnancy, a circumstance that prompted a rash of the usual columnists' stories pondering over the temerity of her 'choosing' her year of build-up to first rank box office fame. Deborah's impending motherhood also drew forth Esther Williams' celebrated remark about how much more satisfactorily she managed such matters.

*If Winter Comes* was finished in late summer of 1947: Melanie Jane was born on 27 December in the Cedars of Lebanon Hospital, Los Angeles, and the release of the Victor Saville film delayed until summer of the following year, the time when Paramount decided, finally, to put out *Hatter's Castle* in the US, cashing in on the American public's increased conversance with the names of Kerr, Mason, Newton and Emlyn Williams.

## V

The year 1948 was a good year for Deborah, beginning with Melanie Jane plump and contented—she grew out of her 'little porker' stage all too fast, says her mother—with loving care all around her and a beautiful home on the sunny slopes of Pacific Palisades. In this ideal setting they all thrived, with the added benefit of unlimited supplies of the meat, butter, milk, fruit and fresh green things still in short supply in England.

*Picturegoer*'s W. H. Mooring, who lunched with her in the studio restaurant, reported that 'Deborah Kerr looks younger and much better in health than she did when she first came to California'. She was, in fact, testing for the rôle of *Young Bess*, a proposed film version of the novel by Margaret Irwin, and could, said Mooring, have easily passed for eighteen. The New York critics' award for her work in her last two British films had delighted the studio heads, to the extent of their being prepared to wait for her to be ready to film with Tracy in England, and, in the foreseeable future, dangling before her the intriguing possibility of playing Elizabeth I of England in her days as a young and romantic girl. The casting was not by any means set—Elizabeth Taylor was another name being considered—but Deborah Kerr was one of the very few stars prepared to reveal to the press that she was actually *testing* for a part.

Mooring, at that time one of the most important links

116

between Hollywood and the British film magazines, explained that most 'names' would be careful to conceal the fact that they were testing because 'they fear that if it is announced and then later it is learned that the rôle was given to someone else, their reputations may be brought into unfavourable comparison with others'. This judgment contained unconscious irony, in view of subsequent developments in the Kerr career. It is certain that at this time Metro were full of good intentions about choosing the best parts for their new star: two previously announced vehicles, one with Gable, to be called *Day Before Yesterday*, the other a film of Rosita Forbes' book *The Running of the Tide*, about witch hunts in Salem, were abandoned, and the Bartleys, sped on their way at a press tea party held by their good friend Malvina Pumphrey, arrived in London in June with Spencer Tracy and George Cukor to start work on *Edward, My Son*.

Before leaving Hollywood they attended one of Louis Mayer's parties, and Deborah met Ann Todd again for the first time since *Perfect Strangers*. Todd, in the USA to film *The Paradine Case* for Hitchcock, has remained an avid Kerr admirer from the time of *Heartbreak House*, in which she described her performance as 'superb'.

Ann says: 'To me she is a full, completely rounded person with such warmth, an extraordinary quality of spirituality and a deep understanding of people.' The latter quality must have come in handy at the Mayer party. Ann Todd describes it as 'one of those elaborate affairs where everything in the house had been changed especially for the occasion: they had mimosa flown in from the South of France, all laced on to trellis-work around the dining-room—special white covers on the chairs, and so on, and when Deborah and I went up to the cloakroom together, which was, in fact, our hostess's bedroom, we were both still raw enough in Hollywood to be simply gaping at the number of famous faces we had seen up there on the screen. At least, maybe it was I who did most of the staring—Deborah had arrived in Hollywood a little while before me—when somebody extremely well-known came up, rolled up her sleeve, produced what looked like an enormous lipstick all covered in jewels, and gave herself an injection. I naïvely said "What's *that*?" and the lady answered: "Well, you don't think we can keep going all evening on those martinis our hostess keeps sending round!" Deborah and I were *speechless*.'

# VI

*Edward, My Son* had been one of the biggest stage hits of the West End stage the previous year. Robert Morley and Noel Langley were the authors, and Donald Ogden Stewart adapted the screenplay. Deborah Kerr as Evelyn, wife of wealthy businessman Edward Boult, followed Peggy Ashcroft, who had created the part in the theatre, while Spencer Tracy succeeded the play's part-author, Morley, in the rôle of Boult, who stops at nothing to give his son Edward, unseen in both stage and screen versions, a life of luxury and ease. Boult's ruthlessness spares neither his friend and former partner Dr Larry Woodholt (Ian Hunter), who loves Evelyn, nor Boult's former mistress Eileen Perrin (Leueen MacGrath, brilliantly repeating her stage rôle), and eventually drives his wife to an alcoholic's death. Mervyn Johns, father of Glynis, was particularly fine as a pathetic ex-convict, Harry Simpkin, driven to suicide, and others in a distinguished cast included James Donald, Felix Aylmer and Walter Fitzgerald.

Evelyn, Lady Boult, was a part with which Kerr was able to extend her talents, and her delineation of the character, from happy youthful marriage to disillusionment and alcohol addiction, due to her husband's callous neglect, was entirely convincing and moving. Acting with Tracy remains a highlight of her film career: she was delighted to play opposite one of her most admired actors, who, although not entirely suited to a rôle tailor-made for Morley, gave a powerful and straightforward interpretation of the character as he saw it. 'If he sometimes appeared grumpy,' says his co-star, 'it was because he was not altogether happy about himself as Boult. Fortunately we had a wonderful director in George Cukor, who knows more about directing human beings than almost anyone else I've worked with. It was such a good movie, and though Tracy didn't want to do it he was darned good in it. But they just didn't get round to promoting it properly: it wasn't in the genre of films they were used to, and they really didn't know what to do with it.'

The critics were almost unanimous in their praise of film, direction and actors. Britain's *Picturegoer*, restrained and fair as usual in their assessment, said: 'Spencer Tracy is at his best ...Deborah Kerr equally good...the direction brings out in full the poignancy of character.' Across the Atlantic Douglas McClelland wrote: 'Deborah Kerr is gifted with a magnificently mobile face and her hands are the most expressive of any film actress ... extraordinarily eloquent in her closing scene when, as the embittered, aged and drunken mother of the worthless deceased Edward, she conveys the pathetic despair and degradation of this once fine woman ... not only with voice, posture, make-up and clothes, but with relentlessly nervous hands that claw at her raw person with the devastation of a tiger.'

Louella Parsons, as enthusiastic a film critic as a gossip columnist, when the mood took her, said: 'That "Lady Boult" portrayal has to get a special paragraph all to itself, because, as etched with bitter realism by Deborah Kerr, it approaches close to art. What a devastating expression of a woman's degeneration she gives: despite her youth and beauty Deborah is a true character actress; her pitiable "Lady Boult" starts with refinement and delicacy, and then, before our eyes, sinks into a drunken harridan, whose voice, face and very looks exude the sour fumes of stale alcohol.' Parsons went on to say how ironic it was that after this superlative performance Deborah had returned to Hollywood to play another cardboard glamour girl in another run-of-the-mill comedy.

By the time *Edward, My Son* was generally released in Britain in April 1949, with a re-issue of Fred Astaire and Judy Garland in *Easter Parade* as second feature, bearing out Deborah's contention that Metro were not at all sure how to handle their unconventional play-into-film property, she herself was back in Hollywood filming *Please Believe Me*, whose main point of interest was that Val Lewton was the producer. Known for his low-budget horror movies, of which *Cat People* is perhaps the best remembered, this late incursion into light comedy proved to be Lewton's last film. Norman Taurog was the director, Deborah Kerr was top-billed, and her attractive trio of leading men were the late Robert Walker, Mark Stevens and Peter Lawford. Her auburn hair, mostly covered by a succession of wigs in *Edward, My Son*, was trimmed to shoulder length for her rôle as a much courted heiress, Alison Kirbe, an English girl who inherits a ranch in America, and becomes involved with a charming, ingenuous youth (Walker), who turns out to be a con-man after her money. A millionaire playboy (Lawford) also reveals himself as worthless, and his taciturn lawyer (Stevens) is the one she eventually marries.

Of this likeable but mediocre comedy she remembers most vividly the genuine appeal and charm of Robert Walker, whose tragically early death two years later robbed the cinema of one of its most attractive light comedy actors. *Picturegoer*, as usual, had the film in perspective: 'Comedy, full of promise, which never succeeds in being more than pleasant, lightly entertaining nonsense. Deborah Kerr gives a more than competent portrayal', which was slightly less than adequate compensation for the Oscar she failed to win for *Edward, My Son*, for which she nevertheless received her first of several nominations for her subtle and delicate portrayal of Evelyn Boult.

Her mother's assessment of the Lady Boult performance was gently disapproving. 'I'm sure it's very good acting, dear,' she wrote, 'but I just don't like to see you like that.'

120

# CHAPTER EIGHT

# 'JOIN METRO AND SEE THE WORLD'

## I

The lack of a suitable promotion policy for *Edward, My Son* was partly due to the internal changes taking place at MGM. Mayer found his ideas clashing with those of his production chief, Dore Schary, and matters came to a head when Mayer referred a dispute between himself and Schary to the studio's president, Nicholas Schenck. Astonishingly the president sided with Schary, and the reign of Louis B. Mayer was over: Dore Schary replaced him as Head of Production in 1951. He had previously served in that capacity at RKO. Less awe-inspiring and far more approachable than the great 'L.B.', Schary was, nevertheless, a man of instant decisions and considerable power.

'And that,' says Deborah, 'is how I got myself to Africa for *King Solomon's Mines*. I was asked to dinner with Dore Schary one evening and said "I know the most marvellous book that I'd like to do—C. S. Forester's *The African Queen*. The part is that of Rose, a high-minded missionary jaunting through Africa with the disreputable captain of a broken-down river boat, and I wouldn't mind going to Africa at all—it's such a marvellous part." Schary said: "Oh yes, it's a *very* good story, but I have a feeling that Warner Brothers own it, and, if you want to make a picture in Africa *we* happen to have a property that would be ideal for you." I had won a battle over a part only recently, when Mayer was still in charge and wanted me to play a sixty-year-old nun in *The Red Danube*. My Scottish blood was up and I firmly declined the rôle, which eventually went to Ethel

Barrymore! There was no gainsaying Dore's suggestion, though: I'd walked straight into it with both feet, and the next thing I knew I was on location twenty-five thousand miles into darkest Africa, in what was then called Meru in Kenya.

'As a trip, at the film company's expense, it was an unforgettable experience. My first glimpse of our camp was one of the most thrilling and exciting sights I've ever seen. We drove in at dusk: there was a huge bonfire, surrounded by rows and rows of tents. Dimly in the background we could still see the mountains, fantastically coloured by the lights of the fire. To one side of the camp were the natives, each with his smaller fire, chanting in exciting rhythm, and strolling around, gun in hand, were the white hunters—to protect us from the wild animals.'

There was need for protection from other quarters, too. In one scene five hundred Masai danced, chanted and yelled for two days, the tempo rising all the time: the natives were making the most of their ancient ceremonial dance, banned under the laws of the day, simply because once they did get wound up there was no stopping them. The dance had been allowed on this occasion, for the benefit of the film unit, and the result was bedlam. Some of the natives went berserk, falling on the ground in fits and throwing their spears around the cameras: their better controlled companions had to calm them, by sitting on their heads. This was where Deborah's early training with the Sadler's Wells ballet came in handy.

'When the spears started to fly I leapt into the air, caught the branches of a nearby tree and scrambled up—there was no time to worry about dignity.' When she—and the technicians—came down from the tree, they removed seven spears from the camera casing. There were other incidents, less dangerous, but no less embarrassing, including one at a film show at the camp. The film was *Perfect Strangers*, and her native porter walked out in the middle. An interpreter explained that he had said: 'Can't be: she up there, she here? Can't be.'

*King Solomon's Mines* was not the most comfortable location. For five months, including the celebration of Christmas 1949 at Luanda in the Belgian Congo, the unit of twenty-four people worked in temperatures ranging from below zero to sweltering heat. This was the same territory to which the *Trader Horn* unit had trekked twenty years previously and where the heroine, Edwina Booth, contracted a rare tropical disease which was eventually to cost her her life.

Deborah Kerr, top-billed, co-starred with Stewart Granger—their first teaming since *Gaslight*. The character of Mrs Curtis, who persuades explorer Alan Quatermain to take her along to search for her lost husband in his quest for the fabulous Mines, was in to provide a love interest in a script that was more Helen Deutsch than H. Rider Haggard, but which proved a big winner at the world's box-offices. Richard Carlson played the heroine's brother: Compton Bennett co-directed with Andrew Marton, and the remarkable Technicolor camerawork, which won him an Oscar, was under the control of Robert Surtees, who remarked of Deborah Kerr 'she acts with her eyes more than anyone else I've worked with'.

Though several critics mocked Deborah's coiffure in a part which called for her 'to sit combing her tresses, variously blonde and deep ginger, in the jungle night' she did put up a fight to attain some degree of realism both in her performance of a rôle that was often supernumerary and unsympathetic, and in her appearance. She held out against the immaculately waved and groomed locks called for in the scene immediately following one in which she had washed her hair. 'This woman, eight thousand miles from civilization couldn't *possibly* keep her hair permanently waved after cutting and washing it herself,' she protested to the director, but he was adamant. 'You can't go through the rest of the picture with *straight* hair,' was the reply. After abortive attempts to reach producer Sam Zimbalist at unit headquarters in Nairobi and Dore Schary by phone nearly thirteen thousand miles away in Hollywood, she capitulated.

Lesley Clay, at that time a journalist in Kenya, found her 'a charming and delightful person, very easy to interview and obviously devoted to her husband and small daughter Melanie'. Miss Clay was friendly with Michaela Denis, who did some doubling for the star in long shots of the characters wading through swamps swarming with flamingos and other tropical life: Armand and Michaela Denis knew the terrain so well they were able to be of considerable practical assistance technically.

During the Bartleys' first four years in America, Tony was unable to do any gainful work, although by the summer of 1948 he had completed a script on the life of Barnato, the British diamond millionaire, which he wanted to turn into a film. Under American law, however, he was forbidden to work in their adoptive country, having been born in India, and technically in the USA on a visitor's visa. The situation became intolerable for him, and Deborah put pressure to bear on MGM executives to do something about her husband's immigration status. After prolonged negotiations, a private bill was introduced in Congress 'for the relief of Anthony Charles Bartley, in recognition of one of our greatest Allies' greatest heroes', and he was able to put into execution his plans to work in television. Subsequently he achieved considerable success in that field, both in writing and in production, including a series about the French Foreign Legion, *El Tigre*, with Douglas Fairbanks Jnr. There was even talk, which eventually came to nothing, of Tony Bartley producing a film to star his wife with Mel Ferrer, called *South Africa* and to be directed by Carol Reed, but Deborah Kerr was going from film to film so rapidly that it is not altogether surprising that it did not materialize.

## II

In the meantime the 'Join MGM and see the world' sequence continued, with the seven million dollar budgeted *Quo Vadis?* Filmed in Rome's huge Cinecitta Studios in only six months it was a considerable feat by director Mervyn LeRoy, in view of the cast of two hundred and thirty-five actors, plus thirty thousand extras, and the resultant world rentals of twenty-five million dollars, the highest since *Gone with the Wind*. The company had made a start on the subject, also in Rome, in 1949, with John Huston directing Gregory Peck and Elizabeth Taylor, but the project had been abandoned. Sam Zimbalist produced this fourth film version of Henryk Sienkiewicz's novel, for which the script was adapted by John Lee Mahin, S. N. Behrman and Sonya Levien. The adjective 'colossal' was incorporated into the billing, and the filming, although nothing like Africa, had its own discomforts and dangers, particularly as it took place during one of the hottest summers that even the Italians could remember, that of 1950.

Deciding against following the action of the original book where Lygia, the Christian slave girl, is tied to the back of a wild steer let loose in the arena, director LeRoy and his script-writers had her roped to a stake and charged at by a wild bull, to be saved in the nick of time by the prowess of athlete Buddy Baer as Ursus, the gentle-hearted giant. For this trick Baer had been training for months with Portuguese matadors to learn the 'furcado'—the art of taking the bull by the horns, and staying alive. Seven bulls were imported from Portugal, for it was found that none of these animals would play the same way twice: during rehearsals a few people were tossed, and one of the bulls actually had to be shot by a policeman, standing by with a tommy-gun in case of emergencies.

'When I was tied to the stake for the crucial sequence I must confess that I was nervous,' says Deborah. 'I knew, of course, that every possible precaution would be taken, and that Buddy Baer would forestall the bull by catching him by the horns and seeming to break his neck. But, even so...'

In the meantime, Melanie Jane, now nearly two and a half, made friends off the set with some Italian children, not only joining enthusiastically in their games, but learning a few words of Italian. Out of an imposing cast the spectacular opportunities went, naturally, to Peter Ustinov's Nero. During the filming he confessed that his elaborately arranged curls and heavy make-up caused him to feel 'like a terrier raised by an old lady for a dog show'. His richly barnstorming performance won praise from most of the critics; Patricia Laffan, who had played a small part in *I See a Dark Stranger*, also pulled out the stops as the

125

Empress Poppaea, suggesting a combination of her own British sci-fi film *Devil Girl from Mars* and Gloria Swanson involved in the Roman excesses of *Nero's Night Out* (*Nero's Mistress* in America).

Leo Genn's noble Petronius and Italy's Marina Berti, as Eunice the slave girl who shares a tragic love affair with him, were genuinely moving, while Nora Swinburne had her first taste of playing Deborah Kerr's mother, as Pomponia, with the imposing Felix Aylmer as her husband, Plautius. Other familiar British faces in ancient Rome were Adrienne Corri as the young girl Lygia befriends in the Esquiline dungeons, Finlay Currie and Abraham Sofaer as Saints Peter and Paul, and Elspeth March, the former Mrs Stewart Granger, as Miriam. Among the extras you just might spot the teenage Sophia Loren, as a Christian risking her life by praying in the catacombs.

If Robert Taylor's sincerity as Marcus Vinicius, the pagan Roman aristocrat who eventually leads the revolt against Nero, suggested the American campus rather than Rome in its glory his classical good looks helped to overcome this disadvantage. Kerr's performance as Lygia strikingly shows her ability to portray spirituality, contrasted with the outer convention of Hollywood-style beauty, here typified by a make-up as vivid, if less extreme, than Laffan's as Poppaea. Lygia's costumes were particularly inappropriate, in particular a gold dress, lovingly designed by Herschel from a special fabric 'after years of experimentation' and soaked in 14-carat gold to gain unusual effect. Here was Hollywood inventiveness at its most out of place on the unworldly Christian heroine—the conventional glamour girl stamp which director Jack Clayton was to describe as 'ridiculously unsuitable' when imposed on Deborah Kerr. She had the unique combination of beauty and spiritual repose necessary to interpret the saintly early Christian, but at this period in her career had to fight against costuming and make-up and rely on her inner resources to achieve conviction in the rôle. The two sides of the coin were never more strikingly at variance than in her portrayal of Lygia : only her instinctive truth in characterization enabled her to overcome the initial disadvantages of presentation. This is not to denigrate the Technicolor camerawork of Robert Surtees, who achieved some stunningly beautiful shots of Kerr in the two films they made together: it was the fault of neither that the image in the camera was inappropriate to the occasion—the culprit was the Hollywood system, of which both star and cameraman were highly valuable components.


## III


Sad news from home reached Deborah during her extensive travels abroad. Grandfather Smale died on 16 October, 1949, at the age of eighty-seven, at 'Longfords', Weston-super-Mare, which had been home for so long to his daughter, Colleen, now Mrs Tom Purvis. Grandfather was active to the last: in his youth his passion for cricket had taken him into the grand league, and when playing for Lydney he had even found himself batting and bowling against the great Dr W. G. Grace at Thornbury. Ted Trimmer, who naturally saw more of his grandfather in later years than his sister did, was especially fond of the old man, and says:

'One could go on for ever about Charlie, and his incredible old sister, Great-Aunt Polly, who used to put her hat and fur tippet on to look out and see if it was raining. But I must relate two favourite anecdotes about him, one in his youth, and the other towards the end of his life. He once told me he became active in the Temperance movement when he was a young man and was invited to play cricket for Lord Bledisloe's team at Bathurst Park. After the match he was persuaded to have some drinks and finished up very tight in the presence of His Lordship. So ashamed was Charlie that he never touched another drop. My mother used to tell how he bought a new pony for the trap, not knowing that the owner had been one of the biggest drunks in the Forest of Dean. Imagine what Grandma Smale said, and picture Grandfather's scarlet-faced confusion

127

when, on their first drive behind the new pony, the animal insisted on turning into the yard of every pub along the road!
In Charlie's last couple of years he lost his sense of taste, and
my mother and stepfather used to slip a drop of Scotch into
his bread and milk. The old man used to smack his lips and
grin—but he never said a word.

'The other story was about one night in 1942. Deb was away
in London: in Weston the sirens went and we all got up. Mother
was holding court in the kitchen: she used to make pints of
strong tea and dripping toast for anyone likely to call. At the
same time she would smoke, talk and knit. My stepfather Tom
Purvis, his son Roger, who was my best friend, were there, and,
I think, the local ARP Warden. We never bothered to wake
Grandfather because he slept in a downstairs room anyway, and,
by now very deaf in one ear, slept on his good ear. All of a
sudden there was a very loud bang. The house lurched, some
flakes of plaster fluttered down into the dripping toast and tea,
and we all ducked. It was just the odd bomb being jettisoned
on the way to or from Bristol, but it was very close and loud.
As we picked ourselves up the kitchen door burst open. There
was Charlie in his blue and white striped pyjamas; white hair
standing on end, no teeth, no spectacles. "Kathleen," he said
to Mother. "There's someone at the door!"'

Deborah was in Africa when she learned about his death.
Only six months later, the tragic news reached her of her
mother's death in a car crash on 18 April, 1950. Mr and Mrs
Purvis were setting out in their Aston Martin on the twenty-
mile journey to visit her younger sister, Phyllis Jane, in Bristol.
It was raining, and on the way out of the town, on the main
Weston to Bristol road their car skidded sideways into the front
of an articulated lorry, which crushed half the car, in which
were Colleen and Deborah's little terrier, Simon, who always
sat on Mrs Purvis' lap. It happened near the local PDSA: Colleen was killed instantly, and Simon, thrown high into the air
by the impact of the blow, broke his spine. He was put to sleep
instantly by a veterinary surgeon. Deborah's stepfather escaped
with minor injuries.

# IV

Francesca Ann was born in Los Angeles on 18 December, 1951, and was as bonnie a baby as her sister had been. Mary Lee Fairbanks had been godmother to Melanie Jane; Mrs Ronald Colman (Benita Hume) did the honours for Francesca. Her mother's next trek—East this time—took her no farther than Paramount's backlot, on loan for *Rage of the Vulture*. Among her best friends were director Charles Vidor and his wife, Doris, who asked her to dinner one day. Deborah was interested when Vidor said he would love to do a film with her, and he had this subject, adapted by Jo Swerling from Alan Moorehead's novel, for which he was going to try to borrow her services from Metro. The part of a blind girl, Joan Willoughby, was something of an acting challenge: Deborah says, 'It's not really all that easy to convince people you're blind. I know the movie did not turn out to be any great shakes, but I enjoyed doing it, as something of a chance to remind audiences that I could portray something stronger than "just a pretty face".'

The film, shot in 1951 while *Quo Vadis?* was being scored and finally edited at MGM-British, Borehamwood and Culver City, was released under the title *Thunder in the East*. From the Plaza, London, it went out on general release at the beginning of 1952, and it transpired that Kerr's rôle was little more rewarding than that of the majority of heroines in Alan Ladd vehicles. The main interest was in the way the girl pitted her integrity against the cynical attitude of commercial pilot Steve Gibbs (Ladd), who had flown to Gandahar to sell armaments either to the state's ruler, Ram Singh (Charles Boyer) or to the revolutionaries, depending on who made the highest bid. The original story's deeper implications were sacrificed to action and the normal Ladd line, with the hero turning out noblest of them all when trapped with an English colony whose members try to persuade him to fly them home. Ram Singh, in the meantime, after having his hand cut off by the bandits, abandons his principles of passive resistance when he emerges

129

from the palace vaults with a machine-gun in his good hand! Lee Garmes' black and white photography helped with its sense of urgency, and another good point was Boyer, albeit in a watered-down version of the character he could have made of the noble ruler. Corinne Calvet's stock vamp performance contributed nothing of value.

Working with Ladd proved to Deborah that, while he was 'very nice, and, I think, effective in the picture, he was rather withdrawn: always polite and professional, but somewhat distant. I don't think he ever believed in himself as an actor, but he made a tremendous career for himself by working at it. He was awfully good in putting across what he had, in his looks and his manner: he had something very attractive—a definite film personality which he had worked hard to perfect.' She respected the self-discipline he must have had to cultivate, and in which his wife and agent, former film actress Sue Carol, who virtually discovered and developed him, undoubtedly played a considerable part.

The mythical kingdom of Ruritania took Deborah Kerr back to her home lot for the first time since *Please Believe Me*, for the third remake of Anthony Hope's adventure story *The Prisoner of Zenda*. The silent version starred Henry Ainley as King Rudolf, and in 1922 Rex Ingram directed Lewis Stone in the title rôle, with Ramon Novarro as Rupert of Hentzau. The first talkie remake in 1937 starred Ronald Colman with Madeleine Carroll as Princess Flavia, Douglas Fairbanks Jnr. as Rupert, Mary Astor as the villainess, Antoinette de Maubań, and Lewis Stone as Colonel Zapt, under the direction of John Cromwell.

Stone was again on hand, this time as the Cardinal in Metro's 1952 reprise, starring Stewart Granger, Deborah Kerr, James Mason, Jane Greer and Louis Calhern. The previous version, produced by David O. Selznick, is now regarded as a classic of the adventure story genre. The gallant Rudolf Rassendyll, travelling in Ruritania, is kidnapped by orders of Colonel Zapt and persuaded to deputize at the coronation of the weak King Rudolf V, whose excesses are bringing the country to its knees: it happens that the two Rudolfs are exact doubles. When Rassendyll agrees, he finds himself involved with the Princess Flavia, who is engaged to the King. The hero is also the target for the schemes of Rupert of Hentzau, an irrepressible but attractive villain who wants the throne and Princess Flavia for himself.

MGM had 'inherited' *Zenda*, with other properties, from Selznick: producer Pandro S. Berman and director Richard Thorpe had the 1937 version closely copied in Joseph Ruttenberg's exquisite Technicolor photography. The result proved popular with the public, although the critics wondered aloud why the subject had been tackled again. The performances were well up to the standard of those in John Cromwell's film: Madeleine Carroll's pale classical loveliness had been considered perfect for the part of Flavia, the epitome of the languishing heroine of bygone days, yet Deborah Kerr, no less beautiful in her way, exquisitely gowned and photographed, was hardly noticed in the reviews. In *Picturegoer*, Ronald Morris wrote an article entitled 'Fun for Everyone except Deborah' and asked: 'Isn't it time for a change of act, before it becomes a beautiful bore? She gives the impression of an actress with a cruelly restrictive bit in her mouth.'

*Zenda* really decided Deborah that it was time she got away from playing lovely ladies in period clothes. Ideas were being tossed around for a change of pace: Douglas Fairbanks Jnr. wanted to make *Elephant Walk* in India with her, but MGM were not ready to let her go. When the film finally surfaced in 1954, starring Elizabeth Taylor, who had replaced Vivien Leigh when she became seriously ill during the shooting, it proved a providential escape for Deborah Kerr. Fairbanks did not do the film, either, and the late Peter Finch, with Dana Andrews, got the few good notices accorded to the movie.

Cary Grant was anxious to film Terence Rattigan's *Love in Idleness*, which had been a hit for Alfred Lunt and Lynn Fontanne on the London and New York stages, but would only do it with Kerr as leading lady, and the rights were too complicated to unravel. He did get Deborah Kerr as co-star, however, when Dore Schary finally paid heed to her plea for a

131

complete change of style, and personally produced them both in *Dream Wife*, directed by Sidney Sheldon, who had written the original screenplay with Herbert Baker and Alfred Levitt. It was generally released in Great Britain in June 1953, five months after *The Prisoner of Zenda*, with excellent black and white photography by Milton Krasner.

The story line presented Kerr as Priscilla Effington of the US State Department and Grant as Clem Meade, her fiancé, who, finding her always putting her career before himself, falls in love with Princess Taji (Betta St John), daughter of a Persian Khan. 'Effie' sends for the Princess and enlists her aid in disillusioning Clem, but a delegation from the Khan makes the marriage between his daughter and Clem a matter of national importance. In the end Meade sees the true worth of 'Effie' and wedding bells ring in all the right quarters. This very light comedy, with Cary Grant in sparkling form and dozens of elegant costume changes for Deborah Kerr, co-starred Walter Pidgeon, as a faithful admirer, with Buddy Baer and ex-Tarzan Bruce Bennett also in the cast. Deborah herself describes the film as 'moderately funny and moderately successful' and it gave her the chance to play an American career woman with grace and conviction, yet strangely the net result suggested that the spirit of Loretta Young had entered into the physical presence of Deborah Kerr.


# V


Four years after the initial publicity Metro finally put *Young Bess* into production in the autumn of 1952. There had been changes of plan, notably that the film, originally scheduled to be made in England, was eventually shot at Culver City. More significantly, Jean Simmons was cast in the title rôle, to which Deborah Kerr had once looked forward with such anticipation. She was certainly in the film, third-billed, after Simmons and Stewart Granger, but before Charles Laughton's Henry VIII.

132

After the brief switch to sophistication and modern times in *Dream Wife*, her reaction was: 'I'm going backwards'—in terms not only of time, but of progress as well.

George Sidney directed the script, adapted from the Irwin novel by Arthur Wimperis and Jan Lustig, photographed in Technicolor by Charles Rosher and produced by Sidney Franklin, whose 1942 Academy Award for 'consistent high achievement' guaranteed a quality standard motion picture. As such it was chosen to inaugurate the giant panoramic screen at the Empire, Leicester Square, along with stereophonic sound—not entirely successfully, for much of it was blurred and out of focus.

The story had Catherine Parr (Deborah Kerr), sixth and final wife of Henry VIII (a splendid reprise by Laughton of his most famous performance, but soon removed from the plot by death), in love with Tom Seymour (Stewart Granger). Young Bess arranges a marriage between Catherine and Tom after the King's death, although she herself is also in love with Seymour. The latter is devoted to his new wife, but is unable to resist the youthful fire and charms of Elizabeth. In the background Seymour's brother Ned (Guy Rolfe) schemes and connives, and after Catherine's death, Tom is accused of having seduced Elizabeth. The impressive almost all-British cast included Kay Walsh as Bess' governess; Kathleen Byron, whose effective casting as Ann, Ned's trouble-making wife, was suggested by Deborah, and Dawn Addams in a bit part as Catherine Howard. Kerr fitted with dignity into a charming film: she brought great warmth to an intelligently written rôle, which, however, was too negative and too fleeting to give her career the shot in the arm it so badly needed at this stage. Working with Laughton, she found him 'always jovial and amusing and extremely clever at parleying all his wonderful theatrical tricks'. In Britain the film was released in June 1953, the month before *Dream Wife*.

Her part in *Julius Caesar*, while far smaller than that of Catherine Parr, was one Deborah welcomed enthusiastically, as a 'chance to work in Shakespeare, and to grow, artistically, and an opportunity to work with Mankiewicz, so marvellous at welding the disparate actors under his direction into a working team'. Joseph Mankiewicz directed *Caesar* to concentrate on Shakespeare's words, rather than on visual images, and he and producer John Houseman between them achieved notable success in subjecting the camera to long speeches without at any time boring the eye or distracting the mind from the dialogue. They decided, in consultation with cinematographer Joseph Ruttenberg, on black and white rather than colour, which was already starting to become *de rigueur* for major screen projects, because the austerity of the drama seemed better suited to stark contrasts.

The soundtrack delivered the words almost without distraction from the usual 'reaction' close-ups and they come over astonishingly harmoniously from the lips of such fine, but dissimilar, actors as Marlon Brando (Mark Antony), James Mason (Brutus), John Gielgud (Cassius), Louis Calhern (Caesar) and Edmond O'Brien (Casca). The parts of Calpurnia and Portia, played by Greer Garson and Deborah Kerr, are so minute that the way they differentiated them as characters—Garson, as the great Caesar's wife, more used to giving orders and to expect her word to be heeded than Kerr as the mere wife of a Senator—is an achievement for which both actresses have been given less than their due. Both stars had asked to play in what many feel to be the finest film yet made from a Shakespearean play—the great achievements of Lord Olivier nothwithstanding.

Brando's Mark Antony (coached by Gielgud) was an electrifying creation and a highlight in the career of one of the cinema's most distinguished actors. It is regrettable that at least two later projects casting him opposite Deborah Kerr finally emerged with another actor in the rôle originally scheduled for him. She has, in the course of her career to date, acted with almost every leading male star of the thirties to sixties era, in several cases on more than one occasion: Mason's fine Brutus marked their third film together, although only in *Hatter's Castle* and *Julius Caesar* did they actually play opposite each other.

Mankiewicz's masterpiece, cast-wise, was a publicist's dream.

One added titbit was the presence together of Greer Garson and Deborah Kerr. The gossip writers had had a field day hinting at a feud between the two ladies, ever since Kerr's arrival in Hollywood had been presumed to be as a possible successor to Garson, should she turn 'difficult'. Fuel was added to this supposition when Deborah played a part in *If Winter Comes* opposite Greer's most familiar co-star, Walter Pidgeon, *and* it turned out to be a rôle for which Garson had originally been announced. In addition, Garson had been a star at Metro for nine years when her 'rival', some thirteen years younger, made her first film at Culver City.

'The idea of a feud between us was pure poppycock—or rather, gossip writers' fabrication—the stuff their dreams were made on. Greer was going great guns all through the time of my contract with Metro, and our friendship has lasted from that time to the present day. She's a great girl, deeply intelligent, with a degree in English literature, and did a fine job promoting *Julius Caesar* by lecturing in schools and universities when the film went on release. She's happily married to a highly successful businessman, Buddy Fogelson, but still turns in an occasional knock-out performance on film or TV when she has a mind to.'

## VI

By the time *Julius Caesar* was generally released in Britain in March 1954, some four months after the West End première, the Kerr career had received a considerable upward impetus. Out of her five releases back home in 1953, two were highly successful, one moderately so, and two were 'super colossal' hits. One of these, *Quo Vadis?*, went out on general release in September after seventy-nine weeks in the West End, where it had been premièred simultaneously at the Carlton and Ritz. It later returned to London at the Empire, the same month as it set out on its record-breaking assault on the provinces. The other 'super

135

colossal', and, from her personal point of view, far more significant was...

But—back to her home studio: after six years of quiet co-operation over almost every subject they suggested for her, she now went to Dore Schary and asked for her contract to be amended, so that she could freelance between assignments for Metro. The final straw was probably her casting as that gentle and amiable lady, Catherine Parr. Deborah made up her mind to change the agents looking after her career. Since her arrival in the USA she had been represented by MCA, for whose personnel she had considerable affection, especially for the boss, Jules Stein, 'an extraordinarily intelligent and nice man. But it wasn't really him I saw or dealt with' she says. 'It had become a joke between Tony and myself that all my agents did was drop by and ask after the children. Their concern was touching, but not actually worth ten per cent of my earnings.'

She had come to know socially, through their mutual friend, Charles Vidor, the late Bert Allenberg, a highly respected and well liked agent whose policy it was to represent only a very few people to whose interests he could devote himself whole-heartedly. This was in contrast to the inevitably more impersonal approach of a vast international organization like MCA. Over dinner one night at the Vidors' Allenberg had mentioned that if ever she wanted to change her mind over the handling of her business affairs and career he himself would be most interested. Deborah remembered the offer and made the change.

She had not long been under Bert Allenberg's aegis when he called her on the phone and said: 'How'd you like to play Karen Holmes?' naming the free-loving, free-wheeling heroine of the number one best-selling American novel of the time, *From Here to Eternity* by James Jones. Everybody had read it and was talking about its raw frankness and the sexual proclivities of the lady in question. 'They'd *never* consider me: you must be crazy!' was her instant reaction. Allenberg repeated: 'I asked you—would you be interested in playing the part?' 'Of course I would—it's such a magnificent part. But, Bert, don't make a fool of me: Harry Cohn will kick you out of the office.' 'Leave it to me,' he said, and rang off.

Allenberg called her back, after a day of agonizing suspense for his client. 'You were right,' he said; 'he kicked me out of the office.' 'I told you so,' said Deborah; 'you made a fool out of me.'

He rang back the next morning to say Harry Cohn had been on the phone at eight-thirty in the morning, to ask him how much she would cost.

CHAPTER NINE

# *FROM HERE TO ESTEEM*

I

The rest of the story is cinema history, and a page in Deborah Kerr's book which would certainly never have been written if Bert Allenberg, the great strategist, had not taken over the management of her career. The movie heads had in their minds a set 'image' of every star. 'I can see their point,' says Deborah, 'and it was an attitude that worked wonders for a number of very great favourites. In my case, the "image" was poisoning the career with a bad case of galloping anaemia. Besides, who can ever really tell *what* one's "image" is?'

However, one of Hollywood's greatest stars, one with one of the most potent and positive images of all time, Joan Crawford, was already set to play the part of Karen Holmes. In fact, she was within an ace of signing the contract when the tricky question came up of her insisting on having her own cameraman: nor was she enamoured of the costumes envisaged for Karen Holmes. Harry Cohn, chief of Columbia and one of the toughest of all the Hollywood moguls, reasoned that, as Crawford was going to be paid a great deal of money she should do as she was told, and let director Fred Zinnemann choose the cameraman. Zinnemann, in any case, was inclined towards casting against type, and Crawford had built a fabulous career out of playing ladies who, if not downright shady, were usually accustomed to having their own way with the gentlemen.

Allenberg had planted the seed overnight in Cohn's brain. First thing in the morning Cohn sent for producer Buddy Adler and Fred Zinnemann and said: 'Can you imagine, that sonofa-bitch Allenberg came in here and suggested that English virgin from Metro, Deborah Kerr, to play Karen Holmes?' Producer and director looked at each other in frank astonishment and echoed: 'What a *fantastic* idea!'

So that was that, and the 'English virgin' undertook a triumphant test for the part of a heroine who, if not actually a nymphomaniac, certainly did not make heavy weather out of controlling her appetite for the opposite sex. Deborah also posed for leg-art for the first time in her Hollywood career, and astonished the film world, including, presumably, Miss Crawford. 'She was very sweet about it when we met later at a party,' says Deborah. 'She took my arm and said: "You were *much* better than I would have been!" I don't know whether she was actually sweet to Harry Cohn—but that's another story, and anyway he was more than capable of looking after himself in any situation.'

Shortly before embarking on the plane for Honolulu, where the location work for *From Here to Eternity* was filmed, Deborah Kerr received the script of a play which was to be as significant to her career as the controversial movie which she was about to undertake. In 1948 she had gone to New York to do a play by Robert Anderson for radio's Theatre Guild of the Air. It was called *Remember the Day* and the author had told her after the show how marvellous it would be if they could do a play together. She told him that she knew Metro would not release her to do a play on Broadway. In fact they had recently refused her permission to play Anne Boleyn opposite Rex Harrison's Henry VIII in *Anne of a Thousand Days*—a part in which Joyce Redman was to make a big success at the end of that year. Deborah said, 'Try again in five years.'

Five years later, in 1953, she was in New York again for more radio, Shaw's *Man and Superman* with Maurice Evans. Her memories of the occasion are hazy, as she had a bad case of 'flu, and played the show with a temperature of 102. She was packing to leave when the hotel pageboy came in with an envel-ope, which she threw in the suitcase and forgot about. The next

139

morning, as the train drew into Chicago, she remembers hearing her husband say: 'Look here . . . I don't know . . . I think you ought to read it.' He handed her a script, with a note clipped to it: 'I wonder if you remember me. I spoke to you about appearing in a play . . . you said then, "in five years' time, perhaps . . ." Here is the play.—Bob Anderson.'

Deborah had considerable faith in Tony's judgment, read the play and thought it wonderful, then had second thoughts about its suitability for herself. Being a person who immerses herself in the work in which she is currently engaged, and finding it virtually impossible to divide her concentration, she laid the script aside and deferred judgment. At the time *From Here to Eternity* was claiming all her attention: having won the part of Karen Holmes, against formidable opposition and all the probabilities, she was now having to fight her own self-doubts about her ability to play the character. Would her accent, her figure and so on be up to it?

The name of Bob Anderson's play was *Tea and Sympathy*, and when Kerr finally agreed to do it, it broke down as many conventions and shibboleths for the theatre, and did as much for her in that realm as a performer as *From Here to Eternity* did in the movie world.


# II


'What Zinnemann did in that movie, at that time, with its more than outspoken attack on the American army, was a very brave thing,' says Deborah. 'And his encouragement of myself, in playing against type-casting, was a deciding factor in lifting me out of the rut of ladylike rôles from which I'd begun to feel there was no exit.' Her ability to change her appearance, and even her shape—although that had been eminently suitable for pin-up photos before the public were allowed to become aware of the fact—in her interpretation of a part, transformed her into the American conception of how a sexy blonde should look.

140

Marilyn Monroe was currently at her peak in films like *River of No Return* with Robert Mitchum, and some of the publicity stills of Deborah Kerr at that time could actually be taken for Monroe herself. Kerr's British accent has never made her unacceptable in American parts—to this day many people are surprised to find she was not born and bred in the USA—and, as Karen Holmes, virtually all traces of the home country disappeared, in her presentation of a woman driven by disillusionment with her marriage to embark on a series of minor affairs, and hence alleviate the unhappiness and boredom of her life.

Karen falls for Sgt Milton Warden (Burt Lancaster), running the infantry unit in which her husband, Captain Dana Holmes (Philip Ober), orders him to make the life of bugler Robert E. Lee Prewitt (Montgomery Clift) as unbearable as possible, merely because he has refused to join the boxing team. Clift, as well as Kerr, were two of the nominees for Oscars who thoroughly deserved to win: he as the sensitive and tortured soldier, and she as the sad and vulnerable human beneath a tough, glossy exterior. Crawford was right: Deborah Kerr's performance *was* better, because it was full of surprises—the senior star, on her showing in the 1946 *Humoresque*, could have played Karen Holmes with consummate ease, but Kerr brought a fresh approach which contained its own magic.

In the Academy Awards, however, she was up against the newest and most exciting star from England, Audrey Hepburn, who, after a few minor rôles in her own country, garnered the Best Actress Award for her American film début in William Wyler's *Roman Holiday*. Entrancing as she undeniably was, an honour of this stature, purportedly given for acting, seems questionable when what Hepburn was doing was presenting her own novel and unique personality. Ken Doeckel, interviewing Deborah Kerr for *Films In Review*, writes that Wyler, one of the few major directors for whom she has not worked—a project for him to direct her in a TV version of *The Letter* never materialized—commented: 'Audrey Hepburn may be the Princess, but Deborah Kerr is the Queen!'

Frank Sinatra's Award as Best Supporting Actor as the tragic Private Maggio, who befriends Prewitt and is beaten to death for his pains by Sgt Fatso—Ernest Borgnine in one of his earliest rôles—is another piece of cinema history, while Donna Reed, born the same year as Deborah Kerr, and also a fugitive from an MGM contract, richly deserved her Best Supporting Actress Oscar as Lorene, Prewitt's girlfriend. Other Academy Awards went to Fred Zinnemann as Best Director, a fitting acknowledgment of his genius and his first since the 1938 short *That Mothers Might Live*, and to Daniel Taradash's scenario and Burnett Guffey's superb black and white photography.

The year 1953 was one to leave Columbia Pictures and Harry Cohn laughing (a quaint image); for Deborah Kerr it meant an almost infinite scope in the parts she could command. It was as well that *From Here to Eternity*—released in England towards the end of the year—had not actually been previewed when she asked for her release from MGM. Her contract was almost due to run out, and Bert Allenberg was able to negotiate a release, at a financial loss to her of about thirty-three thousand pounds, swapping the remaining year of the original deal for an agreement to do three films in the future, thus leaving her free to return to the theatre. Had the tremendous impact of her performance as Karen Holmes been fully realized at the time of this negotiation, it is unlikely that Metro, which remained under Schary's control until 1956, would have been so accommodating.

Deborah had many worries, apart from the thousand pounds a week she was giving up—with her agent's blessing—from her home studio. She went to New York alone, as Tony was then in London, working on his television films, and she turned up for rehearsals at the theatre in the height of summer, outwardly cool and collected as ever, inwardly the victim of conflicting emotions, not the least of which was that this was the moment the gossip-mongers chose to revive an old rumour that while making *Eternity* in Honolulu she had fallen in love with the ubiquitous Mr Sinatra, who was at that time reputedly courting the lovely Ava Gardner. Deborah's husband read the items with amusement and commented: 'Now, you *have* arrived!' Her Scottish hackles arose and caused her one of her rare moments of real anger. 'If I were unattached,' she said, 'what would it matter what anyone said or wrote? But this is a slander on my husband, and that's quite another matter.'

She had enough to cope with in worrying about her wisdom in agreeing to do the play, without *canards* of this kind from professional gossip-writers. Robert Anderson, author of *Tea and Sympathy*, says: 'My only problem in speaking of Deborah will be curbing my enthusiasm for your subject. After our initial meeting in New York, I wrote *Tea and Sympathy* after some time had passed: oddly I did not have Deborah in mind when I wrote it. I never have any actor in mind when I write, but when the Playwrights' Company decided to produce the play (after most other producers had turned it down) I told all and sundry that I would like Deborah to play the part. I immediately sent her a script.

'Then the fun began. Elia Kazan, who had agreed to direct it, said that he did not want a glamorous movie star in the play, for at least two reasons: one, this was my first play to be produced, and he wanted it to be a discovery of me and my play and not of a movie star. Second, though I don't think he had ever seen Deborah on the screen, he felt that a film star would bring the wrong qualities to this part, which required that a lovely but modest and moral woman finally came to the point where she could give herself to the boy at the end of the play.

'Deborah also wrote and said that she did not think it was the play for her, and when she made her American stage début, she would like it to be in something a little more off-centre of the stereotype she had been cursed with in films.' Deborah's own initial reaction was 'Here was another good woman—and that if I played Laura, there I would be, back in cashmere sweaters, being good, noble, and supremely sacrificing. The fact that Laura had an affair with a seventeen-year-old boy escaped me altogether. I wrote and told Bob Anderson that I didn't want to play another good woman and wear out one more cashmere sweater.' Says Bob Anderson: 'A nice problem for a first-time playwright. I wrote her several letters telling her that I thought she was wrong about the woman . . . that she had a considerable amount of guts and I still felt she was the one to do the play. Meanwhile I kept talking to Kazan about Deborah, as we saw other stars for the part, and as we went about casting the other players. Finally, Kazan was due to go to California on other business, and I asked him to see Deborah. I also wrote to her that he would be in Hollywood in May and asked her to see him.

'They met . . . had tea, I believe, and he wired me: "You're absolutely right, and she's going to do the play."'


# III


Anderson went on to say: 'Gadge (as Kazan's friends all call him), creates a sort of climate of friendship in all his works. He works happily. He is happiest when he is working. He is exuberant, full of joy and fun and contagious enthusiasm. With the delight of a child he guides each person to realize the quality of self, the best that is in him . . . "Walk a ways with me" is an innocent enough suggestion, but is likely to lead to a whole afternoon of peripatetic discussion. Deborah Kerr's first introduction to her part came on one of these walks. Gadge suggested they walk a little ways; an hour later they were still walking and finally ended up watching the seals in the zoo and discussing the underlying facets of the character.' Kazan still had to persuade and reassure her that she could be Laura, and, on the opening night, with the curtain about to rise, she fell prey to the torments of self-doubt she conceals so completely from the outside world. Van Johnson once said: 'She's not really an extrovert: she just makes herself that way. She's a triumph of will over nature.' On this occasion she felt the blood drain away from her head and would have passed out had her mentor not applied the old remedy of making her sit down and forcing her head between her knees till the feeling flowed back to her brain and she willed herself to make her first entrance.

144

*Tea and Sympathy* opened at the Barrymore Theatre on her birthday, 30 September, 1953. Anderson says: 'What a birthday she gave us all! As everyone knows, she was magnificent in the part of Laura Reynolds; she received a standing ovation and Broadway took her to its heart. In addition she was an exemplary STAR, never letting down, an example to the rest of the cast. It was a very happy company, and she played for two seasons, one on Broadway and one on the road, without missing a performance.

'It is now closing in on twenty-five years since the play opened, and I can still see her as the curtain rose, luminous with her great beauty in the warm and cosy set by Jo Mielziner ... listening to John Kerr playing the sad tune *The Joys of Love*. And later, in the second act, in the lustrous dark green dress, trying to keep Jack from going out to the prostitute. And finally, in the last act, first blazing away at Leif Erickson with "I resent this judgment by prejudice" ... to her last quiet moments with the boy in his bedroom as she undid the top button on the famous pink blouse as the lights irised out.

'It was an enormously satisfying experience. I think rarely has a play and a playwright been so faithfully and lovingly served as by Deborah, John Kerr, Kazan and Mielziner. I was certainly spoiled for the rest of my life. I'm sure Deborah won't mind my mentioning a little organization which Kazan and Jack Kerr and I had, the ALDK's: this stood for the Associated Lovers of Deborah Kerr.'

The critics gladly joined the association for the occasion: F. Mawby Green in *Theatre World* explained the plot to the English public, who were not allowed to see the play until 1957 as a club production at the Comedy Theatre with Elizabeth Sellars, as the Lord Chamberlain's powers of censorship still lay heavy on the land. 'In a New England boy's school a student is assumed by classmates, faculty, even by his father, to be homosexual, having been discovered nude on the beach with a teacher long suspected of being one ... his sole defender is the housemaster's young wife, and she is asked to remain a bystander, for her only function in the school is to invite the lonely students in occasionally for a sip of tea and a spot of sympathy. Too outgoing for that she tries to guide the boy through this tragic time ... Deborah Kerr is enjoying a triumph for the awareness of her performance and the apparent ease with which she transfers this across to the audience. Every possible nuance in the wife's character and the situation she catches and records with the sensitivity of a seismograph needle.'

John Chapman (*Daily News*) called hers 'an exquisitely sensitive and thrillingly warm performance'; *Life* said that the play 'launched (her) as a powerful and sensitive new stage star'; and Brooks Atkinson (*New York Times*) stated that she had 'the initial advantage of being extremely beautiful, but she adds to her beauty the luminous perception of an artist who is aware of everything that is happening all around her and expresses it in effortless style'.

The 1953/54 period earned her more than enough Awards to atone for her failure to get the Oscar for *From Here to Eternity*: *Billboard* gave her two Donaldson Awards, one for Best Début Actress (shared with Audrey Hepburn for *Ondine*) the other for Best Actress; *Variety* Drama Critics' Poll voted hers to be the Best Performance by an Actress in a Straight Play. In addition, the New York Publicists' Guild voted her Star of the Year for 1954, and she won the 1954/55 Sarah Siddons Award for Outstanding Performance.

The Bartleys moved to New York for the run of *Tea and Sympathy*, a time when the press dubbed her 'Broadway's Favourite Star', when the name Deborah Kerr was literally dominating the entertainment scene, with four 'marquees' (theatres in which she was billed): apart from *Tea and Sympathy*, the films *Dream Wife*, *Julius Caesar* and *From Here to Eternity* were running simultaneously. She withdrew from the play at the end of May 1954 and left with Tony, Melanie and Francesca for England, where she was due to start work on a film for Columbia producer David Lewis.

Despite rumours that Joan Bennett would be her replacement on Broadway, it was Joan Fontaine who took over, with Anthony Perkins inheriting the part created by John Kerr, who

146

had been accorded the *Variety* Drama Critics' Award for the Best Performance by an Actor in a Supporting Part. Fontaine made a big success on her own account for her very different interpretation of the part of Laura: the similarity of appeal between her and Kerr, commented on years before by Emlyn Williams, has persisted, but Joan Fontaine never had such a positive opportunity as Deborah Kerr to break away from the nobly suffering image she had originally established in *Rebecca*.

Joan was one of the stars, with the Taylors, Robert and Elizabeth, of Metro's first big British-made box-office smash since pre-war days, *Ivanhoe*, in 1952, and the studio announced, as a follow-up for Coronation Year 1953, *Magna Carta*, to star the Taylors again, with Stewart Granger, Michael Wilding, Greer Garson and Deborah Kerr. This was one of the projects from which her new deal with the studio would have protected her. In fact, the film was never made, and another one for which Radie Harris in the *Hollywood Reporter* tipped Deborah Kerr and Greer Garson as the 'strongest contenders', the life story of the late Gertrude Lawrence, did not emerge until the late sixties, as Julie Andrews' *Star!*

IV

One of the most interesting offers Deborah had to refuse through sheer pressure of work was the female lead in Alfred Hitchcock's *Dial 'M' for Murder*. Grace Kelly played the part with her customary cool competence, but it was not one which afforded the actress opportunities in any way comparable to that of the star rôle in Graham Greene's *The End of the Affair*, a remarkable novel dealing with the author's attitude towards sex, sin and redemption. During the filming Deborah Kerr talked to *Picturegoer*'s Paul Holt.

'I didn't fight Hollywood because I soon realized that if I did I would wear myself out, and maybe destroy myself. I learned when I was a girl that the golden rule in life is *not* to fight about things that aren't important. Save up your strength and fighting spirit for the time that something comes along that is important to you. Then fight . . . and fight hard. There were compensations for the last two years in Hollywood: I did without the parts I needed as an actress, and in exchange I won three things. I am free. I'll never again play the part of a woman who never existed—though in a way they, too, are a challenge, as you have to reach within yourself to produce something that will make them appear alive. In the future parts I choose are going to be about real women; they may not be pleasant, but they will be real people.' Her second achievement, in order of writing, but first in order of importance, was the family. Melanie, aged six, and Francesca, two, were present, playing happily, at the interview.

'I had them in Hollywood. They grew up in the sun. They had all the shelter children need and I watched them grow strong. I watched them being happy in an atmosphere of peace and riches. And while I was waiting for another of those parts to come along, I had the leisure to be with them. I shall always be grateful for that. The third gift from Hollywood was that it taught me to act for the screen. When I got there I didn't know. It is so different from the stage, which is a flexible art. Acting for the screen is simply a matter of complete concentration, poured into the raising of an eyebrow or the dropping of an eyelid', and she named the three actors who had taught her most in that respect: Cary Grant, Spencer Tracy and Burt Lancaster.

Of Van Johnson, her co-star in *The End of the Affair*, she said: 'Van is like me. He, too, had seven lean years in Hollywood—and now he is free. It's going to be a very interesting film to make, for he plays a real man and I play a real woman.'

On the set she found herself with old friends from her British film days, including lighting cameraman Wilkie Cooper, Britain's premier film dress designer Julie Harris and Chris Noble, now an established First Assistant and permitting himself the familiarity of calling his star by her first name. He found her 'more glamorous, in the Hollywood manner, more mature and perhaps more approachable', though he admits that any lack of *rapprochement* in the past probably stemmed from himself. A year later he left the film industry, after working on a film called *Star of My Night*, starring Griffith Jones. After a successful venture into real estate, he went into the restaurant business with the Little Anchor at Itchenor, near Chichester, approximately a score of miles from Alfold.

Whenever Deborah returned to England she visited Grannie Jane Trimmer regularly: the affection between them grew with the years, but her granddaughter, after attaining her majority, did not mince matters with the old lady, trying to bring home to her the fact that she had made her daughter-in-law's life a misery after Jack Trimmer's death. Old Mrs Trimmer seemed genuinely surprised, though she came near to acknowledging Ceciley Rumble's contention that 'Deborah's grandmother liked to rule'. As time passed and the occasional visits of a district nurse were no longer sufficient to prevent her from being a danger to herself, living on her own in Pound Cottage, Deborah prevailed on Grannie Jane to move to the comfort and security of her own room at Mount Alvernia, a nursing home run by a Catholic order of nuns near Guildford. Her spirit remained indomitable: during one of her granddaughter's weekly visits she announced: 'Deborah, you're not getting any younger—you're thirty-two. I hope you've made provision for me in your will!' Mary Jane was then ninety-two; she survived to ninety-six, and her ashes were returned to the churchyard of St Nicholas, Alfold, where so many of her family were buried.

The other Jane to have played a major part in Deborah's life, her aunt, Phyllis Jane Smale, visited the set during the filming of *The End of the Affair*, and she brought her daughter Harriet, aged ten. The child watched the shooting of the scene where Van Johnson is badly injured in an air raid, and could not be convinced that it was not real blood gushing from the wound on his head. She was so distraught she had to be led from the set: later Van tried to persuade her that it was only make-up: 'Look—it washes off!' He was so likeable she allowed herself

149

to be calmed, but her doubts remained with her for a long time afterwards.

On this film Deborah Kerr found herself with a new stand-in, who has worked with her since then on all her British films. Esmee Smythe, former ballet and ballroom dancer, had married Anthony Ostrer, youngest son of the late Isidore Ostrer, sometime chief of Gaumont-British; after their divorce she went into film work as an extra. One of her first calls was to Shepperton Studios to stand in for Deborah: Esmee proved to be so suitable, as far as colouring, size and even walk were concerned that she has doubled for her in several films, and to this day will drop any occupation she may be following to work with her. Few stars are heroines to their stand-ins, but Esmee Smythe's assessment is unequivocal: 'She is the least temperamental person I know—nothing ever seems to get her bad-tempered, and that's quite a statement when one has known somebody for over twenty years. She's a lovely person and a very great artist, because she never lets her feelings show; she may be tired, she may be thoroughly fed up with the whole thing, but this never comes over. She's never late, she's always there, and a perfectly professional person, which is more than one can say for lots of people, in any walk of life.'

Director Edward Dmytryk brought out all the nuances of mysticism, pathos, humour and dignity of Graham Greene's story, as far as the bowdlerized screenplay by Lenore Coffee—forced upon them by the censorship of the day—allowed. Kerr as Sarah Miles falls in love with writer Maurice Bendrix (Johnson) when he comes to interview her shy and retiring husband Henry (Peter Cushing), seeking material for a book he is writing on the Civil Service in wartime London. When Sarah finds her lover apparently dead after a flying bomb raid she makes a bargain with God that she will give Maurice up if He will let him survive. By an apparent miracle Maurice recovers, she keeps to her pact and he turns bitter, employing a private detective, Albert Parkis (John Mills) to watch her. In her distress she turns to Fr Crompton (Stephen Murray) for guidance, but returns to Maurice when he discovers why she left him from a diary found by Parkis. She leaves Maurice again, and is drenched in a rainstorm, contracting a fever, from which she dies; when her ex-lover meets her mother (Nora Swinburne) she tells him that Sarah had been secretly baptized a Catholic, and he finds a letter from her, telling how she fell into belief 'like I fell in love'.

Deborah Kerr's sensitive interpretation of the woman reclaimed by God through her mortal, though adulterous love, was subtle and delicately moving, and brought out a responsive sincerity in the playing of the hitherto all-American college boy type, Van Johnson, who, though basically miscast as Maurice, is a much better actor than he has ever been given credit for. John Mills was splendid as the sleazy detective and Peter Cushing just right as Sarah's husband, Henry Miles. The edges of Greene's profoundly held beliefs were somewhat blunted by the fact that the subject could not be treated entirely honestly. As Deborah says:

'Today, or even just a few years after we filmed it, the screen play could have benefited from being more explicit. I loved the book, but that's sometimes a trap you fall into: when you come to do the film you find so much is interior thought that it can't be put into dialogue.' Her own performance effected something of a miracle by sketching in what Lenore Coffee's screenplay had had to omit, and Kerr herself got some excellent notices. Summing up, *Picturegoer*'s Sarah Stoddart wrote: 'It's an unusually distinguished film that provokes and excites. It may irritate, too, but you won't breathe freely until the end of this affair.'

Deborah Kerr finished filming at Shepperton in the summer of 1954, returned to the USA for a short rest, then toured *Tea and Sympathy* throughout the country for eleven months, with the late Alan Baxter, one of Hollywood's most neglected actors, usually confined to playing gangsters, taking over as Bill Reynolds, Laura's husband, and Don Dubbins as Tom Lee. Reviews were again ecstatic and houses full.

151

# V

Location work in the summer of 1955 in the Virgin Isles for
*The Proud and Profane* was torrid, one of the roughest Deborah
had encountered, *King Solomon's Mines* notwithstanding. 'It
wasn't just the heat,' she says: 'whenever it began to rain you
thought "Ah! Blessed relief"—then the heat rose up out of the
ground and nearly choked you.'

Paramount producer William Perlberg and director George
Seaton had decided not to court comparison with *From Here
to Eternity* by including a passionate love scene between her and
co-star William Holden, although the location and the character
played by him ('My pleasures are physical . . . my men call me
the Beast') could well have accommodated such indulgence.

Censorship weakened not only the title, but the whole conception of Seaton's adaptation of Lucy Herndon Crockett's
novel *The Magnificent Bastards*. First this title was ruled out, and
*The Magnificent Devils* substituted, then the whole tone elevated
to indicate that the 'Proud' was Nurse Kerr and the 'Profane'
Marine Colonel Holden. In the circumstances it is hardly surprising that it emerged as sheer woman's magazine story, concerning the wartime love of the Red Cross worker and the ruthless,
indeed 'beastly' officer Colin Black, wearing a fierce moustache
and a mean sneer. He demotes a war hero, mocks at a chaplain's
work and refuses Red Cross help for his wounded men, to say
nothing of his deceitful love affair with a widow, the trusting,
pious welfare worker Lee Ashley, which brings her to attempted suicide and the loss of the baby she is carrying. Colin
pays for his sins by nearly being killed in action, but love finds
a way in the last reel as Lee sits keeping vigil by his bedside.

That the movie worked, even on a 'woman's weepie' level
was entirely due to the acting of the two stars, carrying on
though they believed every word, despite one of Thelma Ritter's more embarrassing performances as a Red Cross Commandant with a whiplash tongue and a heart of gold. To be
fair, though, there were critics who said she 'salvaged the film

with a life-saving draught of humour'. Dewey Martin as a lonely soldier received good notices, too. What saved it all, as far as Deborah Kerr was concerned, was working with Holden, and the feeling was mutual. 'She's the most no–problem star I ever worked with, and she has a salty sense of humour which surprises everyone. She's an unusually charming individual.'

Deborah's next co-star was as great a contrast as could be imagined; after accepting her Sarah Siddons Best Actress Award for *Tea* in Chicago in February 1956, she returned with the family to Hollywood to play opposite Yul Brynner in *The King and I*. He was making his first stunning impact into the world of motion pictures, disregarding a little number he had done and hoped to forget in 1949, *Port of New York*, and had had four solid years of involvement with *The King and I* on stage. After the death of Gertrude Lawrence who created the musical 'Mrs Anna Leonowens' he had played with various successors, and it was he who particularly wanted Deborah Kerr to do the part in the film, although they had only met socially before when he visited her during *Tea and Sympathy*.

'It was Yul who was the solid inspiration behind the movie; he knew and loved every line of the story and every note of the music, and that it came out so well was due to his insistence that this and that be done the way *he* wanted it. He could be difficult, but only because he knew he was right. We lived with *The King and I* for the best part of 1955; first there were six weeks' rehearsal, as in the theatre, then we were filming for five months at Twentieth Century-Fox, so all that vast unit had become really like a family. There was a Christmas party to celebrate the end of production, with a huge tree and presents for all the children, and we just couldn't believe that it was all over and that we wouldn't be meeting again the next day to go on filming. I'd never before been on a picture where there was music going on practically all the time—apart from the acting scenes most of the time was spent on the musical numbers. One just wanted it to go on forever.'

Most of the leading ladies in—and out—of Hollywood were eager to play Mrs Anna, including singer Dinah Shore, one of

Kerr's closest friends since they had shared their initial pregnancies back in the forties. Deborah Kerr had been told she was to start the film after the tour of *Tea and Sympathy*, and she took singing lessons in every town they visited—Boston being a notable exception, as the play was banned there. By the time the film went on the floor she was in good enough voice to handle the lead-ins to most of the Rodgers and Hammerstein songs, with Marni Nixon to handle the high notes and those which needed sustaining. Kerr did the monologue *Shall I Tell You What I Think Of You?* herself, and it remains as a high spot of the LP of the film, but was finally edited out of the released version, due to excess length. She sang the whole of *I Whistle a Happy Tune* as it was within a range she was able to accomplish without strain, under the musical direction of Ken Darby.

'At least, I think I did,' she says, 'but Marni was so brilliant at adapting her voice to mine I could never be entirely sure whether it was she who was helping me on the high notes—with the help of the expert sound mixers, of course—or whether I myself was responsible for the sounds which came out in the completed version. I know she sang all of *Hello, Young Lovers* which is a really difficult song to sing because it's so sustained, and I helped out on *Getting To Know You*. It was a fascinating experience to watch Marni; she is an actress with her voice and exquisitely musical, and I used to sit with her in the sound booth and marvel at the way she managed it all. She became a star in her own right, which is only as it should be—no such talent should be confined to helping out people who are not strictly singers at all. She sings Lieder and those incredibly difficult atonal French songs brilliantly; Marni really deserves her recognition as a unique talent in the musical world.'

Among the LPs still in demand are Gertrude Lawrence and Yul Brynner's stage original and a charming version produced by Jessie Matthews in 1969. Valerie Hobson's recordings with Herbert Lom from the Drury Lane production of the play are heard less often, but the Kerr–Nixon–Brynner version is still the most popular with the disc jockeys. Like Grace Kelly for her few lines of *True Love* with Bing Crosby in *High Society*, Deborah Kerr found herself a best-selling recording star, thanks to a good deal of help from others. She had participated the previous year in an LP made by RCA Victor, *Arias Sung and Acted*: the singing, including arias from *La Bohème* and *Madam Butterfly*, was by Licia Albanese, while Deborah Kerr enacted a scene from *Camille* with Dennis King, evoking shades of Garbo's great performance in Metro's 1936 movie.

Kerr's Mrs Anna was charmingly and movingly her own creation, winning her a third Oscar nomination. The story, of the gentle but iron-willed Victorian governess who takes her little boy with her when she goes to instruct the children of the King of Siam, and remains to instil him with some of her own loving kindness, must by now be one of the best known in the world, having been filmed previously without music by Irene Dunne and Rex Harrison as *Anna and The King of Siam*. The 1956 version is constantly being revived: takings of eight and a half *billion* dollars make it one of the most successful musicals ever filmed. The experience of Walter Lang, an expert in the direction of such disparate musical stars as Betty Grable, Carmen Miranda, Ethel Merman and Marilyn Monroe, and the supporting performances of the splendid Rita Moreno as Tuptim, with Alan Mowbray and Geoffrey Toone amusingly guying British officialdom, welded the whole into sheer entertainment. The brilliant camerawork of Leon Shamroy in Eastman Colour and the costumes of Irene Sharaff, which netted her an Academy Award for best design in the colour section, ensured that Ernest Lehman's clever adaptation of Oscar Hammerstein's play was a visual as well as an aural treat. Brynner won the Oscar for his performance, but Kerr, nominated for the third time, lost out to Ingrid Bergman for her *Anastasia*. She did, however, win the Photoplay Gold Medal as the year's best actress.

Deborah enjoyed wearing the most elaborate period gowns of her film career, and so impressed an admirer from Australia, pianist-entertainer Michael Bolloten, that he wrote: 'with a charmed handful of stars—people like Dorothy Dickson, Isabel

Jeans and Deborah Kerr, clothes become personalities when they wear them. I shall never forget how her crinolines in *The King and I* positively *acted*.'

# VI

Robert Anderson wrote the screenplay of his own *Tea and Sympathy* which went into production, as the first of Deborah Kerr's three-picture deal with MGM in March 1956, the year that her performance in *The King and I* was accorded Best in a Musical by an Actress by the Hollywood Foreign Press Association. Comparisons with Irene Dunne were inevitable, and Kerr's international acceptance in such a wide range of rôles prompted an interesting assessment by David Shipman.

' "The camera," Deborah Kerr once admitted, "always seems to find an innate gentility in me." . . . In the fifties she was offered all the ladies of breeding that might in former days have gone to Irene Dunne, Bergman or Myrna Loy—or to Garbo, Hepburn or Bette Davis. There are little bits of all these ladies within her, but she is less flamboyant, obviously, than Hepburn or Davis, less melancholy than Garbo, less light-hearted than Dunne, not as radiant as Bergman in love, nor as clear-sighted as Loy. Discretion is the keynote of her work.'

Bob Anderson says of their film of *Tea and Sympathy*: 'Of course I am delighted to have her performance preserved in the film. The picture didn't come off as well as we had hoped . . . we had to make too many changes for censorship. We kept fooling ourselves that we were preserving the integrity of the theme, but we lost some of it. I feel that the stage production was indeed beautiful, and brought out the harshness and whatever bite the play possessed, while the film bordered on the pretty. But it serves its purpose in preserving the performances of Deborah and Jack Kerr and Leif Erickson.'

She says: 'I suffered with Bob Anderson who had to make these adjustments in his play. It seems impossible that so recently one couldn't say "homosexual" or imply "queer" or "gay", even, and it took something out of the movie that the boy was persecuted simply because he was not good at sports and games, and preferred sewing on buttons and associating with the faculty wives—who did not figure in the original at all—and playing classical music. The scene with his room-mate, Darryl Hickman, is a marvellous one—where Al says "You walk funny: you ought to walk like this," and proceeds to demonstrate how to be a beefy all-American boy. Bob Anderson has always held that the play is not about homosexuality at all— it's about persecution of people whose ideas are different from yours. Because someone is "different" they're not necessarily a "sissy". "Sister boy" was the quaint euphemism used for homosexual in the movie. The crucial point of the play, that he had been seen swimming with a master everyone assumed to be homosexual, had to be omitted altogether; the boy was so innocent he would not even have known what that meant— he went with the man because he was nice to him—and that was all there was to it.'

Of the director, Vincente Minnelli, she says: 'He was extremely sensitive to the subject; the only thing that might have diffused it a little was that his great talent for making movies very beautiful pictorially might have softened it—lushed it up a little. But it was very difficult to shoot the end. In the theatre in the final scene, so brilliantly directed by Kazan and marvellously lit by Mielziner, the lights just focused on Laura, who was up in the boy's room, trying to comfort him with words. She hesitantly leaves the room and the boy turns his face miserably into his pillows. The door shuts. A few seconds pass, then the door opens again. She comes in and stands by the bed and she says the classic lines: "Years from now, when you talk about this—and you will—be kind." And she just undoes the top button of her blouse, and the lights fade . . . An electrifying moment in the theatre—you heard the whole audience gasp with shock, as short a time ago as it was, that a woman of her age—she's thirty-five—is going to bed with an eighteen-year-old boy to prove that all sexual experience isn't as horrible as he found it to be when he visited the prostitute to try to prove himself a man. You just couldn't do that in the film; though the line is the same, the scene is set out in the open—he follows her into a wood—and is far less explicit.

Nevertheless, the film pleased many who had not had the opportunity to see the play, which was done most successfully in Paris by Ingrid Bergman, and it was also extremely popular in Germany, Italy and Scandinavia. Other world achievements included a highly successful tour of Australia and South Africa from 1956–57, starring Dulcie Gray as Laura. Recently Liv Ullmann asked Anderson to adapt a new screen version for her—one which could now be done without the evasions which faced author and actress at Metro in the fifties. Deborah says: 'The idea of Liv doing a new version today would be wonderful. She is a superb actress and I am an enormous fan.'

CHAPTER TEN

# 'THE WORLD'S FAVOURITE ACTRESS!'

## I

Her world travels often brought Deborah and her family to England, where they were able to keep in touch with their friends and relations. By 1956 she was light miles away from the timid days of her childhood, when she had to take cod liver oil and malt to build her stamina and when her tormentors at school had referred to her as 'farthing face'. *From Here to Eternity* had finally established the only real confidence she had in herself—as an actress, by providing a real character for her to play, and gave the lie to those who had considered her incapable of letting her hair down.

'They were the usual foolish people incapable of separating reality from fantasy. The ones who tagged me an iceberg were now quick to decide that I must be very much the reverse. Why don't they realize that there is something of both in every normal woman?' On final analysis, it has always been Deborah herself who has had to overcome her basic timidity, which remains a permanent feature of her personality.

Her admiration of her more extrovert contemporaries was tempered by commonsense: 'Why is it,' she mused, 'that the actresses who wear the least in public always carry the most luggage?'

Her next film was to give her an opportunity to prove the fallacy of trying to put people into categories with labels like flower-seed packets—*Cool—Motherly—Frigid—Sexy—Bluestocking—Pure*—and so on. *Heaven Knows, Mr Allison* was shot

159

on location on the island of Tobago in the second half of 1956, by John Huston, who was to become one of her favourite directors, and co-starring Robert Mitchum, with whom she established instant rapport, despite the fact that this was one of the occasions when Marlon Brando had originally been announced to play opposite her. Oswald Morris, at Pinewood as assistant to lighting cameraman Wilkie Cooper on *Green for Danger* at the time Deborah was making *Black Narcissus*, was responsible for the stirring Technicolor photography, and the film was virtually a two-hander for Kerr and Mitchum, with Buddy Adler again in charge of the production, with Eugene Frenke, for Twentieth Century.

In the film, Deborah plays Sister Angela, Mitchum Marine Corporal Allison, both washed ashore on a small Pacific island in the hands of the Japanese. The very slight story line concerns their initial antagonism, his attempt to assault her after getting drunk following a raid on a Japanese storehouse, and their growing mutual admiration and respect as they are forced to hide from the enemy, until their rescue by US troops. The director and actors together achieved touching aspects of an unusual relationship, and Kerr played Sister Angela with an Irish accent—'the only one to get across her religious phraseology and have it sound true and convincing. *Heaven Knows, Mr Allison* was such an enchanting idea' she says, 'and John Huston contributed so much to that enchantment. It could have been extremely tasteless, when you think—a marine and a nun. He rewrote a great deal of that scenario himself, though John Lee Mahin was named as scriptwriter, from the novel by Charles Shaw. I would get pages under my door every night, and one never knew which scene one would be playing the next day.

'Of course, the perfect person for the part was Bob Mitchum, because there's a sensitivity that belies the rugged exterior, so he was able to personify the marine with this undercurrent that could make their relationship believable. They were two human beings in a perilous situation, who needed each other to exist; they needed each other's lives, and there was never any

En route for location filming in Honolulu for *From Here to Eternity*. Left to right: Frank Sinatra, Deborah Kerr, Burt Lancaster, author James Jones, director Fred Zinnemann. Columbia, 1953.

With Burt Lancaster in *From Here to Eternity*.

With Yul Brynner in the dressing-room during the run
of *Tea and Sympathy*, 1953. (*Rothschild*)

With John Kerr in the film of *Tea and Sympathy*. MGM, 1957.

Left to right: Peter Cushing, Van Johnson, Deborah Kerr in *The End of the Affair*. Columbia, 1953.

Left to right: Ken Darby, associate to Alfred Newman, MD and conductor (centre) of *The King and I*, at a recording session with Marni Nixon and Deborah Kerr. (*Kerr Collection*)

As Mrs Anna in *The King and I*.
Twentieth Century-Fox, 1955.

With Gladys Cooper in *Separate Tables*.
United Artists, 1958.

As Sister Angela in *Heaven Knows, Mr Allison*. Twentieth Century-Fox, 1957.

Left to right: Dean Martin, Deborah, Francesca (six), Rock Hudson as Santa Claus, Melanie (ten) and a journalist presenting the Hollywood Women's Press Award, 1957. (*Kerr Collection*)

With Jason Robards Jnr in *Th*
*Journey*. MGM, 1958. (*Ernst Haas, Ker*
*Collection*)

As Sheilah Graham to Gregory Peck's Scott Fitzgerald in *Beloved Infidel*.
Twentieth Century-Fox, 1959.

With Megs Jenkins in *The Innocents*. Twientieth Century-Fox, 1961.

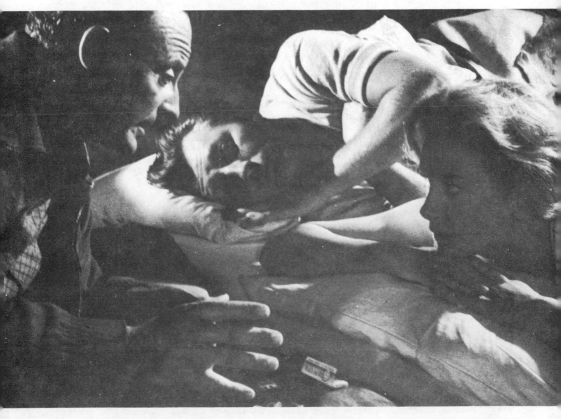

Fred Zinnemann directs Robert Mitchum and Deborah Kerr in a scene from *The Sundowners*. Warner Brothers, 1959. (*Sanford H. Roth, Kerr Collection*)

Wedding in Klosters. Behind Peter Viertel and wife
Deborah are his daughter Christine (eight) and mother
Salka Viertel. Left to right in background: Irwin and
Marian Shaw, Anatole Litvak and wife Sophie, Yul
Brynner, Mel Ferrer and Doris Brynner. (*Comet, Kerr
Collection*)

Deborah and Peter are driven to the reception by Walter Haensli, 23 July, 1960.
(*Fournol, Kerr Collection*)

Left to right: Richard Burton, Cyril Delevanti, Deborah Kerr, Ava Gardner in *Night of the Iguana*, 1963. (*A. Paal, Kerr Collection*)

With Dame Edith Evans in *The Chalk Garden*. Universal, 1963.

Dining with husband Peter and Audrey Hepburn, 1964. (*Kerr Collection*)

hn Huston shows David Niven how to make love to Deborah while on location in Ireland for
*Casino Royale*, 1966. (*A. Paal, Kerr Collection*)

Elia Kazan directing Deborah in *The Arrangement*, 1968: (*Bruce McBroom, Kerr Collection*)

With Julia Foster in *The Day After the Fair* at the Lyric Theatre, Shaftesbury Avenue, 1972. (*Mark Gudgeon*)

Peter and Deborah in Klosters with their Pyrenean Mountain dog, Guapa (Beauty). (*J. Bauer, Kerr Collection*)

Left to right: Deborah, Ed Lyndeck, Tony Musante in *Souvenir*, 1975. (*Eric Skipsey*)

Guest of honour at Leading Ladies Dinner—Gallery
First Nighters' Club, 1973. (*Universal Pictorial Press*)

As 'Candida' with Denis Quilley at the Albery Theatre,
St Martin's Lane, 1977. (*Zoë Dominic*)

Deborah and Peter at home at 'Wyhergut' in Klosters, Switzerland. (*René Burri, Kerr Collecti*

question of its being a sexual relationship. His darling, puzzled face: "But you're a woman—don't you...?" up against her absolute purity: "No, I'm married to Christ." You would think that at the time it was made people would demand more, but they didn't, and they loved it. It was a very successful movie— a real movie, with the action of the bombing of the coconut plantation, the underwater stuff with the turtle; and the Japanese planes coming over: it had everything. John's an incredible director, and so talented in many, many directions. Let's face it, he's one of the best *actors* around. Having now done three films with him I say, when I get stuck, "You do it, John" and he does it impeccably, and I just mimic him in doing it.'

Robert Mitchum wrote to me about his co-star: 'I envy you the time spent with Deborah in sharing her humours and perspectives. It is often lamentable that the association of friends is limited to professional endeavours which occasion a void upon completion. She is a lady of such remarkable and tolerant perception that the resultant communication is a source of joy, in that even the obscure intention finds appreciation in her cheerful translation. One feels 'understood', and, thus encouraged by her understanding, inspired to assist her own happiness.

'She makes it so much easier—so much clearer, and so much more fun. Long may she wave.'


II


To date Deborah Kerr has made three films with Mitchum and three with Cary Grant, the actor who most puts her on her mettle. She says: 'I have never known a man to apply himself so seriously and so ruthlessly to the job on hand. It is only because he can take his job so seriously that he is such a fine comedy actor. You would have to get up very early in the

161

morning to steal a scene from him. I never have. But he plays fair. Comedy is a cut-throat game and many Hollywood comedy actors play it rough, expecting you to take care of yourself. But Cary never cheated. In *An Affair to Remember* we had some wonderful comedic scenes together, and a lot of it was *ad lib*: "But I thought you were going to speak" ... "Well, I'm not—it's your turn" ... "Aren't you going to speak?" "All right, I'll say something ..." and they kept it in the scene. I learned so much from him: he's an absolute genius at comedy timing. He believed in being always what it was his audience expected him to be, and that was why he achieved such enormous success. Things have loosened up since: one can play against type, to a certain degree, but if you go too far, for instance if I tried to play a really ghastly murderess or something like that, audiences wouldn't like it, and they wouldn't go to see it, because it's not me—not what they think of as me.'

In the meantime, Kerr's constantly proven versatility was to win her her fourth Academy Award nomination and her second New York Film Critics' Award as Best Actress for *Mr Allison*. At this time Deborah Kerr's films—all of them on a rising graph of popularity—were released in Britain in a topsy-turvy kind of order: following the late 1956 triumph of *The King and I*, *Heaven Knows, Mr Allison* went the rounds in July 1957 and *Tea and Sympathy* not until October, a month after the most recently filmed *An Affair to Remember*. This was a re-make of the 1939 hit *Love Affair* between Irene Dunne and Charles Boyer, by the original director, Leo McCarey, who wrote the screenplay with Delmer Daves. McCarey had a great flair for sentiment and sophisticated comedy in almost equal proportions, and had won an Oscar for Best Director of 1937 for *The Awful Truth* starring Dunne in one of her classic examples of high comedy acting, and Grant, already well up to his co-star's standard in that respect.

The casting of Grant and Kerr was inspirational, and, for added insurance of a smash hit producer Jerry Wald harked back to his company's recent musical bonanza by having Deborah Kerr cast as Terry McKay, a nightclub singer turned children's coach. (Irene Dunne had played a simple working girl.) She loses the use of her legs in a traffic accident which prevents her carrying out her pact to meet her shipboard romance, playboy Nickie Ferrante, on top of the Empire State Building, six months later. The sentiment got way out of hand at times, but was balanced by the adroit comedy of everyone concerned, and it is the film which, in all her travels, people mention to Deborah as the one they have recently seen again, and how moving it was, and how it made them cry. Leo McCarey knew what he was doing—the picture was another enormous success—and though some of the critics scoffed unrestrainedly, Sarah Stoddart again put the case for the average picturegoer: 'I can't take all this seriously. I don't think you're meant to. The marvel is that these two amazing stars make this weepie *fun* instead of an ordeal. Happily the chuckles drown the tears . . . And Kerr? Warmly sensitive, I knew. But that wry comic touch—it's a revelation.' The same paper's reader, C. S. Davis, of Dartford, Kent, saw Grant and Kerr as the team to replace Tracy and Hepburn as the screen's best adult comedy twosome.

Another bonus for the film was that the title song, written, as were all the others, by Harry Warren, with lyrics by Harold Adamson and the ubiquitous Leo McCarey, went into the Hit Parade. In the film the stars did sing a few bars of the song while dancing cheek to cheek, and Philips Records announced that they would duet together on an LP. When this materialized their duet was vocally conspicuous by its absence, though they were glamorously pictured on the album sleeve: apart from Vic Damone repeating his rendering of the title tune, most of the vocalizing was by Marni Nixon, as it had been when she dubbed Terry McKay's songs for the film, except for the one number Deborah Kerr actually sang in the movie, with the children, *The Tiny Scout* (*He Knows You Inside Out*).

In the original *Love Affair* Boyer took Irene Dunne to see his grandmother who lives on the French Riviera: the late Maria Ouspenskaya acted the part memorably. In 1957 Cathleen Nesbitt played the same scene touchingly; her last contact with Deborah Kerr had been slight, when she was one of the 'Ladies'

163

to Nesbitt's Beatrice in *Much Ado* nineteen years previously in Regent's Park, and *Affair to Remember* was the first time they got to know each other. 'There's a great democracy among film-makers,' says Cathleen Nesbitt, 'and Deborah exemplifies this to a remarkable degree: there's no feeling whatsoever of either class or technical superiority about her. No wonder everybody loves her—she hasn't an unkind thought in her head. I only had one scene with her and Cary, in my "beautiful villa", and all my friends envied me the sunshine of location in the South of France. They were misled: it was all built, most convincingly, in the studio in Hollywood.'

## III

Deborah's next movie, made the summer of the same year, actually was located on the Côte d'Azur, produced and directed by Otto Preminger from Arthur Laurents' screenplay of Françoise Sagan's best seller *Bonjour Tristesse*, and set in La Lavendu, overlooking St Tropez. Kerr played Anne, an attractive widow, engaged to Raymond (David Niven), the rich and promiscuous father of a teenage daughter, Cécile (Jean Seberg), whose way of life Anne attempts to reform. Cécile plots with her boyfriend to reinstate Raymond's former mistress, Elsa (Mylene Demongeot); Anne drives away in distress and is killed in a car crash. Father and daughter resume their former way of life and realize how empty it is. The real star of this undervalued film, which captured admirably the ambiguous Sagan psychology, was Georges Perinal, whose camera fully used the potential of technicolor to paint a breathtakingly beautiful picture of the Mediterranean, in contrast to the grey-green monochrome of the Paris sequences, where Cécile recalls the story of how she virtually drove Anne to her death.

Kerr's portrayal was a striking instance of her ability to create a complete human being, within moments of her appearance on the scene: the attitudes to her fiancé and his daughter of the outwardly sophisticated, but inwardly un-tough fashion designer were expressed in her movements and in her voice, controlled, but with a hint of underlying uncertainty. The climax, when she believed she had overheard Raymond express contempt for her in his reunion with Elsa, was an almost unbearable glimpse of shattered faith and trust. Perinal worked in perfect harmony with the star, in the way his camera moved from the polite observance of her conventionally groomed aspect in the early scenes, to a searching scanning of her unmade-up face, revealing the freckles that give her a touchingly girlish and vulnerable appearance, after her love forces her to drop her defences and disclose herself as the simple person she really is.

Her power as an actress helped bring out the best of the appealingly immature Jean Seberg in their scenes together. The performance of Preminger's 'discovery', still smarting from the critical beating she had taken as 'Saint Joan', varied from the near-perfect to the almost amateur, but overall was very true to Sagan's original conception, as, indeed, was the whole film. Deborah tried to encourage Jean, who was still going through a pretty rough time from the director: 'I told her not to let him "get at" her, and to do what she thought was right. "It's going to be *you* up there—your face, your expression and your way of reading the lines—not the director's."' The rapport between them worked entirely to the benefit of the film, in which Niven was superb as the world-weary Raymond. There was fine support from Martita Hunt, Walter Chiari, Juliette Greco, singing the title song, and Jean Kent as a rich and bitchy socialite. The whole film was brilliantly done and admirably caught the useless, butterfly existence of Sagan's Riviera Jet Set. The fact that the critics had a 'down' on her, as well as Jean Seberg, at the time, robbed a splendid movie of its fair share of appreciation.

At the end of 1957 Deborah Kerr, besides her clutch of honours for *Mr Allison*, received the peculiar distinction of the Photoplay Gold Medal for the World's Most Famous Actress, a significant award, in that she was, at this time, the most in-demand actress in films. Her long-delayed, but highly felicitous teaming with David Niven was repeated the same autumn in Hollywood for the complex organization set up by her old partner, Burt Lancaster, with writer Ben Hecht and business-man James Hill. The subject was Terence Rattigan's highly successful play *Separate Tables*—the casting all-star, and no less complex. Kerr and Niven were the first announced, with Sir Laurence Olivier to co-star and direct, and Vivien Leigh to play his ex-wife. The production began in an atmosphere of cordiality. Cathleen Nesbitt, repeating her stage rôle of Lady Matheson for the film, says: 'It was Vivien's suggestion that we rehearse at one table, so as to get to know each other, rather than at the separate tables which feature in the story. It seemed a great idea, and that was when I got to know Deborah better. Gladys Cooper and I, of course, had been friends in the theatre for a good many years.' The resultant togetherness had one unforeseen and crucial result: producer Lancaster and director Olivier had a spectacular disagreement, which resulted in the withdrawal of the Oliviers from the motley and an urgent search for suitable star replacements.

Cathleen Nesbitt suggested Eric Portman, so magnificent in the original stage productions, and was told 'No good—he's not known in films.' He had, in fact, played both male leads, two utterly dissimilar characters in the two sections which composed the play, while Margaret Leighton had doubled the two female leads with equal success. This was considered impractical for film purposes, in the admirable screenplay which Rattigan himself wrote with John Gay. Eventually the new stars were chosen: Lancaster himself would step into the Olivier rôle, and Rita Hayworth, recently married to James Hill, took over from Vivien Leigh. The action was set in a Bournemouth private hotel, run by Miss Cooper (Wendy Hiller), who is in love with John Malcolm (Lancaster), a writer, now dissipated and being visited by the divorced wife he can't forget, Ann Shankland (Hayworth.) At other tables are the Railton-Bells, Sybil, a shy spinster (Kerr) and her overbearing mother (Cooper), and, sitting on his own, Major Pollock (Niven), whose accounts of his army exploits have been boring the other guests for some time.

166

Sybil is attracted to him through a sympathy which turns to love, and when he is revealed as a fraud, with a penchant for molesting women in cinemas, she defies her mother for the first time, in defending him. Hotelier Miss Cooper gives up what she regards as her last chance of happiness in John Malcolm, realizing the desperate need he and his wife have for each other. Other inhabitants of the hotel were played by Felix Aylmer, Rod Taylor and Audrey Dalton as the young lovers, and the late May Hallatt, using her bullfrog voice to good effect as Miss Meacham, always studying racing form, and more suitably clad in tweeds than in her Indian make-up as the Ayah in *Black Narcissus*. Like Cathleen Nesbitt she was repeating her stage part.

Even in Hollywood, Wendy Hiller's professional path had again crossed Deborah Kerr's, whose Sybil won her her fifth Academy Award Nomination: both David Niven and Wendy Hiller received Oscars, for 1958's Best Actor and Best Supporting Actress respectively. In all, *Separate Tables* gained seven nominations, but neither Delbert Mann's excellent direction nor Hayworth's moving performance as Ann were among them. Never the most self-confident of actresses she felt herself miscast (the director's announcement 'she'd already been cast when I took over,' could not have helped), but Deborah Kerr's opinion of the very good job she made of the part was echoed by few of the critics. Cathleen Nesbitt, however, also found Rita a very likable person and agreed that her performance was considerably under-rated.

Kerr's scenes with the late Gladys Cooper were particularly poignant: 'Someone asked Gladys about Method Acting, and how she obtained her effects. She told me, "I honestly don't know what they're talking about. One just goes on, and one is." That is exactly how I feel: I go on and I am. I can do anything if I am playing a part, but when I have to be just me I'm stiff with nerves. Outwardly I look cool enough, but deep down I'm terribly nervous and very shy, so I responded to Sybil; I have a lot of her in me. Sybil had lived for a long time in a state of negativeness. I had to be careful in playing the scenes in which she reached out for something more: it had to be very

167

tentative, and at the end of the movie you still don't know where her experiences have left her.'

## IV

*The Journey*—the second film on the three-picture deal fixed by Bert Allenberg—was to prove, for Deborah Kerr personally, not only a fateful one, but a turning-point in her life. For the last few years she felt that she and Tony had been drifting further and further apart. He was doing well in his career as European representative of CBS television, while she had been working non-stop as well—usually in places far removed from each other. They were together on increasingly rare occasions.

The location was Vienna and the director the late Anatole Litvak. The story, originally set in China by George Tabori, had been changed to the Austro-Hungarian frontier, in the interests of topicality. However, the central theme, harking back to *Boule de Suif*, and concerning the heroine's voluntary surrender to her captor in order to save the lives of her fellow passengers, remained virtually intact. Litvak, coping with hundreds of extras of all nationalities, and a script which had had its difficulties in transition, sent for his good friend Peter Viertel, whose experience as the writer of screenplays which included *The Sun Also Rises* and *African Queen*, made this salvage work something he could accomplish at his ease. Yul Brynner, who had been so helpful to Deborah during the filming of *The King and I*, was the co-star, and *The Journey* was shot at the Hosenhegel film studio. During breaks in production Deborah spent hours in Vienna's Kunsthistorisches-Museum, revelling in the magnificent collection of Breughels; history of another kind was all too present when the unit shot scenes on the Austro-Hungarian border, and the barbed wire—all known to be mined—and Russian command posts, manned by soldiers with guns, were right there as a reminder of what Hungary had been through less than three years previously.

Peter Viertel was witty, sympathetic and a well-known novelist and screenwriter. It was quite a coincidence that he had adapted the script for Katharine Hepburn and Humphrey Bogart that Deborah had yearned to do at Metro nearly ten years previously. He began to accompany Deborah on the sight-seeing trips round the city she had previously undertaken on her own. They formed a warm friendship and sometimes had dinner together; on one occasion Bob Anderson, who was touring Europe, called and took them out to lunch. In the five years since the opening of *Tea and Sympathy*, actress and author had several times tried unsuccessfully to set up plans to do another play together, a project which remains a joint ambition of theirs, but which to date has not yet materialized.

On 31 May, 1958, it was announced that Deborah and Tony Bartley had separated; the divorce followed a year later, on 10 July, in a Santa Monica Court. On the future of their children, she said: 'We agree completely and absolutely about their care and education and it is my desire still to play the part of a mother.' There was amicable settlement of property, including the home in Pacific Palisades.

The year between Deborah's announcement of their separation 'With deepest regret' and the granting of the divorce was a period of considerable mental torment, and she immersed herself ever deeper in the film work which was flowing in from all quarters. *The Journey*, she says, was 'nearly a good film': the exciting but overlong story concerned a group of passengers on their way from Budapest to Vienna, held at the Hungarian border by the Russian commander, Major Surov (Yul Brynner). He is attracted to Lady Diana Ashmore (Deborah Kerr), who is trying to smuggle her wounded Hungarian lover, Paul (Jason Robards Jnr in his first film) across the frontier. When they are detected, the other passengers urge her to yield to Surov to save them all. He releases them after proving to her that their attraction is mutual, and is then shot by a chance bullet from a partisan guerrilla. The first-rate supporting cast included Robert Morley, E. G. Marshall, Anne Jackson, David Kossoff and Anouk Aimée. Kerr and Brynner again proved themselves a dynamic team, as her ladylike reserve struck sparks from his Mongol flamboyance. The film was released in March 1959, the month after *Separate Tables*.

At this peak of Deborah Kerr's career interesting scripts were available by the gross; choosing one was a problem of some magnitude, since the final result was, inevitably, completely unpredictable. A biopic of the life of the poetess Edna St Vincent Millay, like the earlier mooted *Elizabeth Browning Story*, opposite Tyrone Power, failed to materialize, as did Somerset Maugham's *Cakes and Ale*, adapted by Peter Viertel. Two that were made with other stars, *Hawaii* and *Greengage Summer*, turned out successes, but, in the event, they might not have proved the right subjects for her.

On paper, Nancy Mitford's *The Blessing* must have seemed an ideal subject. The title was changed to *Count Your Blessings*, lest people associate it with Kerr's nun image, and, as the movie was to be shot in Paris, who better to co-star than Maurice Chevalier, along with Italy's current heart-throb, Rossano Brazzi? Not French? Well—at least Continental, and director Jean Negulesco could be counted on to disguise the difference. With beautiful Metrocolor—sometimes a most unflattering process—photography by experts like Milton Krasner and George Folsey, and the wit of Nancy Mitford, how could it miss? But it did. As Deborah said: 'A charming, funny, amusing book—somewhat castrated, because some of the funniest stuff, her beautifully observed sketches of American people in Paris, in government circles, was omitted from the script, because they didn't want to offend the Americans—became just a charming travelogue. I had a lovely location in Paris and beautiful clothes, and Chevalier took me to visit his home, where everything, even the ash-trays, were in the shape of a straw-hat—the ultimate example of an artist being true to his image for ever and ever. Rossano Brazzi is a dear man who exudes charm, though he was too Italian really to suggest a French aristocrat.'

Writer John Douglas Eames summed it up: 'Maurice Chevalier and Deborah Kerr were sparkling players in need of something sparkling to play.' Producer Karl Tunberg was responsible for the screenplay, which dealt with the whirlwind wartime romance of Grace Allingham (Kerr) and Captain Charles-Édouard de Valhubert (Brazzi), and how it takes her nine years to discover his essential promiscuity, on their delayed honeymoon, by which time they have a seven-year-old son, Sigismund (Martin Stephens). Chevalier, as their worldly friend, the Duc de St Cloud, was one of the film's positive assets, along with the character of Grace, so deftly sketched by the star, whose cool detachment, with its underlying sense of real affection, was just right. She had fine support from Ronald Squire as her father, Sir Edward, and Patricia Medina, exquisite to look at, as an old flame of Édouard's, who needs minimal fanning to make her burn brightly again in his life, plus the inestimable Mona Washbourne as a nanny. This wound up Deborah's three-picture deal with MGM.

She was able to spend Christmas 1958, in London, with Melanie and Frankie; her well-earned holiday, touring some of the parts of the globe which her career hitherto had not encompassed, was cut short by a call from Jerry Wald of Twentieth Century, for whom she had another two films to do, to play Sheilah Graham in the adaptation of her own life story *Beloved Infidel*, which she had written with Gerold Frank. Sy Bartlett had adapted the scenario, and the subject was one for which Deborah had high hopes; the life of Sheilah Graham, from deprived childhood to fame as one of the best known columnists of the day, was a real story of triumph over circumstances, and offered a challenge to whoever played her. Things did not work out that way, because Gregory Peck, when asked to portray Scott Fitzgerald, the great influence and love of Sheilah Graham's life, would only agree to do it if the story were adapted to start where he came in.

The result was one of Deborah Kerr's least happy ventures, although the veteran Henry King, who had directed some of the great action-cum-musical movies of the past, besides, more recently, *The Sun Also Rises*, did his best to weld together the disjointed elements. Leon Shamroy handled the Cinemascope photography (great for dawns and sunsets) handsomely in De

Luxe Colour, but, with the emphasis shifted from Graham to Fitzgerald, a prime piece of miscasting for Gregory Peck, it is not surprising that, in the words of *Picturegoer*'s Margaret Hinxman: 'Deborah Kerr here never suggests the orphanage-reared, English-born go-getter who dragged herself out of the gutter, invented a dream family background for herself, and was always conscious of her lack of education.'

In the final scenes some impression of her love for the great writer, whose addiction to alcohol was inevitably to destroy him, did come through—their fight and touching reconciliation was as gripping as the whole film should have been—but it was as though Kerr was having to act for both of them. There were minor compensations in the performances of Eddie Albert, as the faithful friend Carter, and Karin Booth as the late Constance Bennett—with the name changed to 'Janet Pierce'. In her life story Bennett had acidly told Graham: 'It's hard to believe that a girl as pretty as you could be the biggest bitch in Hollywood.' Kerr's Sheilah handled the rejoinder: 'Not the biggest—only the second biggest' with splendid effect, which was somewhat diluted by the word 'witch' having been substituted for 'bitch'.

She says: 'I was heartbroken that the film did not do what it should have done, but, on the other hand, I understood Peck's point of view, and I was happy to work with him. The film wasn't all bad, but it became disjointed, between Sheilah's original story, the film script, and Peck's own writers, and I was unable really to characterize, because half the poor woman's personality was cut out. It was difficult for me to pick up the threads halfway through her life and, for my own self, be genuine. I wasn't able to show where she came from, and what she was, and why she became the way she was later on—it wasn't even explained *why* she took to lion-hunting. It didn't just *happen*, as in the film; it was because of what had happened in her childhood.

# V

Fred Zinnemann had been planning to star Deborah Kerr in *The Sundowners* since 1957: in September of that year he said that he hoped to persuade William Holden to play opposite her, and the next month Gary Cooper was announced to co-star. To picture either as an Australian sheep farmer would have required a good deal of imagination, but an even stranger suggestion was that the director hoped to get Claudette Colbert and Errol Flynn for the two main supporting rôles—eventually played by Glynis Johns and Peter Ustinov. At that time Colbert had not filmed since the 1955 *Texas Lady*, and Flynn was to complete only one more picture, *The Roots of Heaven*, for John Huston, before his death the following year. While it is possible to imagine him in the part of a rolling stone, so excellently played by Ustinov, the idea of Colbert as the widowed publican who sets her cap at him is mind-boggling.

When the film was eventually made, on location in Australia during the second half of 1959—October, November and December, reputedly the best months of the year, although they struck the worst weather ever known in local history—the stars were Deborah Kerr and Robert Mitchum, a combination which blended as perfectly together, and with their director, as they had with Huston two years previously. They were cast as Ida and her husband Paddy Carmody, an Irish sheep-drover in Australia, who travels from job to job, his love of liberty conflicting with his desire to settle down with his wife and son Sean (Michael Anderson Jnr). Having made a great effort by working steadily for a while as a shearer in order to make a down payment on a farm, he gives in to temptation and gambles away their earnings. Ida realizes she can't change the man she married, and they set off again hopefully on their travels.

It's a story of hope and of human fallibility and loyalty, always compelling, despite its length and the slender story line, and Jack Hildyard's Technicolor camerawork excelled even his Oscar-winning photography for the 1957 *Bridge on the River*

*Kwai.* The screenplay by Isobel Lennart, based on Jon Cleary's novel, is full of human touches about real people, such as the sheep-shearing contest which loses Carmody the family savings when a toothless ancient (splendidly played by Wylie Watson) beats him hollow, and the unforgettable scene where Ida sees a stylish and elegantly dressed woman about her own age check her make-up as she sits in a stationary train. When the other woman looks up their eyes meet and they exchange the instinctive wisdom of their sex, with the town lady acknowledging that, for all her advantage of money and elegance, it is Ida who is in possession of the verities which a happy partnership can bring.

In this performance we witness the perfect fusion of human being and actress that is Deborah Kerr's supreme contribution to her craft. Shorn of all trappings of make-up and costuming, the freckles accentuating the perfect structure of her face, she establishes in the little scene just described the identity of Ida in all her toughness and vulnerability; it is as though the actress were recognizing her other self and acknowledging that two sides of the coin are necessary for completeness.

Faultlessly, she captured the Australian hardiness, as well as the coarse-grained quality of Ida; when she complained: 'I got an aching backside', it was for real, as was Mitchum's reply: 'I know all about that backside of yours. It only aches whenever you're losing an argument.' They are Sundowners—people whose home is wherever they are when the sun goes down. Both actors identified completely with their parts; with no concessions to conventional screen beauty, and virtually without make-up, Deborah had never looked lovelier, while Bob Mitchum produced a seemingly casual strength from within which made their love for each other, as well as their marriage, utterly real and true.

The other performances all contributed to the film as a whole: Peter Ustinov's eccentric and lovable Venneker, with his wild and wonderful tales of his past life, Glynis Johns as the jolly bar lady, Michael Anderson Jnr as the Carmodys' fourteen-year-old son—uneducated, but reaching towards something outside the only existence he knows—and Dina Merrill as the 'lady' whose cool beauty and nice dresses Ida secretly envies.

Incredibly, some of the critics did not have too much praise for this great movie, though the public loved it and it was a very big hit in England and Australia. Deborah was still finishing off the studio shots for *The Sundowners* at Elstree when she received the Hollywood Press Association Award as World Film Favourite. The Zinnemann film brought her her sixth Oscar nomination for 1960, although it was not premièred in England until January 1961, at the Warner Theatre in Leicester Square, showplace of the company who made it. Dilys Powell wrote that the film had 'a sense of distance and remoteness which I find exciting . . . (it) adds to my imagination of Australia . . . admiring Fred Zinnemann as I do, I occasionally wished that he had given us less, shall I say, of Australia and more of himself. Still, he is there, recognizable in the humanity of the film, the delicate shading with which even the roughest characters are played. He has drawn an unexpected range of feeling from Robert Mitchum as the itinerant drover, but the strength of the story is in Deborah Kerr as the wife, stubbornly clinging to the dream of a home with a kitchen and a stove—never sentimental, never mannered—a performance with a heart.' This won Deborah her third New York Film Critics' Award.

Her explanation for the general underrating is that 'It was a little before its time. It was a no-story movie—an observation of life, with a marvellous cast. I loved working with Glynis again, for the first time since *Perfect Strangers*. We've always remained friends, though, again, she is one of the people, like Jean Seberg, I don't see as often as I would like. Ustinov is one of the funniest people I know, and the experience of working in Australia a happy one for us all. There's a good deal of Ida in me: I can settle down anywhere and call it home. The whole cast were plunged into gloom by that weather in Cooma—the little town in New South Wales which was our base—as cold as an English winter, the rain pouring down day after day, varied by enormous hailstones. But Peter joined us there for

a few weeks, and while everyone was grumbling about the restricted gastronomical resources of the location, he started to
forage. Exploring the back streets where the foreigners lived
he found a German baker who made wonderful black bread
and an Italian woman who made ravioli. After that eating
became a pleasure. Peter Ustinov, Bob Mitchum and Fred Zinnemann all had their wives with them and we used to have dinner every evening in one another's houses. The Ustinovs produced some marvellous meals, and Bob Mitchum had a way
with steaks, but we all decided that Peter was the best and most
imaginative cook.'

## VI

Deborah was home in England with the children for the Christmas of 1959, and remained there for her next film, which took
her from the wide open spaces to the 'impoverished' gentry of
Hugh and Margaret Williams' comedy *The Grass is Greener*,
from their play of the same name.

Deborah was cast as Hilary Rhyall, married to the conventionally British and correct Victor (Cary Grant). Mitchum
was there again, this time as Charles Delacra, an American visiting her stately home, at the invitation of her husband. Despite
her elegant and staid background—the part of Hilary on the
stage had provided Celia Johnson with an ideal chance to be
'British to the core'—she falls in love with Charles and spends
a week in London with him.

It is only when her sex-mad girlfriend Hattie (Jean Simmons)
sets out to take Victor away that Hilary realizes her love for
her husband is still there, though dormant and needing to be
awakened. Stanley Donen's lightly witty touch as producer-
director, Christopher Challis's handsome Technicolor photography and the Williams' own screenplay sensibly did not try
to disguise the film's stage origins and the result was a very
funny and enjoyable entertainment, acted with style through-

176

out. The advantage went to Jean Simmons, as it had in the theatre to Joan Greenwood, with the small but showy rôle of Hattie. Simmons was a revelation in her first completely zany part, even though she lacked Greenwood's adorably off-beat quality, in a character which had been written for her. Moray Watson was hilarious as the usual impossible butler who so often seemed to act as good fairy in Williams-land.

Kerr's performance, in the company of two of her favourite co-stars, was radiant: 'Between Cary's superb timing and Bob's instinctive awareness of what you're trying to do, this was a very happy film.' The inclusion of some of Noël Coward's music and lyrics helped the atmosphere considerably, and the name 'Grandon Productions' provided the clue that Grant and Donen were the joint owners of the venture, which was not released in Britain until March 1961.

It was during a location in South Audley Street, London for *The Grass is Greener* that Deborah Kerr met the girl who was to become perhaps the most active of her English fans, Mary Johnston, who had written to her during the making of *The Sundowners* and had been invited to watch some of the shooting of the Stanley Donen film. Mary, then Donaldson, was at Southgate County Grammar School when she first saw and was deeply impressed by the star in *The King and I*, in 1957, an admiration to which the seal was set by *An Affair to Remember*.

Mary went into film work as a secretary in Wardour Street and eventually at the studios, and was interested in forming a Deborah Kerr Appreciation Society—a suggestion which was sympathetically but firmly turned down. Deborah explained that a Fan Club had been formed for her in the USA, and she had been obliged to ask that it be wound up, as she literally had no time to devote to it. She told Mary that she would never undertake any project to which she could not give her full attention. Nevertheless she was, and remains, the most approachable of people, and makes it a point of honour to answer all letters. Her attitude is: 'It's the least I can do, if anyone is kind enough to write.'

Many of the letters Deborah Kerr receives are highly intelligent, some offer constructive criticism, and some are sad. At the time of *Tea and Sympathy* she had a few from young men who wrote that if only they had met someone as helpful and sensitive as Laura Reynolds when they were at school, their lives might have turned out more happily.

# CHAPTER ELEVEN

# FRESH FIELDS

## I

With the last shot of *The Grass is Greener* completed Deborah Kerr took off for Switzerland and her marriage to Peter Viertel in Klosters, in the canton of Grisons, was solemnized on Sunday, 23 July, 1960. The simple ceremony was performed by the Clerk of the Court, Herr Joos, in the Gemeindehaus, which could be likened to a cross between a British Town Hall and a Registrar's Office. In Switzerland it is the place where all the local government takes place; it is also where one goes to be married, to call the police, and a thousand other things. The entire population of Klosters, all dressed in their traditional Alpen finery—blue smocks and gaily coloured dirndls—turned out for the occasion. The bride had had to brush up her German for the occasion, while the groom, having been born in Dresden, Germany in 1920 and lived there until he moved with his family to California in 1927, was not only as fluent as the natives, but, having been a resident in Klosters since the forties, a personal friend of almost every one of them as well.

Peter Viertel, son of two brilliantly gifted parents, Berthold Viertel, Austrian poet and director of theatre and motion pictures, and his wife Salka, actress and screenwriter *par excellence*, has, like his wife, the rare gift of putting people instantly at their ease; his marriage in Klosters, which exemplifies the kind of classlessness unique to Switzerland, evoked the warm-hearted response of a full village wedding, with all the citizens turning out to throw confetti and rice and to cheer the happy couple as they were driven away in a pony and trap by the picturesquely garbed Walter Haensli, one of the village's richest native sons, to the reception at the mountain home of Irwin Shaw and his then wife Marian, a few hundred yards away.

The moving and romantic setting was obviously not considered quite dramatic enough to do justice to the union of an international star and a best-selling novelist. Probing behind the scenes, the *Sunday Express* reported that 'A double hitch almost forced film actress Deborah Kerr and Hollywood scriptwriter Peter Viertel to call off their wedding ... The first hitch was when Miss Kerr's cyclamen pink sheath dress, with a jacket of embroidered organdie and matching turban, the gift of Audrey Hepburn and her husband Mel Ferrer and created specifically for her by Givenchy, failed to arrive in time. With the bride in tears (*sic*), urgent calls were made to Paris, Lucerne, Zürich and Geneva to try to trace it. A postman eventually delivered it less than an hour before the ceremony was due to begin. The wedding was postponed for half an hour to give Miss Kerr time to dress.

'The second hitch was when personal documents which had been sent for verification to Chur, the cantonal capital sixteen miles from Klosters, and without which the couple could not have been married, were delayed. They arrived only five minutes before the ceremony began. The witnesses were American novelist Irwin Shaw, author of *The Young Lions* and the film producer Anatole Litvak ... After the twenty-minute ceremony Miss Kerr and her husband were driven in a pony cart to Mr Shaw's home. There Mr Viertel said: "All I hope now is that Deborah will have six months free from filming so that we can be together." '

Deborah's own comment on the occasion is: 'You mustn't believe everything you read in the papers, you know, and I was certainly *not* in tears. It was a charming wedding, with just a few of our very close friends at the small reception in Irwin and Marian's lovely house: Peter's mother, Salka, Anatole and Sophie Litvak, Yul Brynner and his then wife Doris, Mel Ferrer

(Audrey was busy becoming mother to their son Sean), Adam—the Shaws' son, Harry Kurnitz, Irving Lazar, Hans and Doris Guler, who run the charming Chesa Grischuna Hotel and Restaurant in the village, various other locals, and Peter's eight-year-old daughter Christine, of his first marriage to Virginia Ray Schulberg, the divorced wife of writer Bud Schulberg.'

Peter had been in Klosters for some months, supervising the finishing touches to what was to be their home. 'Wyhergut' (literally 'Good Weir' because it stands near a weir) was constructed on the mountainside, by local builders, from blocks of rough stone individually chosen by master stonemasons, so that it glows with subtle colours and green lichen. The woodwork inside is beautifully intagliated and bevelled, and the chalet, from the outside, gives the appearance of having evolved centuries ago from the mountainside around it. Peter Viertel, as adept a builder of houses as he is novelist and scriptwriter, lived and worked with Herr Thut—a very fine architect—and the builders until the home was completed in six months, something which could not be accomplished today as handsomely as it was in 1960.

## II

Peter's wish for Deborah to have at least six months free of commitments was indeed to be fulfilled. After several years of virtually non-stop travel and filming, she was able to relax in the family atmosphere of their delightful mountain home.

Her next return to a cold England was early in 1961, to face the squally Eastbourne seafront for locations on United Artists' *The Naked Edge*. For her the main interest in working on this film was that, at last, she had Gary Cooper as her co-star; he would certainly not have been well enough to face the rigours of the Australian locations for their first announced partnership in *The Sundowners*, and by the time he made *The Naked Edge*

181

he was a very sick man. He died of cancer before the film was released, and Deborah, who had been friendly for years with 'Coop' and his wife 'Rocky' in Hollywood, says: 'He was a darling man, and always extremely thoughtful to work with, but sometimes he seemed withdrawn and remote, as though he were no longer with us.'

Ann Todd, who was working on the next set, feels that Cooper must have been grateful to be working with Deborah Kerr at that time, 'because of the positive sense of peace she brought to every film with which she was connected'. Todd had arranged to watch some of the shooting on *The Naked Edge* on a particular day, and checked with Deborah, who advised her that it would not be a good day for him. Ann deferred her visit to a more propitious time, when she found Gary Cooper the epitome of charm and courtesy.

The film has been dismissed in some quarters as being only of interest because it was 'Coop's' last film, and Michael Anderson's direction as 'sub-Hitchcock', which underestimates the genuine sense of mystery and the mounting tension he achieved, as well as the haunted and moving final performance by Cooper and the compassion and concern of Kerr's interpretation of the rôle of his frightened wife, Martha. Cooper was cast as George Radcliffe, a sales representative whose reluctant evidence at the trial of a colleague for robbery and murder causes her to fear that he himself was responsible for the crimes. A blackmail note accuses him of this, and in the climax Martha becomes convinced that he is out to kill her as well, until the dénouement discloses the mysterious Jeremy Clay (Eric Portman) to be the guilty man. Kerr's performance, her only one to date in this well-tried movie genre, was even more effective than Crawford's hitherto definitive acting in *Sudden Fear*, in that the potential victim appeared infinitely more vulnerable. Portman, whose death robbed British films of their most subtle exponent of sinister charm, was genuinely frightening in his final moments as Clay tries to murder Martha, and there was splendid support from Hermione Gingold as her wildly improbable aunt, with further light comedy from Michael

Wilding and an incisively bitter cameo from Diane Cilento as the wife of the murdered man. Peter Cushing, Ronald Howard (son of Leslie) and the late great Wilfrid Lawson rounded off a quality cast.

'Quality', in every department, was the keynote of Deborah Kerr's next film, also made in England in 1961, Jack Clayton's *The Innocents*. Truman Capote, with some extra dialogue by John Mortimer, adapted the play by William Archibald, based on Henry James's story *The Turn of the Screw*, and it is one of the films with which Deborah is proudest to have been associated.

She says: 'It was also one of the hardest; in a very long schedule I was in virtually every shot. I remember being very tired by the end, having worked every single day of the sixteen-week schedule, but it was so fascinating to work with Clayton and to watch *him* working with everyone. The subtlety with which he and his team established the atmosphere of the two worlds—the everyday and the spirit world—was so evocative of decadence, in the most delicate manner, that it completely escaped the majority of the critics. Today, a new generation of young movie "buffs" realize how extraordinary were the effects he achieved. One instance is the way the edges of the screen were just slightly out of focus, as though seen through a glass, perhaps. Now it is acclaimed as a great work of art; then they didn't push it because they didn't know how to respond to something so genuinely spooky—so interwoven with reality that it could be real—and that's something people didn't like. Today they love to be frightened: they can revel in *The Towering Inferno* or *Earthquake* because they *know* it isn't real, but even so, they still hesitate about frights and horrors that come too near home.'

Her interpretation of the extremely complex part of the governess, Miss Giddens, trying to cope with two young charges who appear to be under the spell of a pair of dead lovers, represents for many the supreme achievement of Deborah Kerr's film career. She managed with razor-sharp precision to suggest the moral rectitude of a well-bred Victorian governess—or was it the fevered imaginings of repressed sex? Miss

Giddens remains an enigma, and one of Deborah Kerr's subtlest characterizations. The down-to-earth solidity of Megs Jenkins' housekeeper, Mrs Grose, was always a welcome presence in the film to contrast with the eeriness of the children, Pamela Franklin and Martin Stephens, from whom Jack Clayton drew performances of astonishing effectiveness. The male ghost materialized convincingly in the person of Peter Wyngarde.

If Miss Giddens emerged as an enigma, that was what both the director and Deborah Kerr intended. She says: 'I played it as if she were perfectly sane—whatever Jack wanted was fine; in my own mind, and following Henry James' writing in the original story, she was completely sane, but, because in my case the woman was younger and physically attractive—Flora Robson had played her wonderfully on the stage—it was quite possible that she was deeply frustrated, and it added another dimension that the whole thing *could* have been nurtured in her own imagination.'

Jack Clayton, en route for Hollywood, talked in his London office about *The Innocents*: 'Deborah had one film to do for Twentieth Century, and so did I: that was the one we both wanted to do and which we had discussed when we met the previous year. I had admired her work in two films with that very underrated actor, Robert Mitchum—*Heaven Knows, Mr Allison*, which showed her at her best without make-up, and *The Sundowners*, in which her freckles were so attractively in evidence. I swear she gets more beautiful as the years pass: she is certainly more so now than she was in 1961, and her beauty in the past has only apparently become less when imposed into the set Hollywood mould, which she could not avoid when she went there, because that was the way a "proper film star" was supposed to look. Yes, she's indeed a "proper person", and such a lovely contrast to some of the "proper film stars" I've met.

'When we were about to go into production I found that the film had to be in Cinemascope—a process I'd vowed never to work with—and it was a case of having to adapt the process to suit our own purpose. Freddie Francis is a great cameraman; if you remember the slightly blurred edges of the screen which lent a kind of other-worldly feeling to the composition of scenes—that was something he achieved which worked for the general atmosphere of the story. Into this Debbie brought a subtly understated neurotic quality that no other actress could equate—on a knife-edge between possible menace to the children and their own "wickedness".

'Her professionalism is complete. To achieve what we wanted in the monochrome photography the arcs had to be of considerable intensity, and the atmosphere on the set, with fifteen "brutes" burning away, often stifling. During a long schedule, imprisoned in those voluminous Victorian dresses, she never complained, never showed a trace of the discomfort she had been feeling. During one day's shooting she had to carry the boy, Martin Stephens, in her arms—he was twelve, and a very heavy load. She carried him uncomplainingly for all the takes necessary until we called "Cut!" at the end of the day's work. The next day she mentioned that she had been running a temperature and feeling like death the day before—but she had given no hint of that while we were filming.

'Debbie has a spirit of total generosity to every actor she is associated with, and certainly to every director, besides, basically, to everyone around, spiced slightly, in certain moments of acute provocation—I can't say "stress", because that's one thing she never shows—by displaying suddenly the most marvellous, biting sarcasm, which, to my mind at least, is so much more effective coming from such a lovely, generous lady. But it's extremely rare, and over as soon as said.'

During the filming of *The Innocents* my friend Lyn Fairhurst went to interview her for his radio programme, *Movie-Go-Round.* I asked to be remembered to her, having had no contact with Deborah since she left for Hollywood. Lyn returned and reported that she had thought for a few moments, then said, 'I do remember him: he was always so *enthusiastic!*' An immediate flashback came to mind, about neglecting her morning call, to worship at the shrine of Kay Francis: never had reprimand been so gently administered, nor so salutary in its effect.

Another close associate of Deborah's on *The Innocents* was

185

Gordon Bond, who over a period of seventeen years looked after her hairdressing in every film she made in England. David Niven was instrumental in getting him on to *Bonjour Tristesse*: Gordon and Deborah struck up an immediate working friendship, and from then on, until he left the film industry in the late sixties, she asked for him to do her hair.

One day, on the set of Jack Clayton's film, Deborah asked him to accompany her to watch the 'rushes', as she was worried about her appearance. The entire production unit was packed into the small preview theatre and Bond sat down beside the star, slightly concerned, as he knew she rarely attended her own rushes. The lights dimmed, and on to the soundtrack came a peal of bells, followed by a commercial on sound, mentioning Gordon 'Bubbles' Bond—the nick-name she had given him soon after their first meeting. Following a scene from the rushes there came a similar commercial, another peal of bells from the soundtrack, and finally the announcement: 'The management of this theatre and all the company of *The Innocents* wish "Bubbles" Bond a Happy Birthday!' He says: 'This was Deb: full of fun off set, and with a wicked sense of humour. She can make me laugh more than any other star I worked with over a period of twenty-four years in the business. But once on set it was *work*, and no nonsense; everyone really loved this woman on every film we've done together. I think she is the tops because she's sincere in everything, work and play, on and off set, and because she is always so grateful for what life has given her.'

### III

*The Innocents* was released in Britain early in 1962, and Deborah Kerr was away from the cinema screen until 1963. During that time she was at home in Klosters with Peter and the children, apart from the periods when they were away at boarding-school. His daughter Christine was then eleven, Melanie fifteen

186

and Francesca twelve. Deborah told Sheilah Graham: 'Tony and I have a warm and affectionate relationship over them, which is as it should be.'

Television drama demands a change of pace, somewhere midway between film and theatre, which Kerr found both exciting and frightening. Arthur Penn was producing a 'spectacular' for Associated Rediffusion in London with Fred Coe and offered her the starring parts in their *Three Roads to Rome* which Ronald Marriott was to direct.

'I liked the challenge and the opportunity of doing something you can't do either on the stage or in films—in this case to play three different characters in three different periods inside three days. We rehearsed for three weeks and then taped in three days. The rehearsals were fine, but with the taping terror set in. Suddenly, I found myself confronted by seven cameras: men were crouching on the floor and were sending signals and signs in all directions. Before long I had no more than a quarter of me under control and I was praying I wouldn't forget my lines. One had to know them—or else.'

This Anglo-American production was made in 1961, the year in which Deborah received her first ever Award from her own country, from the Variety Club of Great Britain, for her performance in *The Innocents*. *Three Roads to Rome* was not, however, put out on English television until 30 December, 1963. It has, to date, never been shown in the USA: after it was made the bottom fell out of the market for expensive TV plays of this kind, and the sponsors were just not prepared to pay the money for it. The three playlets were written by Tad Mosel from stories by Martha Gellhorn, Edith Wharton and Aldous Huxley: the first, *Venus Ascendant* presented Deborah Kerr as a thirty-year-old Englishwoman, Moira Shepleigh, an eccentric, rather frumpish girl who has never married and is staying in Rome with friends and driving them mad. She falls in love with a gigolo, played by Anthony Newlands, and it all ends rather sadly.

Set in the present day, the second play *Roman Fever* gave her the rôle of a sixty-year-old called Grace Ansley. Grace is staying

187

with her friend Alida Slade (Celia Johnson, also making her ITV début) in the same hotel in Rome as in the first story, which took place in the thirties. Ostensibly devoted friends, the ladies exchange barbed remarks which reveal rivalry over an old lover, now dead, and over the way life has dealt with them in general.

The third play, *The Rest Cure* set at the turn of the century, cast the star as Miranda, a romantic young girl who runs away to the country the day her stuffy fiancé, played by Allan Cuthbertson, is due in Rome. She falls in love with a handsome young innkeeper, Tonino (Jeremy Brett). The fiancé tracks them down, and the story, in common with the other two, has an ironic twist in the tail.

Richard Sear in the *Daily Mirror* wrote: 'Deborah Kerr made a romantic and entrancing entrance into British television . . . she proved to be made for TV close-up, displaying the most subtle range of expressions of any leading actress to date. Her three rôles—frumpish, middle-aged and romantically young—allowed free range to these expressions—the droop of an eyelid or the twitch of a lip and another mood came vividly to life.'

Jeremy Brett recalls the way in which Deborah shed more than twenty years in a matter of minutes at the end of a long day's filming, when Arthur Penn suggested the change into her period dress and character of Miranda to tape the introduction to the playlets. There was ominous muttering on the set over the proposed extended working period, but she just observed, 'It won't take me a minute to change' and was back in a flash, looking sweet sixteen and ready to start work again.

'Well—it had to be done some time, so it seemed sensible to get it over there and then,' she replied to Jeremy's enquiry about how she was able to take the inconvenience in her stride so calmly. 'Her professionalism and cooperation were so complete they altered the mood on that set immediately,' he says.

She met again an old friend from wartime, when Guy Deghy found himself cast for *Three Roads to Rome*. 'It was only a small part,' he says, 'and I wondered as I walked into the rehearsal room if after all these years Deb would remember me at all. After all, we weren't really close friends and I never had any illusions about my own professional importance. But as soon as I came through the door I heard that unmistakable voice cry out "Hello, Guy!" All the old warmth was there and I felt right back where we had left off. Seventeen years of Hollywood stardom could not corrupt that lovely and lovable character. Deb is not only a great actress but a great human being.'

Early in the New Year, 1964, she received a much treasured letter from her friends, Ursula and Roger Livesey: 'Roger and I feel we simply have to write and tell you of our unbounded admiration for your performances on television on Monday night. All three were quite lovely, and your comedy in the one by Gellhorn utterly delicious. It's always been pretty obvious what a splendid actress you are, but it was driven home even more deeply by your TV appearance.'

Deborah was delighted to be able to work with Arthur Penn, whom she already knew socially in Hollywood, and it is regrettable that *Three Roads to Rome*, which generated so much genuine enthusiasm all round has never been repeated, nor shown in America. That, to date, is the sum total of her television experience, apart from 'Chat shows galore. You name them—I've done them, including Johnny Carson, Dick Cavett, and, on innumerable occasions, my friend Dinah Shore.' They have done comedy routines together by the dozen, but, to date, never raised their voices in song.

# IV

Back in England in early 1963 to start work at Borehamwood for Ross Hunter on *The Chalk Garden* Deborah was able to spend a few days in Bristol, where Phyllis Smale was enjoying extended popularity during her nineteen-year run as Mrs Luscombe in Denys Constanduros' radio serial *At The Luscombes*.

In April, Mary Johnston visited the studio and suggested Deborah Kerr might like to become an honorary member of the Judy Garland Club, having heard her express great admiration for the talented Judy, with whom she had become friendly during the days at Metro. She was delighted to do so and her then secretary, Mrs Myrtle Tully, wrote to confirm Deborah's acceptance of the honorary membership, which she has retained ever since, with permanent billing in the Garland Club magazine, run by film and theatre buff Ken Sephton.

Kerr was directed by Ronald Neame, for the first time in all the years they had been friends, in the film version of Enid Bagnold's fine play *The Chalk Garden*, adapted by John Michael Hayes and Douglas Heys. The Technicolor photography was in the expert hands of Arthur Ibbetson and costumes designed, as in all Deborah's modern day dress films, by Julie Harris. The character of Miss Madrigal was another governess and another enigma, but one whose reticence and strangeness turned out to be firmly rooted in the fact that, years before the story began, she was Constance Doris Wakeland, a convicted murderess. She is hired by the eccentric and dominant Mrs St Maugham (Edith Evans, re-creating her original stage rôle) to try to cope with her unruly sixteen-year-old granddaughter, Laurel (Hayley Mills), who is given to fantasies: she swears that she had seen her father shoot himself and that she was assaulted at the age of twelve. The girl's resentment of the new governess turns to affection and she makes a pact with her ally, Maitland, the general factotum (John Mills) to conceal the facts they discover about Miss Madrigal's past. The governess persuades Mrs St Maugham to let Laurel join her mother, played by Elizabeth Sellars, from whom she has been kept apart since early childhood. Miss Madrigal stays on as companion to the lonely old lady.

As a photographed stage play this worked well, in its contrived and sentimental way, mainly because of the sheer ingenuity of the plot's construction and the high quality of the actors involved. Richard Whitehall wrote in *Films and Filming*: 'Deborah Kerr, following in the wake of Peggy Ashcroft,

Pamela Brown and Gwen Ffrangçon Davies, gives a reading which owes nothing to her illustrious predecessors and which is, in its way, every bit as good.' He omitted to mention Siobhan McKenna, who had played the part in New York, opposite Gladys Cooper's Mrs St Maugham, a characterization Dame Gladys was to repeat in the 1971 revival at the Haymarket Theatre, London, when Joan Greenwood provided yet another intriguing variation on the theme of the mysterious Miss Madrigal. At the end of its West End run, while preparing to take the play to the Lincoln Centre, Toronto, Gladys Cooper contracted pneumonia and died after a short illness. Cathleen Nesbitt completed the tour in her place.

Edith Evans repeated her fine performance in the film version, although some of her best lines had been cut, in the interest of building up the part of Laurel for Hayley Mills, then at the peak of her film popularity. John Mills did something to readjust the balance in his scenes with Deborah Kerr: he was excellent as the wise butler, while Felix Aylmer brought great authority to the rôle of the judge who reveals the truth about Madrigal's past. Kerr was awarded the Prix Femina Universal du Cinéma in Belgium as the year's Best Actress for 1964, and the following year the Exhibition Laurel Award Top 5, as Top Dramatic Star.

Enid Bagnold revealed in her autobiography that she disliked the film and in particular the casting and performance of Hayley Mills. She also felt that Deborah Kerr was wrongly cast. An off-beat piece of casting was when Esmee Smythe, standing in for the star, was also asked to double for Edith Evans in a car-driving sequence. As no wig was handy at short notice, the make-up department powdered down Esmee's hair and no one, seeing the completed film, could detect the difference: from Kerr to Evans in one afternoon made an intriguing double take.

Another successful play, Tennessee Williams' The Night of the Iguana, emerged, after a traumatic location at Puerta Villarta, Mexico, as a fine film, and one which, due to the explosive elements involved in its making, had reaped world-wide publicity on a staggering scale. From a unit including John Huston,

191

Williams himself, Ava Gardner, a star who continues to attract international headlines just by being herself, and Richard Burton with Elizabeth Taylor, who accompanied him on the location, and Sue Lyon, in her first film since *Lolita*, the world's press were ready and eager for something explosive to happen, with Ray Stark, the producer, doing his best to see that it did. Michael Wilding, ex-husband of Taylor, was also on the spot, acting as PA to Burton. Deborah Kerr who, with her husband, was expected to have a soothing effect on the potential cauldron, and almost certainly did, says:

'John Huston has always loved to choose difficult locations, but this was *the* most. To begin with, there was no road at all to where they had built the necessary set for the film, which could actually have been done in any studio, anywhere, *and* it was black and white, so they never used the lushness of the surroundings, but perhaps he was right in that, as far as the subject was concerned. Anyway, it meant you had to go by boat, forty-five minutes each morning, and if the sea was rough it was unimaginably uncomfortable.' She recorded her impressions of the location in *Esquire*, 'The Days And Nights Of The Iguana— a Journal by Deborah Kerr', which earned her eight hundred dollars and at least as much satisfaction as the two hundred and fifty thousand dollars she received for her work in the film. The amounts received by the individual stars were headlined everywhere: five hundred thousand dollars, for Burton, four hundred thousand dollars for Gardner and a hundred and seventy-five thousand dollars for Lyon, for whom Deborah acquired quite a soft spot. She was just a year older than her daughter Melanie, and, because the press, and a number of others, were waiting for her to be catalyst to an eruption (which never actually happened) was 'rather put upon. I think she was sweet, and in a way, unjustly used.'

The worst drama was occasioned by the instability of the cottages built on the beach to house the stars: these 'homes' were all falling down by the time they arrived, having been built with beach sand. One of the balconies gave way and caused a serious accident to two of the boys and one of the assistant directors, who injured his spine, among other disabilities. The guest contributor to *Esquire* spoke her mind on the subject of a certain type of journalistic output, having warned the magazine that she was not going to add to the sensational 'news' that was being pumped out daily, and that she would write of her fellow-actors as she saw them, rather than the way the world's press might have wanted her to see them:

'I am revolted by the mass of moronic muck that is printed almost every day in almost every newspaper and magazine, and even more revolted by those who assure me this is *only* what people want to read, and how they *tried* writing nice, pleasant and interesting pieces about famous personalities, but that it just hasn't worked . . .

'I feel more and more like Hannah in this movie. Nothing human disgusts me unless it is unkind or violent. I do loathe and detest unkindness and violence and gossip and troublemaking and envy and malice. It does disgust me as well as depress me.' Her summing up of her fellow-actors included the following: 'Ava is funny and rich and warm and human as well as beautiful . . . John said what a real disadvantage it is sometimes to be so beautiful. It has been so for Ava, and she has well and truly paid for her beauty. It has made her appear publicly as a person she is not and her work has made her appear the kind of person she is not. Elizabeth is such a generous and sweet woman, friendly and warm and impulsive . . . and Richard easy, sensitive and great fun, with the sense of humour and humility of a really good artist.'

The rôle of Hannah Jelkes (acted by Margaret Leighton in the American theatre) in John Huston and Anthony Veiller's screenplay, is that of an artist, who roams the world with her grandfather of ninety; as 'expatriated Americans' they eke out an uneasy living by selling her sketches and by him reciting his poems. They arrive at a shabby hotel in Mexico run by Maxine Faulk (Ava Gardner), a promiscuous widow (originally played on the New York stage by Bette Davis), who keeps a couple of beach boys as pets and who is also putting up an unfrocked clergyman, Laurence Shannon (Richard Burton). He has been accused of interfering with a young girl, Charlotte (Sue Lyon), by her enraged and Lesbian schoolteacher Miss Fellowes (Grayson Hall).

Shannon's spiritual crisis has driven him almost to madness, but he begins to recover his peace of mind thanks to Hannah, who expounds to him in his delirium her philosophy—the most benevolent and positive points of view ever expressed by Tennessee Williams, making some strikingly true observations on human relationships. When her grandfather, 'Nonno' (the late Cyril Delevanti), dies after reciting his last poem, Hannah decides to continue her wandering life, realizing that Maxine loves Shannon too, and that she will be able to look after him better than she. Kerr's quality of repose and inner calm has never been more movingly deployed than in this performance with its semi-mystical aura, which surprisingly failed to win her even an Academy Nomination, when she should assuredly have carried off the Oscar this time at last, but she was awarded an unofficial one in a National Poll in Australia—the first of its kind.

Her own reservations about the film echo what happened in the adaptation of Nancy Mitford's *The Blessing*, when the filmmakers cut scenes of social comment in order not to offend the nationalities involved. 'In the play the party of German tourists, talking about Fascism and Hitler, represented the forces of evil which Hannah Jelkes was fighting spiritually, and it was shown how she humbled herself to go and sell the drawings to them, because she needed the money for her aged grandfather—and what it cost her to do that. This theme was removed, so as not to offend Germany, and the Lesbian schoolteacher substituted, or rather, her part was built up to represent the evil and violence in the plot—which, of course, it didn't: it wasn't enough. This took away from the part of Hannah, and was, I think, a weakness in the film's total effect, but it was still a damn good movie.'

She recorded this opinion in her published Journal, although she values her own contribution only for what it brings to the film as a whole. She thought Burton and Gardner both 'marvellous, Ava in particular bringing to the part of Maxine just the right self-mocking quality.'

194

# V

En route for Switzerland in November 1964, the Viertels appeared on some TV chat shows, including Johnny Carson's, and Dinah Shore's again: the limelight was on Peter and his best-selling novels, *Love Lies Bleeding* and *White Hunter, Black Heart*. Since their marriage, after the run of filming in England, they had had leisure not only to stay home in Klosters with their daughters but to go for holidays at a house they used to rent in St Jean de Luz, France, in the Basque country, not far from Spain. For the first time in twenty years Deborah was really able to relax, see friends and family in England, and 'just potter', a proclivity she thinks she must have inherited from her father, the inventor, rather than from her always industrious mother.

Her leisure was interrupted by the arrival of a script, *Community Property* from her old buddy, Frank Sinatra. There was a delay before filming could start and she hesitated, then asked advice from another long-time friend, David Niven. She had at this time decided to ease off her filming activities—really to pick and choose her rôles—but Niven advised her strongly to take the offer. Then Sinatra called her on the phone again and said: 'Come on: let's do this picture together. Why not? Let's have fun.' And they did, with Dean Martin and a cast which included the indestructibly handsome and funny Cesar Romero, the West End's unique comedy character actress Hermione Baddeley and Frank's daughter, Nancy Sinatra.

'We had a ball,' says Deborah: 'it was so much fun—a joke, and all quite ludicrous. Frank would come in one morning and say "We don't need this scene!" and just tear it out of the script and throw it away. Then Dino, perfectly happy and absolutely relaxed, would murmur: "What a great way to earn a living; what other business is there where you can come in every morning and meet lots of people that you absolutely adore, do something you like doing—and get paid for it?"'

Unfortunately, this on-set fun and bonhomie did not really communicate itself in the completed film, released by Warner

Brothers late in 1965, with its title changed neatly to *Marriage on the Rocks*, and ploddingly directed by ex-choreographer Jack Donohue. The movie had a few very funny moments, but was bogged down by a story which had worked hilariously in the past for stars like Betty Hutton and the late Rosalind Russell, but did no service to Deborah Kerr in 1965. She played Valerie, neglected wife of tycoon Dan Edwards (Sinatra), whom she persuades to come on a second honeymoon to save their marriage. Instead they get divorced after a tiff, and having arrived back at the point of remarriage Dan, delayed by sudden business, sends his bachelor friend, Ernie (Martin) to explain. Ernie and Valerie get accidentally married after a night out, and she refuses to have the marriage annulled, to make Dan jealous. He, however, is forewarned and pretends to be looking forward to a riotous bachelor existence... and so on, until the inevitable happy ending.

Dean Martin gave the film what little style it possessed—where he goes style follows—and Baddeley got a few laughs, as a Scottish mother-in-law, addicted to wearing a kilt and playing the bagpipes. Nelson Riddle's score was delightful, but Cy Howard's screenplay did nothing for Kerr, who, entangled in the meshes of its asinine plot, gave the one and only embarrassingly skittish performance of her career—'unsuitably kittenish', said the *Monthly Film Bulletin*. She was, however, gorgeously photographed in Technicolor by William H. Daniels, Garbo's favourite photographer in the past, and one of her loveliest gowns, a green chiffon evening dress, provided Sinatra and Martin with a running gag during the filming. 'I'm very tall, and both Frank and Dino very short. When they saw me in this dress they called me "the Jolly Green Giant", after the popular brand of peas. Whenever I came on the set it was: "Ah—here comes the Jolly Green Giant!" The movie was a laugh to make from beginning to end, and not to be taken seriously by anybody.'

The same might justly have been said of her next to be seen, the over-publicized, over-loaded and only occasionally funny *Casino Royale*, Charles K. Feldman's send-up of the James Bond

196

films—a project the former gambler and Hollywood actor's agent had been trying to get off the ground since 1954, when he was unable to get backing for the first spy story by the then little-known Ian Fleming. The subsequent financial jackpot which Cubby Broccoli and Harry Saltzman hit with Sean Connery as Bond enabled Feldman to raise the finance he needed, but by 1966 most of the gimmicks of the first book had been used up in the previous films, so *Casino Royale* had to be done as a spoof. Deborah Kerr's location scenes, directed by John Huston, were shot during the summer in Ireland, with the Wicklow mountains standing in for the Scottish highlands, where some of Sir James Bond's (David Niven) adventures take place. Studio scenes, with their long list of guest stars, moved to Pinewood, Shepperton and finally to Metro's Borehamwood Studios, although the picture itself was distributed by Columbia. The Technicolor photography was handled mainly by Jack Hildyard, with additional work by John Wilcox and Nicholas Roeg.

Deborah Kerr obliterated the memory of *Marriage on the Rocks* by giving an altogether delightful comedy performance as the lusty Secret Agent Mimi, masquerading as Lady Fiona McTarry, Scottish chieftainess, in Huston's hilarious sequence—the only one in the film really to come off—which presented him, wearing a carroty red wig, waving in the full glory of Panavision, being blown up in an explosion. Mimi, having set out to seduce Sir James and failed, gets uproariously drunk and sends her teenage 'daughters' to accomplish the task which had proved beyond her. (They are all SMERSH agents, who have done away with the McTarrys and replaced them, with the intention of sullying the hitherto incorruptible name of Bond.) Agent Mimi then renounces the world and takes the veil, thus sparking off the plot (?) of the main part of the film, with its farcical quest for James Bond. She reappears, be-wimpled, several reels later to tell Bond that his daughter has been kidnapped, her wink implying that the holy lady has not entirely forgotten her earlier self—at the same time sending up the other high-principled religious and tutorial ladies Deborah

197

had played so well in the past. Her comedy was as rich as her Scottish accent—the only time she has been called on to revert to the brogue of her forefathers. There were four other directors and guest stars from Ursula Andress and Woody Allen, via Jean-Paul Belmondo, Charles Boyer, William Holden and Peter O'Toole, to George Raft, Peter Sellers and Orson Welles.

*Casino Royale* was released at the beginning of 1967. Deborah Kerr's next film to be shown in Britain, *The Eye of the Devil*, which had the most chequered career of any with which she has been associated, arrived at the Ritz, Leicester Square, at the beginning of March 1968, seven months after it was first seen in America, where it did not enjoy a very wide release. In England it went out on circuit as a second feature. It was actually filmed, as far as Deborah was concerned, during the winter months of 1965–6: she received a call at Klosters to work over Christmas to replace Kim Novak, originally set to star with David Niven. Philip Lorraine's novel *Day of the Arrow* was passed from scriptwriter Terry Southern to Robin Estridge and Dennis Murphy, while the directorial rein went from Sidney Furie, Arthur Hiller and Michael Anderson to J. Lee Thompson, who worked on the film with the title *13*. Julie Andrews was initially mentioned for the lead, but shooting started with Kim Novak, who had almost completed her rôle when a back injury caused her to withdraw, with eighty per cent of the one million pounds production already in the can at Borehamwood. The insurance company guaranteed a further six hundred thousand pounds and David Niven set to work with his co-star of *Separate Tables*, of whom he said:

'Playing opposite Deborah is as delightful an experience as an actor can have. I've always felt I won my Academy Award because she made me look so good. That sort of thing makes for a warm and relaxed screen relationship. Kim, on the other hand, while highly professional—all Hollywood-trained actresses are—worries about her looks, her scenes, her individual lines—everything.' He told the *Daily Mail*'s Harry Weaver 'I don't think I would be betraying any confidences if I said that Kim often told me: "I think I'm not right for this part. I think

198

I'm a sex-pot!'' I'm not trying to de-sex Deborah, but the part does call for a marquise who's the mother of two children, rather than a blonde bombshell!'

Novak would arrive at the studio at four-thirty a.m. and often do her own make-up: Kerr came at seven-thirty and left it to the make-up department. She usually arrived alone, while her opposite number had an entourage of dialogue coach, press agent and a personal secretary, with whom she rehearsed her lines before going on set. Deborah Kerr just walked before the camera and did them; stand-in Esmee Smythe occasionally would hear her lines—'*Very* occasionally, because she always knew them'—and once in a while help out if the dresser was not on the spot, but says it is her policy, although they invariably share a portable dressing-room on set or location, not to hang around the star all the time. 'She's entitled to her privacy: after, say, making her a cup of coffee and having a morning chat, I go about my business and leave her to hers.'

*The Eye of the Devil* posed a few possible snags for the newcomers, having started work on the film so far into the schedule. After the weeks in the studio when the unit were making plans to return to France to re-shoot the location work Esmee Smythe discovered that the other stand-ins were not included in the itinerary. She mentioned to Deborah Kerr that she anticipated being left behind as well. 'Oh?' was the reply: 'What do they think I'm going to do—stand-in for myself?' Esmee said that obviously the company would save the money she could ask for doubling as well as standing-in and get a substitute out in France. 'I don't think they will,' said Deborah quietly. A few days later one of the assistant directors asked Esmee how much she would require to go to France. She enquired what was entailed: it included horse-riding, driving and cavorting about on the battlements of the castle where much of the action took place. She named her price. The assistant sighed and said: 'Well, I suppose we'll have to'—and so the stand-in went to France.

The location was in the wine country, at Brives les Gaillards in the Périgord, and the château bore the same name. The weather there during the previous filming had been very cold, and Deborah organized winter woollens for the January–February shooting. When they arrived it was like summer and they had to borrow shirts from the technicians to keep cool. From then on they had a pleasant location in the sunshine until it was time to return home to finish filming at Borehamwood. From Brives to London entailed an overnight train journey, and the production office made it clear that they expected the company back at work on the set the next morning. Deborah Kerr suggested that this was out of the question. 'We must have rest,' she said; but the office remained adamant. 'If I were you,' said Esmee, 'I'd be absolutely raving mad.' 'It's not worth getting mad—it only ruins oneself. But I'm just not going to do it, and you won't either—don't worry.' They did not work the day after their all-night journey.

The film received few kind words from the critics and was sadly underrated as one of the sixties' most gripping studies of the occult—worthy to rank with the best of Roger Corman, and a salutary illustration of the insidious spread of evil once it has taken root anywhere. Deborah Kerr on the side of the angels was no novelty, but she portrayed brilliantly a woman gradually discovering that her husband is in the grip of demoniacal forces against which he is powerless—a sensitive and moving performance for which David Niven received little or no credit. They were cast as Philippe, Marquis of the Château de Bellac in the Dordogne and his wife, Catherine. He is called back from London to do something about the failure of his vineyards. Despite his discouragement Catherine follows with their two children and finds herself up against the sinister Père Dominic (Donald Pleasance), who supervises black masses in which Philippe seems to be the central figure. She also encounters twelve hooded men who kidnap her when she goes to investigate the family vaults, besides a mysterious blond youth, Christian (David Hemmings), who haunts the castle grounds shooting doves, with his beautiful sister Odile (Sharon Tate), who is obviously a witch and tries to kill Catherine. On her side are the Countess (Flora Robson), who refuses to leave her quarters, and Philippe's father Alain (Emlyn Williams), who

200

is in the same position, having faked his own sudden death in conformity with a family tradition. In the end the Devil, in the shape of Père Dominic, wins, and Catherine drives away from the castle a widow, unaware of the hold he has already established over her son, played by Robert Duncan. The faithful Jean-Pierre (Edward Mulhare) is waiting to comfort her.

Emlyn Williams says that Deborah faced 'her daunting job of re-shooting with courage and humour'. Irwin Hillier's black and white photography did her proud, although a few long shots of Kim Novak were left in the final film. Deborah foresaw a great future for the beautiful and talented Sharon Tate, 'given the right breaks, and a reasonable amount of luck'. The poor girl's luck ran out all too soon after, when she was murdered by the Manson gang in 1969. There were two other casualties after the completion of this most jinxed of films: one member of the location crew was crushed by a car, and the castle of Brives les Gaillards was burned down some three years later.

## VI

Two projects announced for Deborah Kerr in 1967 failed to materialize. Terence Young's re-make of *Mayerling*, Anatole Litvak's classic love story filmed in 1936, starred Omar Sharif and Catherine Deneuve in the parts originally played by Charles Boyer and Danielle Darrieux, with James Mason and, in the event, Ava Gardner in the Empress Eugénie rôle for which the director had wanted Kerr. Nor did she make *Les Cygnes Sauvages* for René Gainville in Paris, feeling that the theme of the older woman with a young lover had been given more than its share of exposure over the years.

Instead she returned to England to make *Prudence and the Pill*, adapted by Hugh Mills from his own novel, for Twentieth Century. She flew with Peter to Madrid to stay with friends, after initial wardrobe tests, to enjoy a short break before the actual filming began at Pinewood. While unpacking, she suddenly felt the room spinning round—a terrifying experience for someone who had, until then, virtually never had a day's illness in her life. Doctors diagnosed that she had developed a virus infection, wherein a tiny drop of water had become displaced in the bone cavity of the ear, completely destroying her sense of balance. There was nothing to do but await developments and go for further tests, which entailed travelling by train to London: flying, in the circumstances, was out of the question.

From Madrid, her husband notified the producers, Kenneth Harper and Ronald Kahn, that Deborah's starting date on the film would have to be delayed until the condition had resolved itself. Specialists told her it was something from which many people suffer in the course of their lives. It is sometimes brought on by a blow on the head, but often with no tangible cause, inducing an imbalance in the level of the fluid in the ears which, for normal health, has to remain perfectly equal on both sides. One expert said that to date they had been unable to find any reason for the displacement and added: 'Unless we have the good fortune of your leaving this office, being knocked down by a bus and killed—enabling us to do a quick autopsy—we shall never know what caused it!'

She wrote me from the Connaught Hotel in June 1967, where she was 'sitting it out, nursing a beastly case of labyrinthitis, which affects one's balance and vision,' and 'am tottering around like a drunk!' In her letter, she thanked me for an article I had sent. 'I am rather a self-effacing person, and it is always a big thrill when someone writes of my work and evaluates it.'

The unit publicist for *Prudence and the Pill*, Lily Poyser, had arranged for me to meet Deborah again at Pinewood, in connection with a career story for *Films and Filming*, but she was still not well enough to return to work by the end of the following week, so I went to see her at the Connaught: in a russet velvet trouser suit, with touches of white at the neck and sleeves, she was more beautiful than I remembered her. The hair was the same warm auburn and her eyes seemed bluer, but they were part of a more mature human being than the pre-Hollywood, always friendly, though sometimes austere star of the forties.

During four hours of the frankest and most enjoyable interview of my days in film journalism the idea for this book was born and we have corresponded regularly ever since.

*Prudence and the Pill* was premièred in New York in July 1968, and at the Carlton, Haymarket the following month. The plot fairly defies any simple break-down, but cast Deborah Kerr and David Niven as Prudence and Gerald Hardcastle, whose twelve-year-old marriage has become static, and not only because he has had a mistress for several years (Elizabeth, played by Irina Demick). Gerald's brother Henry (Robert Coote) is happily married to Grace (Joyce Redman), who finds she is pregnant after their daughter Geraldine (Judy Geeson) has been substituting aspirins for her mother's birth control pills to ensure that she herself can safely copulate with her boyfriend Tony Bates (David Dundas). This alerts Gerald to the fact that Prudence has been taking Thenol and has a lover, a Harley Street specialist, Dr Allen Hewitt (Keith Michell).

Prudence shares the final fade-out with Allen, by which time everybody who is physically capable is discovered to be pregnant, with the notable exception, presumably, of Dame Edith Evans as Tony's grandmother, Lady Bates, whose march across Brands Hatch in the middle of a race, clad in a full-length feathered pink creation, was the funniest moment in a film which a large public found greatly to their liking.

The critics were, in the main, not amused. *Variety* said: 'The obvious attempt was to incorporate a lot of unique personalities, all affected by the pill and contemporary changing sex customs, but the result is a lack of unity. The whole film, then, is less than the sum of its parts.' Less reasonably, Margaret Hinxman in the *Sunday Telegraph* gave Deborah Kerr scant credit for her stylish comedy delineation of a part the actress herself admitted to be 'a bit of a bitch'. 'There's a shrewish performance from Deborah Kerr which is disturbing, not because it's out of character with Deborah, who is a very versatile actress, and as such capable of any change of mood, but because it's out of character with the attitude of bedroom farce which relies on the charm of its protagonists to excuse their moral turpitude.'

203

The lack of unity may well have been due to the change of control more than halfway through the filming; Fielder Cook, the original director, did not seem at ease, and, in particular was at loggerheads with the usually equable David Niven. After directing sixty per cent of the shooting, Cook walked out after a row with the producers, and Ronald Neame took over, carrying on, officially, 'in the style of Fielder Cook'. A message from Twentieth's publicity department, regarding my article on Deborah, said: 'Please do not use Mr Neame's name, as the final credits show only Mr Fielder Cook.'

Deborah Kerr says: 'He's a director who has done some fine things, but perhaps was going through a difficult time privately, and it was just an unfortunate case of him and David not getting on together. It was very nice of Ronnie to take over, and fine for us as we both knew him so well.' The stunning dresses Julie Harris designed for her and which Ted Moore's camerawork in De Luxe colour showed to such glowing advantage, brought further praise from Michael Bolloten in Australia: 'She looked a veritable mannequin, yet so *human*; having dabbled in "dress" I was taken with the lovely clothes which she wore with genius, even to parading the two "startling" slits in a long evening gown with such aplomb.'

Julie Harris told David Castell of *Films Illustrated*. 'Deborah Kerr is an actress of great natural elegance. I didn't design her clothes for *Separate Tables* (which called for her to look dowdy) . . . I can imagine how difficult it would be to make her look sloppy and shapeless. She just rises above whatever you put her in.'

# CHAPTER TWELVE

# *FULL CIRCLE*

## I

Throughout her career Deborah Kerr has garnered, arguably, more rave notices than any other star of her generation. Yet the subject of critics is one of the few that can raise her Scottish hackles. '*Constructive* ones help,' she says, 'but there are damned few of these; so many critics nowadays should really be writing "want-ads".' Her favourite quote, from Edmund Burke, who was writing about politics—which she maintains, have a lot in common with acting—is: 'Those who would carry on the great public plans must be proof against the most fatiguing delays, the most mortifying disappointments, the most shocking insults, and worst of all, the presumptuous judgment of the ignorant upon their designs.'

Yet, professionally, Kerr virtually never 'loses her cool': 'I absolutely cannot *work* in disharmony with anyone, and consequently I will perhaps wrongly put up with jealousies and suffer fools gladly in order to work happily and establish CONTACT—so important is any acting, to me, anyway.'

History records two fools who were just too much for her to suffer gladly: they probably made theatrical history during *Tea and Sympathy*. She says: 'Even now I get butterflies in my stomach when I remember what happened when a couple of men in the stalls who had obviously been celebrating talked loudly all through the first act. I put up with it until the second act, when there is a very touching scene between Laura and the boy. The silly maudlin voices went on . . . "No head's wife in

205

my school was ever like that to me." "No, nor in mine." I could bear it no longer. I stared straight at them and said "BE QUIET!" There was an audible gasp from every part of the house. The two drunks were so shattered that they got up without another word and shuffled meekly out of the theatre. When I realized what I had done I was so horrified that I "dried" and John Kerr had to prompt me.'

Her complete lack of any kind of temperament helps to make her 'someone totally loved', as Jack Clayton said. Frank Sinatra wrote, after I contacted him about this biography: 'I love Deborah. She's a marvellous lady, a good friend and an absolutely brilliant actress.'

There may have been occasions when her inability to lay down the law has harmed her professionally. There was considerable controversy about her 'nude' scenes with Burt Lancaster in John Frankenheimer's *The Gypsy Moths*, which she started back at Culver City for Metro after an absence of ten years, in July 1968. She explains: 'Actually, I didn't do them. That was the only bone of contention. I said, "I'm not going to do those scenes. I think it's totally unnecessary and unreal that these two people would strip stark naked in the living-room—in reality they simply wouldn't do it." But it was a period when nudity was just starting in films: *every* picture had to have a nude scene—for no reason. It boomeranged, because it was gratuitous. I had no say, obviously, though I should have stipulated that I wouldn't do the movie, if those shots are in—but I really didn't think Frankenheimer would do it. So they used somebody else's nude body. To do it there in the living-room, on the couch—to have this stark naked backside staring at you was, quite frankly, just laughable. In doing that you overstate so much you spoil the point. I said to Burt, my old friend from way back: "Do you think they're really going to show this?" He didn't think so either, but it was the girl who got the maximum exposure, with Burt front view—not much below waist-level—to the camera, and all of her breast and bottom in various shots, with him masking such portions of her anatomy that they didn't think, at that time, they could get away with.'

Apart from this scene—and it is significant that in recent TV viewings it has been cut discreetly, to the benefit of the film as a whole—*The Gypsy Moths* received sharply divided press. Critics decided it represented either the best or the rock bottom work of John Frankenheimer. There was a similar reaction to her next film, *The Arrangement* for Elia Kazan which she started immediately afterwards, in October. At one time the schedules clashed, but she was able to do both pictures, as the filming of the Kazan movie was postponed, due to the indecision of Marlon Brando, originally set to co-star with Kerr and Faye Dunaway. Both films, on reassessment, have since been recognized as true—and even inspired—reflections of the sections of American society with which they dealt: respectively small town Kansas and the affluent Los Angeles executive advertising belt.

*The Gypsy Moths* are a trio of sky-divers who arrive for a brief stand in Bridgeville—Burt Lancaster as Mike Rettig, the leader, Gene Hackman as Joe Browdy and Scott Wilson as Malcolm Webson, the youngest, whose aunt and uncle, Elizabeth and V. John Brandon (Deborah Kerr and William Windom) invite them to stay. Rettig shows contempt for the uncomfortable atmosphere in their household, but finds himself attracted to Elizabeth. They go walking in the evening, and eventually make love. Browdy spends the night with a topless go-go dancer (an incisive cameo by Sheree North) and Malcolm makes friends with Annie Burke (Bonnie Bedelia), the Brandons' student lodger.

Before the aerial show Rettig asks Elizabeth to go away with him; she refuses and denounces the futility of their affair. At the climax of their performance Rettig performs his spectacular and dangerous cape jump, and plummets to his death. Refusing Elizabeth's offer to pay for the funeral, Browdy and Malcolm stage a memorial show to raise the money, then leave town. The ending shows Elizabeth with her apparently uncaring husband, who has observed her nocturnal affair with Rettig—and others—and asks her why she did not agree to go away with him. She replies: 'The thought terrified me.' He answers quietly: 'And me'—an inspired ending, which encapsulates the understanding behind their seemingly loveless marriage.

This subtlety is present at several levels of William Hanley's screenplay, finely photographed in Metrocolor by Philip Lathrop, which, wrote Gordon Gow in *Films and Filming* 'conveys the essence of the novel by James Drought from which it was adapted, particularly in the enigmatic nature of Lancaster's interpretation of the Rettig character, whose philosophy is: "To face death is hard, but to face life is harder." ' This arid philosophy is implicit in every scene of the movie and probably accounts for its unpopularity with the few audiences who went to see it. In Britain it went out in November 1969, as the top half of a double feature with James Garner as Raymond Chandler's *Marlowe*. Gow continued: 'It seems ages since Deborah Kerr has been given a rôle so worthy of her talent. It requires great skill in the playing, especially since Frankenheimer surrounds it expertly with realistic notations of the small town mentality, against which she fortifies herself in her own pathetic way . . . she is permitted a neat little speech which sums up her formative years and the things that went awry . . . she tells Rettig her tale with a concise and heightened terminology, in a few minutes so impeccably controlled by Frankenheimer, so beautifully spoken by Kerr and so "perceptively" listened to by Lancaster that the dimension of the medium is expanded to contain the speech—virtually a thing of the theatre.'

She herself thought Frankenheimer's handling of the relationships 'very interesting' and the director himself 'a strange bird—kind of a driven person, brilliant and highly individual'. Of the nudity in *The Arrangement* she says: 'I always said I would do it if it was *really* a part of the action; after all, I can't go on pretending for ever that I don't have a body. There it was real, because they were in bed together and they had no clothes on.' There was a brief scene of her disrobing to step into the bath, which was also discreetly done, in a medium shot, diffused by steam, yet the film reaped maximum advance publicity from the nudity implicit in the story. *Variety* reported gloatingly: '*Arrangement* Sneaks Will Reveal the Facts about Film's Daring-do ... for months rumours have been swirling that the film, produced, directed and written by Elia Kazan from his own best-selling novel, is the most sexually daring feature yet to come from a major studio. In rushes and rough-cut form, at least, the genitalia of some of pic's leading players were plainly shown, according to reliable sources (*sic*). Kirk Douglas, Faye Dunaway and Deborah Kerr are topcast ... The picture, its more daring footage cut even before submission to the Motion Picture Association of America, will go out with a rating of "R"—persons of sixteen not admitted unless accompanied by parent or adult guardian'—a more enlightened view than the British 'X' certificate which effectively barred young people from attending under any circumstances, although the film has since reached the universal audiences commanded by television.

*The Arrangement* opened at the Warner Cinema in London in January 1960, to excellent notices. Deborah told me how happy she had been with the way people had understood the aim of the director and players, and that she herself felt it was one of the 'truest' things she had done in the cinema. Gordon Gow wrote that the part of Florence was 'perfectly and succinctly drawn by Deborah Kerr as the wife whose belief in her husband's ability to achieve anything he sets out to do has turned into a consuming desire to see that he does it'. Eddie Anderson (Kirk Douglas), a successful advertising executive, leaves home to drive to his office and, following some compulsive inner urge, lifts his hands from the steering-wheel of his car and deliberately collides with a truck on the Los Angeles highway. From then on he goes into a state of withdrawal, trying to evaluate his life, refusing to communicate with his wife and his business associates. He is still tormented over his relationship with his mistress Gwen (Faye Dunaway), herself a victim of sexual exploitation, who has left him before the story starts. They go back to each other, then he returns to Florence; holding one in his arms in bed at night he sees the other in his mind's eye. His feelings towards his father, a stubborn and ailing old Greek immigrant, played by Richard Boone, are another source of stress. Eddie tells his wife: 'I don't like my life. I don't like what

I've done with my life. I don't like my home. I'm in a trap that opened when I had my accident. That accident was a success. It gave me a breather, a little trip to another country, a few quick minutes to think for the first time in my life.' 'Then what do you want now?' she asks; his reply is that he hasn't the vaguest idea.

Deborah Kerr found *The Arrangement* a fascinating movie to make. She comments: 'Of course it didn't go down well in America, because it's too near the knuckle in the direct shots it took at the very basis of the American way of life, which came just a little too close to home to be comfortable. The book was, of course, a number one best-seller, but a lot of people didn't like it, and the deliberately diffused manner of shooting in the movie, with subliminal cutting all over the place, confused certain audiences. Florence was not all that nice a woman. Well—"nice" she was, but rigid—very human and *adoring* her husband. I know so many like her; they say: "But, darling, what do you want? You've got everything in life; we, together—we have everything. Why do you want something else—why do you want this terrible little tramp? I've given up everything for you; I've stood by you; I don't like living in Hollywood—I've done it for you ..." Then off he goes with an eighteen-year-old and wants to live a crazy existence. I've seen it all, and it's so true to life.'

Elia Kazan elicited from Kirk Douglas the performance of his career—'One,' says Gordon Gow, 'to be set alongside the magnificent acting of Lancaster in *The Swimmer*, another important study of man in decay.' Of acting with them Deborah Kerr says: 'Working with both is very interesting. They are totally different people, but have the same *enormous* intensity in application to their work. Whereas all comes naturally to Mitchum *they* both apply themselves more cerebrally.' Dunaway she considers 'a blazing talent. She's an extremely bright girl—a bit crazy, but that's marvellous. I love her looks and I love her most interesting mind and I think she's a terrific screen personality. But now the studios simply don't have the facilities to build up talent and see they get the right parts. I was a product

210

of a machine that just doesn't exist any more, so these girls get put into parts which mean nothing, simply because there are so few films being written with good rôles for women. I hope it will be different for Faye after *Network*, but I don't find it surprising that they are not doing it for people of my age group, when you think they aren't even writing parts for her or Julie Christie or Karen Black. Today it's *all* men: you've got to have Robert Redford, Al Pacino, Steve McQueen, Paul Newman, Dustin Hoffman—and preferably all of them together, and then you'll get some funds to set up a movie!' She instances 'the magnificent Streisand' as the only female to hold rank alongside this all-male Chorus Line, with, just possibly, Liza Minnelli and Tatum O'Neal creeping up into position on the distant horizon.

Elia Kazan has his own opinion on the subject of female talent on stage and screen: 'Deborah Kerr is a great lady. Let that stand by itself. She is also a fine actress, a joy to work with, devoted, understanding and gifted with a sense of humour. She is outstandingly fair to her fellow-performers. She is regally handsome. That's enough. If I say any more it might embarrass her or swell her head. And I wouldn't want that.'


## II


Late in 1971, Deborah slipped quietly into London to rehearse the part of Sybil Railton-Bell for an all-star Midnight Matinée tribute to Terence Rattigan at the Haymarket Theatre on 10 January, 1972. For her it was a happy reunion with Trevor Howard—very moving as the bogus Major—and Celia Johnson, who took over splendidly where Gladys Cooper left off in the film, as the formidable mother. Wendy Hiller also repeated the rôle she had played in the movie; Nigel Patrick directed the second part of *Separate Tables*, and also in the cast were Richard Briers and Beatrix Lehmann. The occasion was to be a spring-board to another facet of the Kerr career, one that was to bring her full circle back to the British stage.

211

Playwright Frank Harvey finished *The Day After the Fair*, an adaptation of Thomas Hardy's short story *On the Western Circuit* from *Life's Little Ironies*, at his home in Devon during the postal strike of 1971. He got it up to his agent via the legal bag sent daily from Exeter to London, and in due course it was accepted by producer–director Frith Banbury and his associates. One morning Harvey switched on Pete Murray's radio programme *Open House* in time to hear Deborah Kerr, during an interview about the Rattigan Benefit, say she would like to return to the London stage. He mentioned this to Frith Banbury, who was about to direct Nigel Patrick in the West End production of *Reunion in Vienna*, and he invited him to the dress rehearsal of *Separate Tables*.

Banbury says: 'I had only been sitting in front for a minute or two before it was obvious to me that Deborah had not lost the knack of playing before audiences in the thirty years that had passed since I saw her in *Heartbreak House*. I sent the script of *The Day After the Fair* down to the Connaught Hotel that Wednesday evening. She went back to Klosters the next day and rang me at the weekend: "I may be mad, but I love the play and the part. I'm very interested." ' She sent Frank Harvey the telegram authors dream about: 'Adore the play.'

Frith Banbury asked her to give him ten days to get *Reunion* on, then flew to Switzerland and spent four days in Klosters discussing all aspects of the production and presentation and reading the play out loud with Deborah. When he returned to London he got his associate Arthur Cantor (in his individual capacity) to put up the greater part of the money, while Banbury's company made a reciprocal agreement with him for an American production.

In June I had a letter from Deborah in Los Monteros, Marbella, where she was applying herself 'to the gigantic task of learning the very long part I have in the play'. She went on: 'We start rehearsals in August and take it out of town for three weeks and open at the Lyric the first week in October. It is a good part and a charming play and we have Julia Foster playing the young girl, which is really terrific, as she is a marvellous

212

actress. It will be an exciting adventure and I am really looking forward to it ... of course, I hope it will not be too harshly received critically, but even if it is, I feel very strongly that it will afford people a very good evening in the theatre, and I think that has been lacking for a long time.'

At the beginning of rehearsals she appeared on the Michael Parkinson Show on BBC TV: he had said that he found her 'unsullied quality much sexier than Raquel Welch, because you feel there is so much beneath the surface—and that is always much more exciting than having all the goods on show'. The interview went splendidly, and a reunion with Edith Evans turned out more funny than nostalgic, as the Dame had at this time taken to chat shows like a duck to water, and assumed command of the situation, like Lady Bracknell at a charity garden fête. 'How are the gels? Quite well? Good...'

At rehearsals Frank Harvey said, 'Deborah created about her an atmosphere of non-anxiety which enveloped the whole company. One of her chief qualities is courage. After all, to return to the West End after such a long break in a very taxing part in a play somewhat old-fashioned in technique, the sort of play they don't write any more, took a bit of doing.' There was, however, no mistaking the genuine feeling of anticipation and goodwill at the Theatre Royal, Brighton, that Monday, 11 September. I had cycled to nearby Peacehaven the day before and put up for the night; although less than sixty miles from London the trip to Brighton by pushbike tends to make one arrive not always at one's most alert for a first night, and I was taking no chances on this occasion.

The only face I recognized among the capacity audience was that of Ursula Jeans. Applause at curtain rise greeted Reece Pemberton's stylish set, representing the Victorian drawing-room of Salisbury brewer Arthur Harnham (Duncan Lamont). Avice Landon, giving a performance of subtlety and delicacy as his sister Letty, set the scene, talking about the young servant girl, Anna (Julia Foster), whom Arthur's wife Edith had taken under her wing, and preparing the way for Deborah Kerr's entrance in an exquisite period costume by Berman's—to tumultuous and

213

sustained applause. The story, set in 1900, dealt with Edith's frustrated affection for her upright but unimaginative husband and her sympathetic interest in the bucolic Anna, who meets a young barrister at the City Fair, falls in love with him and finds herself pregnant after a single intimacy. She persuades her mistress to ghost-write the letter she herself is incapable of penning to the young man, and Edith takes him in so completely by her vivid expression of her own inner feelings that he marries the girl, only finding out the true author of the letters after it is too late.

The company took innumerable curtain calls, and I dashed backstage after the show, briefly, to add my congratulations and to tell Deborah how true I felt the play and her performance to be. Brighton's enthusiasm was repeated by the London audience at the Lyric on 4 October, and her dressing-room was overflowing into the corridor with friends and relatives. Instantly recognizable were Dame Sybil Thorndike, who had appeared, arms opened wide and declaiming 'I must see my Deborah!', Lauren Bacall, in town for *Applause!* and Phyllis Smale, who had seen it all begin for her niece, so many years before. I stayed in the corridor and talked to Deborah's brother Ted, before cycling home to Twickenham, happy in the certainty that the play would be set to stay in London for many months to come. And so it was: every box-office record at the Lyric Theatre was shattered in the first week and the play ran to often capacity houses until May 1973, when, faced with the alternative of signing for a further year in England or taking the play to America for a national tour, opening in September, Deborah opted for the latter.

Of the rôle of Edith she says: 'I felt that it was a part I could play well, and that gave me the confidence to beard the lions in their den. I didn't mind a bit if they hated me or loved me, and it proved itself by the takings—the whole venture muchly helped by Julia, as it was essential to have a really good actress, as well as a beauty, in the part of Anna.'

London critics, though in the main enthusiastic about Kerr and Foster, were cool towards the play. A notable exception was B. A. Young in *The Financial Times*. 'One of the most enjoyable evenings I've had for a long time ... a "well-made" play ... Deborah Kerr must not be allowed again to stay away from the stage so long. In her solicitude for the girl she has a radiance that is almost tangible, in her grief she is agonizing, and all with a fine economy of means.' Michael Billington in *The Guardian* also praised play and players: 'A solid, sedate, wholly literate piece of narrative drama ... the play also gives Deborah Kerr a chance to display that nervy thoroughbred gentility for which she is cinematically famous. Indeed she offers us the enthralling spectacle of an apparently serene, self-contained woman gradually cracking open like a shell because of the pressure within ... it's a classy performance and well-matched by Julia Foster's as the bubbling, ringleted voluptuous serving girl. I also liked Ducan Lamont, with a voice like rough cider, as the purple-faced brewer, and Frith Banbury's production, like the play itself, is a trifle slow, but extremely safe and sure.'

Julia Foster says that she doesn't think the play would have been right for her 'if it had been any other lady than Deborah Kerr in the lead, and I don't think I would have done it. I had a feeling about her, and the play, and myself, and that if those three things worked it could make an enchanting evening. In fact, I was right. I had never met Deborah before we both got together with Frith Banbury, though, of course, I had seen many of her films; as both she and I are rather shy people, I don't remember much about the first meeting, except thinking how extraordinarily beautiful she was—much more so than she has ever looked on the screen.

'Rehearsals were not, for me personally, a particularly happy time, though it was lovely rehearsing on the Embankment, by the river: the part I was playing was very simple and straightforward and I always try to make things more complicated then they are, so it wasn't too easy a time as far as I was concerned. The Brighton opening was a nightmare for me, because I'm always a disaster for the first two weeks of a play, but everybody who came thought it wonderful entertainment, and the reason

215

for the success of the play was *entirely* Deborah: when you're with her, either sitting in a theatre, or in a room with her, you just get a warm, welcoming feeling, and I think anybody coming to watch her in the theatre shares that feeling. If she's playing a sympathetic part, which she was, you can't fail to have a delightful time. A critic said she "cast a glow over the whole evening" and that glow enveloped not only us, in the company, but the audiences as well.

'Not only is there something about her that is definitely soothing, but, despite her years in Hollywood, she's completely unspoilt. I once asked her "How is it you've remained so totally unaffected by everything you've been through?" and she said she'd been properly brought up, and if you have a proper upbringing you never lose the standards you've been set. I have named my second daughter, Tamara Deborah, born 20 January, 1976, after her, and know that if one particle of her quality rubs off on to the baby she will grow up a fine human being.

'She is the only star I know who genuinely treats each and everybody exactly alike. There are those who work at it because it's good for their "image", but her attitude comes from the heart—she has time for anybody and everybody. She's always in the theatre an hour after the show, entertaining people in her dressing-room; she enjoys doing it—I think she sees it as part of the work, which is why she doesn't resent the time—it's a kind of continuation of the performance and the right thing to do. She's very good with people and has that knack that Tommy Steele has, of being able to be the right thing to all people.

'Deborah was a witness at my wedding to Bruce Fogle on a lovely April day in 1973. The reception was given to us by a great friend of mine, Marvin Liebman, who was the other witness, at the Carlton Towers Hotel. Among the guests were Ingrid Bergman, Carol Browne, with whom I've been friendly for years, and her husband, Vincent Price. Upstairs in the powder room there was this marvellous attendant lady, who caught my arm on the way out and said: "*Oh—what* a recep-

216

tion: Deborah Kerr, Ingrid Bergman, Coral Browne—they're *legends* in their own time!"'

## III

During the nine-month run at the Lyric Deborah and Peter Viertel stayed in a roomy and pleasant flat in Upper Grosvenor Street. Predictably, it was a time of family reunions and meetings with old friends. Harriet Forster had gown up to resemble her cousin Deborah to a marked degree, particularly vocally: she had attended the same drama school in Bristol, did a little professional acting on leaving the Guildhall School of Speech and Drama and took up teaching children after she married an osteopath, Michael James Robinson. Their two daughters, Shauna Harriet and Victoria Jane, then aged eight and two, met their second counsins, Melanie and Francesca for the first time. Ted Trimmer's six-year-old daughter Deborah, of his second marriage, spent a day with her aunt, whose theatrical propensities she already showed a marked aptitude for emulating. Ted's first wife Pamela died in 1961 and he married Toni Bass, a colleague from TWW, where he was head of newscasting in Bristol, until moving in 1968 to ATV, Birmingham, where he is now Editor of News and Current Affairs.

Uncle Arthur Smale and Aunt Gre brought their family up from Goring-by-Sea for the day—daughter Shelagh and her husband John Broderick with their children, Philippa Clare, aged fourteen and Stephanie Jane, aged eleven. They all saw *The Day After the Fair* and were entertained by Deborah and Peter. Mrs Smale says: 'Deborah slipped at once into talking of family matters and made us so much at ease it didn't seem possible she had been away so long.' Another visitor from Goring was her first agent, John Gliddon and his wife Irene; for them, too, it was as though she had never been away: 'We found the same warmth and friendliness I had known in her all those years ago.'

Deborah's number one fan, Mary Johnston left her two-year-old son Robert at home with his father, Brian, and took a party of friends to the theatre. I went again several times with various friends, including Dorothy Dickson, who, with Edith Evans had been one of the handful of stars working in the theatre— afternoons only in the revue *Diversion*—during the Blitz of 1940, when Deborah was playing her first film and stage rôles. I also took Irish singer Ruby Murray—the only girl to have had five discs in the British Hit Parade at the same time. Her daughter, Julie, was tremendously impressed when she told her about going round to meet Deborah Kerr in her dressing-room. 'Tell me, Mummy,' said Julie, then thirteen, 'What did she think of you?'

Deborah had a visit from Theyre Lee Elliott, whose painting of Toumanova had influenced her to rent the ballerina's house all those years ago in Hollywood. Two dear friends from the past were sadly absent. Ursula Jeans had died suddenly shortly after she and Roger Livesey went to see the play in Brighton. He was not long able to survive without her, and was to follow her 'much too young, and so much mourned' early in 1976. Another sad break with the past was impresario Hugh 'Binkie' Beaumont's death in March 1973: Deborah and Peter were at the memorial service in April at St Paul's Church, Covent Garden, where Paul Scofield, Lord Olivier and Sir John Gielgud were among the readers.

The Viertels fulfilled a long-standing date with the Gallery First Nighters Club on 11 March: first invited, at Sir Terence Rattigan's special request the previous year, she had had to decline at the last moment and wrote a letter of regret from Spain. Her speech, at the dinner in honour of 'Our Leading Ladies' at the Europa Club, was a big hit with all present, especially the Club's President, Jack Rossiter, who was 'captivated by her beauty, modesty, sincerity and charm, with not the slightest hint of Hollywood stardom'. (This status seems to infect everyone in the vicinity with an apprehension that its holder is liable to go off suddenly, like an alarm clock.) The other guests of honour included Dame Anna Neagle, Wendy Hiller and Constance Cummings.

Deborah made her first appearance on Yorkshire Television's *Stars on Sunday* on 26 November, 1972, reading a passage from the Bible: this curious semi-religious programme has retained an enormous nation-wide following and presents a gloriously indiscriminate roster of stars of all kinds, from the Archbishop of Canterbury to Eartha Kitt. Deborah Kerr has, at different times, been featured with Yehudi Menuhin, Hughie Green and Gracie Fields, who was tempted out of semi-retirement in Capri to record a number of songs, spread out over odd Sundays during the years. There's no knowing when the songs or Bible readings will be repeated: Deborah and Dame Anna seem to be the most requested 'lesson' readers among the female stars.

Before she left the country to prepare for the American tour of *The Day After the Fair* I had tea with Deborah and Peter at their flat, and she talked about some of the film parts she had either missed through doing the play, or turned down due to their unsuitability. As far back as 1969 *Variety* reported her set to star in the film of Bryan Moore's novel *The Lonely Passion of Judith Hearne*, about an Irish spinster addicted to the bottle, for director Irvin Kershner, but the project had not got off the ground, due, she thought, to the very downbeat ending. *Travels with My Aunt* was mooted strongly for both Kerr and Katharine Hepburn; when it emerged Maggie Smith played the part, for which she was manifestly too young—as indeed was Deborah, but she would have been happy to work under George Cukor's direction again. There was talk about the Lady Nelson part in *Bequest to the Nation*, but this was during the run of the play, and was eventually done by Margaret Leighton, her performance being one of the enlivening factors in a none too brilliant movie.

'I couldn't think of trying to do a film and play at the same time,' said Deborah. 'After acting on the stage one doesn't unwind until the early hours of the morning, and then to be in the make-up room for six am is unthinkable.' At the time she was very interested about a proposed movie for Paul Newman's company—from Iris Murdoch's book *A Fairly Honourable*

219

*Defeat*, to be retitled *Mirror, Mirror*—with Joanne Woodward, James Mason, Louis Jourdan and Peter Ustinov, but to date this has not materialized. Neither has the projected film version of *The Day After the Fair*, which, opened up, could be an ideal subject.

Other offers varied from the obscene to the ridiculous. 'There seems to be an occasional inspiration like "Let's do something really *awful* and put Deborah Kerr into it." Some of the scripts are *unbelievable*; one had me vying with my daughter for the love of a young man and ended by my castrating a pig in front of her. I sent it back with a note: "You must be joking. D.K." That's where I think so many films today go wrong; any situation or subject is valid as a subject, as long as it bears resemblance to some sort of reality, but all too often it seems to be a case of "Let's see how far we can go to make a fast buck." This is when the time comes for anyone who cares for the profession to say: "No, thank you very much." '

## IV

The US tour of *The Day After the Fair* opened in September 1973 at the Shubert Theatre, Los Angeles to a rave review from Dan Sullivan of the *Times*: 'Lovely... not only marks the return of Deborah Kerr to the stage, but the reappearance of a kind of play that has practically become an endangered species. Call it the intelligent comfortable play. The kind that speaks to our love for well-turned theatrical surfaces rather than to our deeper selves, yet doesn't deny that we have a brain. Frank Harvey's play may be teacup drama in the old phrase, but it's not empty. Miss Kerr's is a subtle and intelligent characterization, a look at the "good" Victorian woman from a not especially flattering angle. Yet it is her personal warmth, grace and honesty that strike us first and strike us last, too. She is a superb technician and an accomplished actress, but basically she's one of God's great women. Is that sexist? Sorry.' There was similar enthusiasm in San Francisco, Chicago, where they sold out in advance for their month's run, Boston, Toronto and Washington, where they closed, at the beginning of March 1974.

Frith Banbury summed up the play's appeal: 'It was very much appreciated by the great majority of playgoers...underrated by the critics in London, though not in the States. I think this was due to the fact that it was an old-fashioned kind of play—just the kind that the present generation of critics think should be banned from our stage, but to which the still predominantly middle-class audiences are addicted—when they can get it. However, it was always obvious to me that, without Deborah's name, drawing-power and performance it would never have had the success it did. I particularly admired the way she adjusted her performance in the American production to the demands of the enormous theatres in the US. Her ability to enlarge was quite remarkable.

'It is now obvious to me that critics working in a less class-conscious society like the USA were far more able to judge the play on its merits, without those overtones of inverted snobbery with which we have to contend in several London critics. The situation in the play between a middle-class woman and her maid is presented in an *ironic* light (*Life's Little Ironies*). This seemed to escape the notice of some critics, who resented the fact that the bourgeois assumptions about life and the middle-class canons of behaviour towards social inferiors (period 1900) were not commented on or criticized from the point of view from which we would see them today.'

Vickery Turner replaced Julia Foster, who was expecting a baby; Brenda Forbes played Letty; Avice Landon, who gave such a moving performance in England, was ill during much of the run and died in June 1976. The fine contributions of Duncan Lamont and Paul Hastings as the husband and the girl's barrister lover were well matched in the US by W. B. Bryden and Michael Shannon. Vickery Turner had made a good impression as another flighty maidservant, in another era, safeguarded by the 'pill' in *Prudence and the Pill*.

221

Deborah Kerr was given the Los Angeles Critics' Circle Award for her acting as Edith, and also the Press Club of San Francisco's 'Black Cat' Award for 1973.

During 1974 Deborah did some relaxing in Marbella and accompanied Peter on a promotion tour for his book *Bicycle on the Beach*, during which he demonstrated on the *Dinah Shore Show* his ability to make a Spanish tortilla. This was live, on camera, but the results were sufficiently succulent to have won Fanny Cradock's unqualified approval. Later in the year Edward Albee interrupted Deborah's 'breather' when he went to Klosters to see her about his play *Seascape*. I had a card from her in December, from the Watergate Hotel, with 'The Renowned Watergate Complex' gleaming glamorously, reflected in the waters of the Potomac: she wrote that she was doing *Seascape* at the Kennedy Centre, Washington, prior to opening in New York on 26 January, 1975.

Originally the play consisted of three acts, but, after the first reading, Albee, who was directing his own work, came to rehearsals the next morning and said: 'Well, it's quite obvious— Act II does not exist!' The theme was played out entirely on a beach between four characters; James Tilton did a magnificent job of creating an entirely self-sufficient stretch of sand dunes and cycloramic blue sky. Two of them are husband and wife, Nancy and Charlie (Barry Nelson), both over forty: she is painting and he just trying to relax in the sun. He is a teacher, content with life as it is; she, the driving force of the two, is not satisfied with 'having had a good life' and a good marriage. She wants to continue to have a good life and to extend their horizon—she's full of plans to get up and go and do everything. While they are having a terrific argument about liver paste sandwiches they are joined by the other two characters, a male and female lizard who have come up from the bottom of the sea, because they felt they no longer belonged. Nancy and Charlie continue their argument until they suddenly become aware of apparent death threatening them from these two human size figures. Nancy insists they lie down on their backs before the monsters: 'Go on—get down; do as I tell you. Animals, you see; it's submission—they'll think it's submission!'

This brings the curtain down on the first act, and they are still 'submitting', while the sea creatures sniff them all over and are not sure what to make of them at the start of Act II. Eventually the four of them, animal and human, discourse on evolution—the lizards are in that process, which has caused them to make for dry land—sex, morality and all the topics with which people, if they are honest with themselves, are inextricably involved. In the end the creatures don't care for what they have learned about life above the sea, and they want to go back, but the humans plead with them to stay: 'Don't go back—you have to stay; you've no alternative!'

Notices were mixed: Deborah Kerr says: 'Albee is never easily categorized; this play is full of the unexpected, the ambiguous. *Seascape* is part fantasy, part satire, part comedy, part drama. Reactions to it are diametrically opposed: people seem to either respond completely or not at all.' Clive Barnes, whose power to make or break a play by his notices is something that does not have a direct counterpart in the British theatre, wrote in the *New York Times* that the play was 'a major dramatic event...a play of great density, with many interesting emotional and intellectual reverberations...Mr Albee is suggesting that one of the purposes of an individual human existence is quite simply evolution—that we all play a part in this oddly questionable historic process. So that the purpose of life is life itself—it is a self-fulfilling destiny...With that spare, laconic language of his he probes deeper and deeper into the subterranean seascapes of our pasts, presents and futures...Deborah Kerr starts beautifully and diffidently as a no-nonsense English matron, and then slowly slips off her pretences and becomes a very warm woman. Barry Nelson who, like Miss Kerr, and this is not truly a fair criticism, looks a little too young for the rôle, is a complete master of the off-hand. His accomplishment is so charming and so unforced, and he works with Miss Kerr as if they had been married for years.'

George Oppenheimer in *Newsday*, said it was 'Albee's finest play in a long while . . . Miss Kerr, looking young and lovely, is pure enchantment . . . as for Frank Langella and Maureen Anderman they are sinuous and singularly effective. The movements of the lizards, Leslie and Frank, are amazingly balletic and lifelike, so much so that I suspect that Albee, who has directed as superlatively as he has written, must have had a lizard as technical adviser.'

When *Seascape* opened in April for a season at the Shubert, Los Angeles, she told an interviewer over a lunch of Eggs Benedict—a favourite of hers, at home and abroad—that she would return home after the run, 'because it would not be fair to Peter to expect him to spend another year moving from one hotel to another. Perhaps a writer can write anywhere. But it is not the most convenient lifestyle.'

## V

In point of fact, travelling has formed as much a part of Peter Viertel's lifestyle as it has of Deborah's. He served in the United States Marine Corps from 1942 to 1945 in the South Pacific and the European Theatre of Operations. His first novel *The Canyon* was published in 1940, six years after his father, Berthold Viertel, established himself as a success in the British cinema, comparable to the esteem he had previously enjoyed in German films. In 1936 he directed the excellent *Rhodes of Africa*, starring Walter Huston, whose son John both Peter and Deborah were to work with in Hollywood years later. His mother Salka, also known in the German cinema, as actress and writer, began her long association with Garbo when Salka played the Marie Dressler part in the German version of *Anna Christie*. Thereafter she worked on most of her scripts and began a close friendship which is as strong today in Klosters as it was in Hollywood.

Peter's screen credits include *Saboteur* for Hitchcock, and, among his work for John Huston, *The Old Man and the Sea* and

*Beat the Devil*. There were so many friends in common in their work that the only wonder is that Deborah and Peter Viertel did not meet earlier in their careers than *The Journey*. In *The Sun Also Rises* (1957) there was not only Ava Gardner, going through a turbulent time in her life, whom Peter reputedly was able to influence and calm more effectively than anyone else on the movie, but Mel Ferrer, who, with Audrey Hepburn, was to become very friendly with the Viertels in Switzerland. Peter first worked with Katharine Hepburn five years earlier, during *The African Queen*; in 1974 she came to stay with Peter and Deborah in Klosters during the winter ski-ing season. Despite the fact that she had not joined in the sport since her debutante days, Hepburn insisted that Peter take her up into the Alps for a day's ski-ing, borrowing for the occasion an old pair of boots from Deborah, and continuing up and down the slopes until the light faded. When she returned her feet were bleeding, and her hostess tended them, applying Scholl's pads to the wounded areas. The next morning Katharine the Great, one of the fittest women in the history of Hollywood, went out again with Peter to the ski-slopes, without a murmur of complaint, and repeated the process. A few weeks after her return to the US, to film *Rooster Cogburn* with John Wayne, a large package was delivered at 'Wyhergut'—Scholl's plasters, 'with love from K.H.' One of Deborah's most prized garments is an old polo-necked pullover Hepburn gave her in 1959.

Francesca for some time attended a school in the Alps opposite Noël Coward's chalet at Les Avants. While the distance from Klosters as the crow flies is minimal, the journey for a human entails crossing the Alps; consequently Deborah mainly saw Sir Noël when she went over to the school for prize days or similar occasions. He was, however, very friendly with her daughter, who spent much of her free time at his home, with his friends Graham Payn, Cole Leslie and Gladys Calthrop, when they were in Switzerland. If she missed her visits for longer than he thought proper Deborah would receive a card: 'Why hasn't "Brown Bloomers" been to see me?'—referring to the brown uniform the girls all wore at the school. She says:

'He was an adorable man—so affectionate and genuine. He always retained great generosity towards other people in the business—which a lot of people don't—a generosity only matched by the great Thorndike, who always had time for people, well into her nineties: "You want to see me—right, I can fit you in at three-thirty, for tea." We all miss Noël terribly; sometimes, even now, one thinks: "I must call ... oh, no ..."'

Salka Viertel and her daughter-in-law are extremely close friends. Peter's mother continued to work in California for many years after Garbo retired, and wrote the adaptation of Dumas' *La Duchesse de Langeais*, which Garbo had actually signed to do for Cukor in 1948, and for which James Mason had received a substantial portion of his fee, before negotiations broke down. Salka settled in Klosters shortly before Peter and Deborah's marriage, and there she wrote her entrancing auto-biography, *The Kindness of Strangers*, published in 1970, when she was eighty. Her ex-husband Berthold returned after the war to Vienna's Burgtheater, where he was the leading director until his death in 1953. One of his most successful productions was Tennessee Williams' *A Streetcar Named Desire*, the source of the quotation that provides the title of Salka's autobiography. Another link in the family chain is that Fred Zinnemann was, early in his career, Berthold Viertel's assistant.

Garbo often visits her friends in Klosters, where her passion for solitude is understood and respected, and she made one of her rare public appearances when she went to see Deborah Kerr in *Seascape* in New York—a great evening for the entire company who knew, but did not let it be known she was there, and for the Viertels, who value her friendship highly. Garbo went backstage after the play to congratulate Deborah: her exquisite bone structure was unmistakable, despite a fur hood which almost masked her features, but she came and went un-troubled by anyone, and declared herself delighted with both play and performance.

The relationship between Peter and his wife is firmly grounded on mutual respect, affection and sense of humour. She says, 'He is the kindest person I know, and will go to any lengths to help people. He is also incapable of any kind of subterfuge.' They are comfortable to be with, and although he's obviously proud of her, will bring refreshingly astringent humour to bear on the subject: 'I'm married to a goddam movie star, which means we can't just go and get on to planes; we have to have the VIP treatment at the airport, which means all the luggage is lost and the plane leaves without us.' Deborah's comment: 'That's why we get along. He simply refuses to make heavy weather of things.'

Melanie and Francesca have led their own lives, out of the limelight, for the past sixteen or seventeen years—a subject on which their parents were in complete agreement: 'It was fine for them to be photographed wherever we went when they were small and cute; it was fun for them and always makes a nice picture when the children are young. However, about the age of eleven or twelve they become little human beings, with their own lives to lead, and we felt very strongly that it would not be to their advantage to be publicized any longer as So and So's children, or to continue to have photographs taken which could single them out from the other children and perhaps have made it difficult for them to develop in their own way. We've always remained very close, and Peter's daughter, Christine, got on with them from the beginning. For a while my London agent, Anne Hutton, who started with us as a secretary in Klosters, then worked for another of my agents, Christopher Mann, before finally branching out on her own, looked after them in England; she had known them since they were very young, and they stayed with her when Melanie was at London University and Francesca at the Lycée in Paris. Anne has been a dear and good friend for more than fifteen years.

'Neither of them has followed me into the profession, although Francesca did think she might be interested and took a year, after getting her A-levels, working on the technical side of films. She was on *Nicholas and Alexandra*, then decided to go to college, after which she went to work in Anne Hutton's office, helping her in the agency business. Melanie has a

227

degree in sociology—she's always been interested in setting the world to rights, and we certainly need people to do that.

'I don't really involve myself in Peter's work—if he asks me to read anything I'm happy to do so, but wouldn't dream of sneaking into his workroom to read bits of what he is writing. When *Vogue* asked us to write, unbeknown to each other, six hundred words on "First Love" and they were published, I was quite unbearable about it—for days after I kept opening the magazine to read my words in *print*. Peter said: "There's only room for one writer in the family," just as I say: "There's only room for one actor!"'

The article in question was, in fact, used as part of an English class's work in Film Appreciation, by another Deborah Kerr fan in Australia, teacher David Kerry Pitts, who once travelled with two friends to Klosters to meet her: his subjects are English and history, and another section of his class's work was to study *The Innocents, Prudence and the Pill* and *The Arrangement*—an assignment which met with enormous enthusiasm from his pupils, 'though what the actress herself would feel about having her work studied and examined in a high school is another matter,' he writes. Her answer to that is 'very flattered indeed'. She does, in fact, take the devotion of the fans as a responsibility for which she is grateful, but which can be a liability. She is one of a handful of personalities who bring out in their admirers a feeling of dependence: the star becomes a kind of private icon, which is where the liability can arise, in judging the right degree of help and advice it is politic to give, without getting inextricably involved in other people's lives.

'Wyhergut' is regarded by the Viertels as their 'working home'. They have been helped by a succession of beautiful Swiss secretaries who have had world-wide secretarial experience, thanks to a Swiss training scheme which equips young people for such work wherever they may be needed. In Deborah's small office-cum-dressing-room are her nominations and awards, including a 'Citation' from the Association of Suicidology for the television appearances she has made to help the work of the Suicide Premonition Organization, a cause very close to her heart.

'I have always been so disturbed by the number of the very young, as well as women and men in their fifties who get desperate enough to contemplate self-destruction and have no "outside family" help to turn to. The suicides of Charles Boyer's son and Gregory Peck's son, and, more recently, of Jennifer Jones' daughter, just broke my heart, and if my TV "spots" could be of *any* help, then it is the least I can do.'

There are other objects of considerable personal value in her office, including a small watercolour dated 3/2/54, by the late Clifford Odets, the playwright, representing rows of solemn-faced children, old and young, with an inscription by the artist: 'Hoping this will give you a chuckle; "Happiness, they say, is no laughing matter."' There is, too, a lifelike sketch of Deborah by William Holden, and several of her own paintings: a particularly striking one is a village scene where English-type houses are intermingled with Swiss. In the bedroom there is an effective portrait painting which Jean Negulesco had brought from France from the set of *Count Your Blessings*. She liked it so much the company gave it to her for her birthday. She says, modestly: 'I paint, rather badly, but I love it and had the honour of having my paintings stolen; I got them back from the trusty Swiss and German police—you can't get very far in Switzerland. There was a Picasso bull-fight drawing in Peter's study which they ignored: I guess that didn't look as pretty—and as corny—as my paintings did.'

The Viertels are very friendly with Irwin Shaw, with whom Peter collaborated on a play called *The Survivors*, produced in New York in 1948, his ex-wife Marian and director Robert Parrish and his wife Kathy. He directed one of the segments of *Casino Royale* in which Deborah was not involved, and is one of the few major film-makers with whom she has not worked, although they had plans and a script on which he worked very hard, to do Rumer Godden's *Kingfishers Catch Fire*. After months of research the rights turned out to be unavailable, and they had to shelve the project.

# VI

The only drawback to these idyllic surroundings of the Alps is their unsuitability for keeping dogs—for whom Deborah has always had such a soft spot. The most recent, in the days when they were still renting Annabella's farm house at St Jean de Luz for their summer holidays, was an enormous Pyrenean Mountain dog of extraordinary beauty, Guapa, which means just that in Spanish. The land all around St Jean is sheep country, and one day when the family were at lunch, Guapa, with tremendous pride, herded a huge sheep into the living-room, and stood grinning from ear to ear, waiting for praise for what she had done.

'Poor Guapa was only "doing her own thing",' says Deborah, 'and couldn't understand why we were not delighted. There were Peter, my daughters and I all trying to get this sheep out of the room—you have no idea how heavy they are until you meet one socially!' Guapa, alas, had to go, because it was impossible to fence her in, and in the mountainside by 'Wyhergut' there are deer lurking among the pine trees, and cows grazing, whose bells when they come down for the evening in age groups, with mother's bell making the deepest clang, are one of the most evocative sounds for those who have spent any part of their childhood in the Swiss mountains. She found a good home with friends of Annabella's, the exquisite star of *Le Million* and *Hôtel du Nord*, who now devotes her life to helping the needy. Deborah says: 'She does extraordinary good work in rehabilitating people in Paris, or wherever the need is, and has been a friend of ours for many years.'

Peter Viertel, whose Spanish friends include Louis-Miguel Domenguin and his film-star wife Lucia Bosé, has a love of the country that goes back to the fifties; his 1961 bestseller, *Love Lies Bleeding* was a moving study of the decline of a great bull-fighter. The Viertels started to go regularly to Marbella through the renowned generosity of their friends, who were always ready to insist: 'Take our house for the summer!' Their present home there came about quite by chance when Deborah and Peter were doing something they have rarely done in their lives—playing golf, at the Rio Real, with their friend Ignacio Coca, a banker, who owns the whole of the urbanization around Los Monteros.

He remarked that they really should have a house of their own out there, and Peter replied that they did not want to go into building houses again, adding: 'We just want a little cottage like that one'—indicating what looked like a small Sussex farmhouse overlooking the course—whitewashed and tiled, with a little balcony and black shutters, resembling a derelict doll's house. It was almost a ruin, with no road to it, was two hundred years old, and originally the overseers' cottage to a fruit and vegetable farm, which meant that the soil around was exceedingly rich. 'You can have it,' said their host, as it was a part of his property. Peter asked him what he wanted for the cottage, which took some months to be put in working order.

Finally a letter came from their friend, saying he could not sell it to them, because there was no road to it, and you can't sell anybody a house with no means of access. For years after that they used to reach their new home by driving across the golf course in the only Harley Davidson golf car in the whole of the Iberian Peninsula, found, again by sheer luck, in a garage in Torremolinos, where an attempt to market the car had been prohibited by law. The whole process of shopping and transporting the goods by golf car was adventurous, and so was the bliss of having no telephone—until they wanted to talk business from their remote holiday home, twenty feet above the golf course.

Now there is a huge Auto Pista to their house, plus a telephone. They love their retreat and tend to head for Los Monteros when the tourists descend on Klosters or in November to catch the sun, after it has deserted Switzerland. Deborah has filled the small garden with a profusion of oranges, lemons, plums, figs, cherries, avocados, apples and tomatoes; they grow their own onions and beans and peppers, all proliferating with sweet peas and other flowers in the area behind the house, which

231

has wooden beams in the ceilings, thick walls and large open fire-places. There are three bedrooms and Peter himself designed the only concession to modernity, the kitchen, where he prepares most of the meals, revelling in fry-ups, curries and spaghettis, counteracting the potentially fattening effects of these by his addiction to sport, particularly tennis, swimming and surfing.

Near neighbours include Madeleine Carroll who, after leaving films, turned successfully to real estate on the Costa Brava. Comedian Michael Bentine, with his wife Clementina a regular visitor to Marbella, loves to visit Madeleine and listen to her pithy and trenchant conversation about the Hollywood she knew. David Hemmings, calling on Deborah and Peter for drinks with his then wife Gayle Hunnicutt, likened their hide-away to a 'Spanish version of a country cottage in Guildford'.

Towards the end of 1975 the Viertels left Spain to do their first play together. *Souvenir*, written by Peter in collaboration with George Axelrod is about a Hollywood star called Julie Stevens (Deborah Kerr) who never was, but recalled echoes of many who had been. It was an intriguing idea about a woman whose husband had created her stardom and then died, causing her to become a recluse. She emerges from retirement to work again and begins to fall for the young director, Mark Sanders (Tony Musante), with whom she fights, but whom she begins to feel, against her will, she needs. They have an affair and one by one her defences are laid bare; the play is about dependence and patience, and presented the actress first as a woman of fifty, takes her back to twenty and the beginning of her career, then on to thirty, and also shows her as a character in a movie she makes. Arthur Cantor was one of the presenters of *Souvenir*, and Laurence Hugo co-starred as the husband. Gerald Freedman directed.

It became apparent during rehearsals that things were not going to run smoothly, as costs mounted, due to an elaborate production and a large cast. Advance bookings were good before the November opening at the Shubert Theatre, Los Angeles, but an aggressive press put the lid on any chances they had of recouping their losses and *Souvenir* folded after two weeks. Deborah Kerr wrote a letter of appreciation to the magazine *Westways*, which suggested that if the play could survive long enough for certain changes to be made it could turn into a rewarding theatrical experience, but it was off before the article came out. She quoted her dialogue as Julie Stevens:

'If what you're asking is: "Do I want to be a movie star?" the answer is "No."—not a movie star or a sex goddess, nor do I wish Julie Stevens to become a household name,' she says to the director on the day of her first screen test. 'I want to be an actress, that's all. I want to put make-up on my face and pretend to be somebody else. I don't want to be me—that's the whole point. That's what the whole business is about.'

Deborah continued: 'I had a tremendous feeling of *déjà vu* about *Souvenir*—of having been there before. I don't want it to be about me, which it isn't—but it is.' They would like to put it on again one day in a simplified production; at the time it was a very great disappointment.

Across the way at the Westport Playhouse Deborah's old friend Cathleen Nesbitt was suffering a similar experience that November: author–producer Edward Chodorov had phoned her in London to star in his own re-write of his 1935 success *Kind Lady*. On the strength of a script hastily borrowed from Sybil Thorndike, who reported that it had worked well for her forty years previously, Cathleen Nesbitt took the train to Los Angeles and a disastrous production, which netted her personally, at eighty-seven, the biggest personal ovations she had ever received, but foundered on the casting of young Joseph Bottoms, whose enchanting smile and lack of any stage experience utterly belied the premise of the play that he intended to murder the old lady who had taken him into her house. Deborah and Cathleen were able to commiserate with each other at supper at George Cukor's Los Angeles home, while Deborah's PRO, Rupert Allan, also gave a party for them both before they went their separate ways.

In the summer of 1976 Esmee Smythe heard 'through the grapevine' that Deborah Kerr was coming to England in June to play in John Sturges' *The Eagle Has Landed* from the best-seller

233

by Jack Higgins. It was as well that Esmee checked, to find the grapevine had been premature in its forecast. The part of Joanna Grey, an aristocratic WVS worker and secret Nazi agent, had not appealed sufficiently to tempt Deborah from her mountain home, even though the makers offered to tone down the violence inherent in the part. Jean Marsh gave an uncannily accurate portrayal of the way Deborah Kerr might have played the rôle complete to the last details of a look-alike appearance and hair-style, confirming how right she had been to decline the offer, despite the film's enormous box-office success. The rôle in the film—though not in the novel—is utterly without motivation, and to have played it could not have done her any good whatever. She said: 'I have a good life and a marvellous marriage and home—I'm not going to take any offer that comes along, just for the sake of doing a movie. I think I'm incredibly lucky in what life has brought me.'

In November she flew to London, to meet her first grandchild, Joe, the son of Francesca and her husband, actor John Shrapnel. She also presented Peter Sellers with his award on the *Evening News* TV Awards Show for his performance in *The Pink Panther Strikes Again*.

On 18 February, 1977, she opened at the Ahmanson Theatre, Los Angeles, opposite Charlton Heston in Eugene O'Neill's *Long Day's Journey into Night*. She wrote: 'The play is playing to packed houses despite adverse critics—the in-fighting that goes on between *this* particular theatre and the critics is incredible . . . So they slam *everything*. But my true and critical friends find the production excellent and have heaped praise on my particular conception of Mary Tyrone. I have adored rehearsals and Peter Wood is a brilliant director. Looking back, I realize I have nearly always been singularly fortunate in the people—and particularly the directors—with whom I have been privileged to work.'

After a break in Los Monteros to learn the very long part of 'Candida' she flew to England with Peter for the première at the Grand Theatre, Leeds, on 6 June, the start of Elizabeth II's Jubilee celebrations. During my 600-mile cycle ride via the

Malvern Festival I had ample time to reflect on the eventful journey that has been Deborah's from Shaw to Shaw—from the frailty and innocence of Jenny Hill to the strength and wisdom of Candida, via Phyllis Smale's Drama School and the Hollywood Dream Factory.

The West End opening at the Albery on 23 June presented Denis Quilley as Morell and Patrick Ryecart as Marchbanks opposite a Candida who, in the words of the author, 'has the ways of a woman who has found she can always manage people by engaging their affection'.

Critical reactions included Bernard Levin's 'She is played by another of those ageless beauties, Deborah Kerr, and I admit with shame that I have never before realized what a fine actress she is' and the *Catholic Herald*'s conclusion that the combination of her, Shaw and a fine cast is 'irresistible', making for the best entertainment in town. Jack Tinker in the *Daily Mail* encapsulated the fusion of playwright's intention and actress: 'It is impossible not to succumb to (her) spell ... Miss Kerr kindles the fires and the text blazes suddenly into crackling life. She is dominant. She is appalled by the petty jealousy she has aroused. She lifts the lid off beauty and shows us her mind and heart. In short, she *is* Candida.'

# BIBLIOGRAPHY

BAGNOLD, ENID, *Enid Bagnold's Autobiography*, Heinemann, London, 1969.

BAER, D. RICHARD, *The Film Buff's Bible*, Hollywood Film Archive, California, 1972.

CRAWFORD, JOAN (with Jane Kesner Ardmore), *A Portrait Of Joan*, Doubleday & Company, New York, 1962.

EAMES, JOHN DOUGLAS, *The MGM Story*, Crown Publishers, New York, 1976.

HALLIWELL, LESLIE, *The Filmgoer's Companion* (second edition), MacGibbon & Kee, London, 1967; (fourth edition), Paladin, London, 1972.

GIFFORD, DENIS, *British Cinema, An Illustrated Guide*, A. Zwemmer, London, 1968; A. S. Barnes, New York, 1968.

GRAHAM, PETER, *A Dictionary Of The Cinema*, A. Zwemmer, 1968; A. S. Barnes, New York, 1968.

*Kinematograph Year Book, 1922*, Kinematograph Year Book Publications, London, 1921.

LANDSTONE, CHARLES, *I Gate-Crashed*, Stainer & Bell, London, 1976.

MEYER, JIM, *Screen Facts* (volume four, number one), Screen Facts Press, New York, 1968.

MILLS, HUGH, *Prudence And The Pill*, Sphere, London, 1968.

NIVEN, DAVID, *Bring On The Empty Horses*, Hamish Hamilton, London, 1975.

NOBLE, PETER, *British Film Year Book, 1947–48*, Skelton Robinson British Yearbooks, London, 1946.

PALMER, LILLI, *Change Lobsters And Dance*, W. H. Allen, London, 1976.

PARISH, JAMES ROBERT, *The RKO Gals*, Ian Allan Ltd, London, 1974.

*Picturegoer's Who's Who And Encyclopaedia* (first edition), Odhams Press, London, 1933.

ROBYNS, GWEN, *Light Of A Star: Vivien Leigh*, Leslie Frewin, London, 1968.

SHIPMAN, DAVID, *The Great Movie Stars: The International Years*, Angus & Robertson (UK), London, 1972.

THORNTON, MICHAEL, *Jessie Matthews*, Hart-Davis, MacGibbon, London, 1974; Mayflower Books, London, 1975.

*Who's Who In The Theatre*, Pitman, London, from seventh edition (1933) to fifteenth edition (1972).

# FILMOGRAPHY

*The films are listed in order of production: the year of release is given where different from the year of filming. The first name after the production company is that of the director; the producer is listed only where synonymous. The main players are listed.*

Abbreviations    *sc.—Screenplay by . . .*

*B. & W.—Black and White.*

*In films from* Love On The Dole *onwards, Deborah Kerr has been starred above the title, unless otherwise indicated.*

1  *Contraband*   British National   Michael Powell and Emeric Pressburger; sc. Brock Williams; 91 mins; B. & W.   Wartime espionage thriller, with Kerr as cigarette girl in nightclub sequence with Margaret Vyner; subsequently cut. Conrad Veidt, Valerie Hobson. 1939:1940

2  *Major Barbara*   General Film Distributors   Gabriel Pascal with Harold French and David Lean; sc. Bernard Shaw from his play; 121 mins; B. & W.   Kerr seventh-billed as Jenny Hill, Salvation Army lass, attacked by drunken Snobby Price (Robert Newton) in course of her duties at the Major's Hostel HQ. Wendy Hiller, Rex Harrison, Robert Morley, Emlyn Williams, Sybil Thorndike. 1940:1941

3  *Love On The Dole*   British National   John Baxter; sc. Walter Greenwood from Ronald Gow's book; 100 mins; B. & W.   Kerr top-billed as Sally Hardcastle, with Clifford Evans as her lover, victimized over his attempt to improve the lot of his fellow-miners: after his death she becomes the mistress of bookmaker Frank Cellier. Mary Merrall, George Carney, Geoffrey Hibbert as her family. 1940:1941

4  *Penn of Pennsylvania*   (US Title: *The Courageous Mr Penn*)   British National   Lance Comfort; sc. Anatole de Grunwald; 85 mins; B. & W.   Kerr second-billed as Gulielma Springelt, wife of Clifford Evans' Penn, the Quaker founder of the title: she dies in childbirth.

237

Dennis Arundell, Aubrey Mallalieu, D. J. Williams, John Stuart, Max Adrian. 1941:1942

5   *Hatter's Castle*   Paramount-British   Lance Comfort; sc. Rodney Ackland from novel by A. J. Cronin; 102 mins; B. & W.   Kerr second-billed as Mary Brodie, daughter of Robert Newton, the mad hatter: she loves doctor James Mason and is thrown out by father after becoming pregnant by villain Emlyn Williams. Beatrice Varley, Henry Oscar, Enid Stamp-Taylor, Anthony Bateman. 1941:1942. (US 1948)

6   *The Day Will Dawn*   (US Title: *The Avengers*)   General Film Distributors   Harold French; sc. Frank Owen; 97 mins; B. & W.   Kerr second-billed as Kari, Norwegian skipper's daughter, who throws in her lot with British commandos. Ralph Richardson, Hugh Williams, Griffith Jones, Francis L. Sullivan, Roland Culver, Bernard Miles, Finlay Currie. 1942

7   *The Life and Death of Colonel Blimp*   The Archers–UA   Michael Powell & Emeric Pressburger, pro., also sc.; 148 mins; Technicolor.   Kerr second-billed as Edith Hunter, English governess in Berlin during the South African war; Barbara Wynne, a war nurse in Germany, 1914–18; 'Johnny' Cannon, MTC driver, 1939–45: co-starring with Anton Walbrook as a German officer who wins her in the first episode, and Brigadier Roger Livesey, VC who marries her in the second and survives to become the Blimp of the title in the Second World War. Roland Culver, James McKechnie, Albert Lieven, Ursula Jeans, A. E. Matthews. 1942:1943

8   *Perfect Strangers*   (US Title: *Vacation From Marriage*)   MGM-London Films   Alexander Korda, also pro; sc. Clemence Dane and Anthony Pelissier; 102 mins; B & W.   Kerr under title as Catherine Wilson, wife to Robert Donat, solo-billed above. Their anaemic marriage revives after they both undergo naval service. Glynis Johns, Ann Todd, Roland Culver. 1944:1945

9   *I See a Dark Stranger*   (US Title: *The Adventuress*)   General Film Distributors—Individual   Frank Launder, also pro, and sc. with Sidney Gilliat; 112 mins; B. & W.   Kerr top-billed as Bridie Quilty, an Irish girl who spies for the Germans in the Second World War and changes sides for love of British army officer Trevor Howard. Raymond Huntley, Liam Redmond, Olga Lindo, Garry Marsh. 1945:1946

10   *Black Narcissus*   General Film Distributors–Archers   Michael Powell and Emeric Pressburger also pro., sc. from book by Rumer

Godden; 100 mins; Technicolor. Kerr top-billed as Sister Clodagh, with Sabu, David Farrar, Flora Robson. Superior of a teaching convent in the Himalayas, she clashes with the other nuns and gives up her work after the mission is forced to return to Calcutta. Kathleen Byron, Esmond Knight, Jean Simmons, Jenny Laird, May Hallatt. 1946:1947

11 *The Hucksters* MGM Jack Conway; sc. Luther Davis from book by Frederick Wakeman; 115 mins; B. & W. Kerr second-billed as society beauty Kay Dorrance opposite Clark Gable, ad. man out to get her to endorse a brand of soap. Sydney Greenstreet, Adolphe Menjou, Ava Gardner, Keenan Wynn, Edward Arnold. 1947

12 *If Winter Comes* MGM Victor Saville; sc. Marguerite Roberts and Arthur Wimperis from book by A. S. M. Hutchinson; 97 mins; B. & W. Kerr second-billed as Nona Tybar, true love to Walter Pidgeon's suffering hero, divorced by hard-hearted wife Angela Lansbury and held responsible for the suicide of teenager Janet Leigh. Binnie Barnes, Dame May Whitty, John Abbott, Rene Ray. 1947:1948

13 *Edward, My Son* MGM George Cukor; sc. Donald Ogden Stewart from play by Robert Morley and Noel Langley; 112 mins; B. & W. Kerr second-billed as Evelyn Boult, wife to self-made millionaire Spencer Tracy, whose ruthless dedication to pampering their (unseen) son drives her to an alcoholic's grave. Ian Hunter, Leueen McGrath, James Donald, Felix Aylmer. 1948:1949

14 *Please Believe Me* MGM Norman Taurog; sc. Nathaniel Curtis; 87 mins; B. & W. Kerr top-billed as English heiress to a ranch, with Robert Walker, Mark Stevens and Peter Lawford as her suitors. James Whitmore, J. Carrol Naish, Spring Byington. 1949:1950

15 *King Solomon's Mines* MGM Compton Bennett, Andrew Marton; sc. Helen Deutsch from H. Rider Haggard's book; 102 mins; Technicolor. Kerr top-billed as Elizabeth Curtis who persuades adventurer Stewart Granger to include her in his African safari to look for her missing husband. Richard Carlson, Hugo Haas, Siriaque. 1949–50:1951

16 *Quo Vadis?* MGM Mervyn LeRoy; sc. John Lee Mahin with S. N. Behrman and Sonya Levien from book by Henryk Sienkiewicz; 171 mins; Technicolor. Kerr second-billed as Lygia, into whose Christian household Roman General Robert Taylor is welcomed,

although Peter Ustinov's Emperor Nero is after the blood of all followers of Christ. Leo Genn, Marina Berti, Patricia Laffan, Nora Swinburne, Felix Aylmer 1950:1952

17  *Thunder in the East*  Paramount  Charles Vidor; sc. Jo Sterling from Alan Moorehead's book *Rage of the Vulture*; 98 mins; B. & W.  Kerr second-billed as Joan Willoughby, blind girl involved with other passengers in a plane piloted to war-torn Gandahar by cynical Alan Ladd. Charles Boyer, Corinne Calvet, Cecil Kellaway. 1951:1952

18  *The Prisoner of Zenda*  MGM  Richard Thorpe; sc. John Balderston and Noel Langley from the book by Anthony Hope; 100 mins; Technicolor.  Kerr second-billed as Princess Flavia for whose hand Stewart Granger as King Rudolf of Ruritania and his double Rudolf Rassendyll contend. James Mason, Louis Calhern, Jane Greer, Lewis Stone. 1952:1953

19  *Dream Wife*  MGM  Sidney Sheldon; also sc. with Herbert Baker and Alfred Levitt; 99 mins; B. & W.  Kerr second-billed as Priscilla Effington of the US State Department, engaged to Cary Grant: she neglects him for her career and he falls for Persian Princess Betta St John. Walter Pidgeon, Buddy Baer, Bruce Bennett. 1952:1953

20  *Young Bess*  MGM  Sidney Franklin; sc. Jan Lustig and Arthur Wimperis from book by Margaret Irwin; 112 mins; Technicolor. Kerr third-billed as Catherine Parr, sixth and last wife of Henry VIII. On his demise she marries Thomas Seymour, and when she dies he is accused of seducing Bess. Jean Simmons, Stewart Granger, Charles Laughton, Kay Walsh, Guy Rolfe, Kathleen Byron, Cecil Kellaway. 1952:1953

21  *Julius Caesar*  MGM  Joseph L. Mankiewicz: sc. William Shakespeare; 122 mins; B. & W.  Kerr seventh-billed as Portia, wife to Brutus, in the film of the play. Marlon Brando, James Mason, John Gielgud, Louis Calhern, Edmond O'Brien, Greer Garson. 1953:1954

22  *From Here to Eternity*  Columbia  Fred Zinnemann; sc. Daniel Taradash from book by James Jones; 114 mins; B. & W.  Kerr third-billed as Karen Holmes, American officer's wife, embarking on an affair with Sgt. Burt Lancaster in the period before Pearl Harbor. Montgomery Clift, Frank Sinatra, Donna Reed, Philip Ober, Ernest Borgnine. 1953

23  *The End of the Affair*  Columbia  Edward Dmytryk; sc. Lenore Coffee from book by Graham Greene; 107 mins; B. & W.  Kerr

240

top-billed as Sarah Miles, civil servant's wife involved in religious conflict over her affair with writer Van Johnson. John Mills, Peter Cushing, Stephen Murray, Nora Swinburne. 1954:1955

24  *The Proud and Profane*  Paramount  George Seaton, also sc. from book *The Magnificent Bastards* by Lucy Herndon Crockett; 112 mins; B. & W.  Kerr second-billed as Nurse Lee Ashley in torrid romance with Marine Colonel William Holden, whose baby she miscarries. Thelma Ritter, Dewey Martin, William Redfield. 1955:1956

25  *The King and I*  20th Century-Fox  Walter Lang; sc. Ernest Lehman from play by Oscar Hammerstein II; 133 mins; Eastman Colour.  Kerr top-billed as Mrs Anna Leonowens, governess to King of Siam: she brings a measure of gentleness of his life. Yul Brynner, Rita Moreno, Alan Mowbray, Geoffrey Toone. 1955:1956

26  *Tea and Sympathy*  MGM  Vincente Minnelli; sc. Robert Anderson from his play; 122 mins; Metrocolor.  Kerr top-billed as Laura Reynolds, housemaster's wife who proves to student John Kerr that he is not homosexual, as everyone at the college assumes him to be. Leif Erickson, Edward Andrews, Darryl Hickman. 1956:1957

27  *Heaven Knows, Mr Allison*  20th Century-Fox  John Huston, also sc. with John Lee Mahin; 91 mins; Technicolor.  Kerr top-billed as Sister Angela, stranded on a Pacific island with Marine Robert Mitchum, who learns deep respect and affection, which she reciprocates. 1957

28  *An Affair to Remember*  20th Century-Fox  Leo McCarey, also sc. with Delmer Daves; 115 mins; Eastman Colour.  Kerr second-billed as Nickie, a nightclub singer unable to keep a date on the Empire State building with playboy Cary Grant through an accident which loses her the use of her legs. Richard Denning, Cathleen Nesbitt. 1957

29  *Bonjour Tristesse*  Columbia  Otto Preminger, also pro; sc. Arthur Laurents from book by Françoise Sagan; 94 mins; Technicolor.  Kerr top-billed as Anne, a widow engaged to David Niven, whose teenage daughter Jean Seberg sees her as a threat to her way of life and ultimately causes her death in a car crash. Mylène Demongeot, Juliette Greco, Geoffrey Horne, Walter Chiari, Martita Hunt, Jean Kent. 1957:1958

30  *Separate Tables*  United Artists  Delbert Mann; sc. Terence Rattigan from his own play, with John Gay; 99 mins; B. & W.  Kerr top-billed with Rita Hayworth. Sybil Railton-Bell is a timid spinster,

dominated by mother Gladys Cooper, and falls in love with ex-Major David Niven, who is exposed as a fraud and sexual deviant. Burt Lancaster, Wendy Hiller, Cathleen Nesbitt, Felix Aylmer, Rod Taylor, Audrey Dalton, May Hallatt. 1958:1959

31 *The Journey* MGM Anatole Litvak; sc. George Tabori and Peter Viertel; 125 mins; Technicolor. Kerr top-billed as Lady Diana Ashmore, who arouses the interest of Russian commander Yul Brynner when he halts the train on which she is trying to smuggle her wounded lover Jason Robards Jnr across the Austro-Hungarian frontier. Robert Morley, E. G. Marshall, Anne Jackson, David Kossoff, Anouk Aimée. 1958:1959

32 *Count Your Blessings* MGM Jean Negulesco; sc. Karl Tunberg; from Nancy Mitford's book *The Blessing*; 102 mins; Technicolor. Kerr top-billed as Grace Allingham, who takes nine years after her wartime romance with French Count Rossano Brazzi to discover her husband is essentially promiscuous. Maurice Chevalier, Martin Stephens, Tom Helmore, Ronald Squire, Patricia Medina. 1958:1959

33 *Beloved Infidel* 20th Century-Fox Henry King; sc. Sy Bartlett from book by Sheilah Graham and Gerold Frank; 123 mins; De Luxe Colour. Kerr second-billed as Sheilah Graham opposite Gregory Peck's Scott Fitzgerald in re-working of journalist Graham's autobiography dealing with their ill-starred love affair. Eddie Albert, Philip Ober, Karin Booth. 1959:1960

34 *The Sundowners* Warner Bros. Fred Zinnemann; sc. Isobel Lennart; 133 mins; Technicolor Kerr top-billed as Ida Carmody, who longs for her own home but loves her husband, sheep drover Robert Mitchum, enough to settle for the roving existence which is his life. Peter Ustinov, Glynis Johns, Dina Merrill, Michael Anderson Jnr, Chips Rafferty. 1959:1960

35 *The Grass Is Greener* Universal-International Stanley Donen, also pro. and sc. with Hugh and Margaret Williams, from their play; 105 mins; Technicolor. Kerr second-billed as Hilary Rhyall, English lady of the manor, married to Cary Grant, and undertaking a little extra-marital relaxation with visiting American Robert Mitchum. Jean Simmons, Moray Watson. 1960:1961

36 *The Naked Edge* United Artists Michael Anderson; sc. Joseph Stefano from Max Ehrlich's book *First Train to Babylon*; 99 mins; B. & W. Kerr second-billed as Martha Radcliffe, gradually driven to the conclusion that husband Gary Cooper has committed a murder for which another man was sent to jail. Eric Portman, Diane Cilento,

Hermione Gingold, Peter Cushing, Michael Wilding, Wilfrid Lawson. 1961

37   *The Innocents*   20th Century-Fox   Jack Clayton; sc. Truman Capote and John Mortimer from the story *The Turn of the Screw* by Henry James; 100 mins; B. & W.   Kerr solo-billed as Miss Giddens, Victorian governess trying to cope with the eerie other-worldliness of two young charges in a haunted, isolated mansion. Michael Redgrave, Megs Jenkins, Peter Wyngarde, Pamela Franklin, Martin Stephens. 1961:1962

38   *The Chalk Garden*   Universal-International   Ronald Neame; sc. John Michael Hayes from the play by Enid Bagnold; 106 mins; Technicolor.   Kerr top-billed as Miss Madrigal, mysterious governess to the undisciplined and wayward Hayley Mills, granddaughter of autocratic Edith Evans. John Mills, Elizabeth Sellars, Felix Aylmer. 1963:1964

39   *The Night of the Iguana*   MGM   Seven Arts   John Huston, also sc. with Anthony Veiller from play by Tennessee Williams; 118 mins; B. & W.   Kerr third-billed as Hannah Jelkes, an artist who roams the world with her grandfather, selling her sketches and pausing at a remote Mexican hotel peopled by explosive and conflicting personalities, owner Ava Gardner, unfrocked priest Richard Burton, turbulent teenager Sue Lyon. Grayson Hall, Cyril Delevanti. 1963:1964

40   *Marriage on the Rocks*   Warner–Pathé–Sinatra Enterprise   Jack Donohue; sc. Cy Howard, title changed from *Community Property*; 109 mins; Technicolor.   Kerr second-billed as Valerie Edwards, trying to save her nineteen-year-old marriage to Frank Sinatra, but inadvertently marrying his best friend Dean Martin. Cesar Romero, Hermione Baddeley, Nancy Sinatra, John McGiver. 1965

41   *Eye of the Devil*   MGM–Filmways   J. Lee Thompson; sc. Robin Estridge and Dennis Murphy from Philip Lorraine's book *Day of the Arrow*; 90 mins; B. & W.   Kerr top-billed as Catherine de Montfaucon, English wife of Marquis David Niven, who after the failure of his wine crops accompanies him back to the family château and uncovers some fatal devil worship. Donald Pleasence, Edward Mulhare, Flora Robson, Emlyn Williams, Sharon Tate, David Hemmings. 1966:1968

42   *Casino Royale*   Columbia–Famous Artists   John Huston and four others; sc. Wolf Mankowitz with John Law and Michael Sayers, suggested by Ian Fleming's book; 131 mins; Technicolor.   Kerr alphabetically-billed guest star as Agent Mimi ('Lady Fiona

McTarry'), SMERSH member out to discredit David Niven's Sir James Bond, but later, relenting after taking the veil, she helps him out of a tight spot. John Huston, guest stars from Ursula Andress to Orson Welles. 1966:1967

43 *Prudence and the Pill* 20th Century-Fox Fielder Cook and Ronald Neame; sc. Hugh Mills from his book; 92 mins; De Luxe Colour. Kerr top-billed as Prudence Hardcastle, living in a state of polite tolerance with husband David Niven, who, finding she has a lover, Keith Michell, substitutes what he thinks are aspirins for her birth-control pills. But he's wrong...Robert Coote, Irina Demick, Judy Geeson, Edith Evans, Joyce Redman, Vickery Turner, David Dundas. 1967:1968

44 *The Gypsy Moths* MGM John Frankenheimer, also pro. with Edward Lewis; sc. William Hanley, from James Drought's book; 106 mins; Metrocolor. Kerr second-billed as Elizabeth Brandon, disillusioned small-town wife who has an affair with visiting sky-diver Burt Lancaster, after which he plunges to his death. Gene Hackman, Scott Wilson, William Windom, Bonnie Bedelia, Sheree North. 1968:1969

45 *The Arrangement* Warner Bros-Pathé Elia Kazan, also pro. and sc. from his own book; 126 mins; Technicolor. Kerr third-billed as Florence Anderson, trying to re-awaken the love of husband Kirk Douglas after his nervous breakdown due to his work as an advertising executive and an affair with Faye Dunaway. Richard Boone, Hume Cronyn, Michael Higgins. 1968:1969

# DISCOGRAPHY

### Compiled by Mary Johnston

| Title | No. | Composer | Year |
|---|---|---|---|
| Arias Sung and Acted with Licia Albanese from La Boheme, Madam Butterfly, La Traviata Scene from 'Camille' with Dennis King | RCA Victor LM 1801 (US only) | Puccini, Verdi | 1954 |
| Quo Vadis? Dramatic Highlights | MGM ST E 3524 (US only) | Incidental Music Miklos Rozsa | 1954 |
| The King and I With Yul Brynner, Marni Nixon | Capitol SLCT 6108 | Rodgers & Hammerstein | 1956 |
| An Affair to Remember Marni Nixon Title song by Vic Damone | Philips BBL 7200 | Incidental Music: Hugo Friedhofer Music: Harry Warren Lyrics: Adamson-McCarey. Soprano: Marni Nixon | 1957 |
| Bonjour Tristesse | Columbia LOC 1040 (US only) | Incidental Music Georges Auric | 1958 |
| Night of the Iguana | MGM C 994 (UK) MGM E 4247 (US) | Incidental Music Benjamin Frankel | 1964 |

245

| Title | No. | Composer | Year |
|-------|-----|----------|------|
| *Casino Royale* | RCA Victor SF 7874 | Incidental Music Burt Bacharach | 1966 |
| *Prudence and the Pill* | 20th Cent.- Fox Records SSL 10248 (UK) S 4199 (US) | Bernard Ebbinghouse | 1968 |
| *The Arrangement* | Warner Bros WS 1824 (US only) | Incidental Music David Amram | 1969 |
| *Julius Caesar* Highlights from the Soundtrack | MFP 2122 (Reissue of 1954 MGM release.) | Incidental Music Miklos Rozsa | 1972 |

# DEBORAH KERR IN THE THEATRE

*Sadler's Wells Theatre, London*   29 March, 1938: made her début as a member of the corps-de-ballet during the 1938 season in *Prometheus* under the direction of Ninette de Valois

*Open Air Theatre, Regent's Park, London*   3 June, 1939: her straight theatre début as one of the 'Ladies' in Shakespeare's *Much Ado About Nothing* presented and directed by Robert Atkins, with Cathleen Nesbitt and D. A. Clarke-Smith

*Open Air Theatre, Regent's Park, London*   20 June, 1939: 'Page to Pericles, Prince of Tyre' in Shakespeare's *Pericles* presented and directed by Robert Atkins, with Cathleen Nesbitt, Robert Eddison and Cecil Ramage

*Open Air Theatre, Regent's Park, London*   4 July, 1939: 'Attendant to Hippolyta' in Shakespeare's *A Midsummer Night's Dream* presented and directed by Robert Atkins, with Leslie French, Robert Eddison, Romney Brent and Iris Baker

*Open Air Theatre, Regent's Park, London*   31 July, 1939: 'Attendant to Olivia' in Shakespeare's *Twelfth Night* presented and directed by Robert Atkins, with Jessica Tandy, Iris Baker and D. A. Clarke-Smith

*Open Air Theatre, Regent's Park, London*   7 August, 1939: 'Girl in attendance on Sara' in *Tobias and the Angel* by James Bridie, presented and supervised by Robert Atkins, directed by Frank Napier, with Robert Eddison, Edana Romney and Leslie French

*Playhouse Theatre, Oxford*   29 April, 1940: Margaret in *Dear Brutus* by Sir James Barrie, presented by the Oxford Repertory Players and directed by Leslie French, with Pamela Brown, Nora Nicholson and Leslie French

*Playhouse Theatre, Oxford*   6 May, 1940: Patty Moss in *The Two Bou-quets* by Eleanor and Herbert Farjeon presented by the Oxford Reper-tory Players, directed by Leslie French, with Julian d'Albie, Winifred Evans and Leslie French

*Playhouse Theatre, Oxford*   20 May, 1940: soubrette in *The Playhouse Revue*, presented by the Oxford Repertory Players, devised and directed by Leslie French, with Pamela Brown, Michael Felgate, Andre Van Gyseghem, Julian d'Albie and Leslie French

*Cambridge Theatre, London*   19 March, 1943: Ellie Dunn in *Heartbreak House* by George Bernard Shaw, presented by H. M. Tennent, directed by John Burrell, with Robert Donat, Edith Evans, Isabel Jeans and George Merritt

*Theatre Royal, Drury Lane, London*   31 March, 1945: in the launching of an eight-week tour of the Armed Forces in Theatres of War in Belgium, Holland and France, as Bella Manningham in *Gaslight* by Patrick Hamilton, presented by Linnit and Dunfee for ENSA, directed by John Fernald, with Stewart Granger

*Barrymore Theatre, New York USA*   30 September, 1953: Laura Reynolds in *Tea and Sympathy* by Robert Anderson, presented by the Playwrights' Company, in association with Mary K. Frank, directed by Elia Kazan, with John Kerr and Leif Erickson

*Atlantic City, New Jersey USA*   February 1955: toured as Laura Reynolds throughout the USA, closing in Chicago in May 1955, with Don Dubbins and Alan Baxter

*Haymarket Theatre, London*   10 January, 1972: at the Midnight Matinée in honour of Sir Terence Rattigan, as Sybil Railton-Bell in his *Table Twenty-Four*—second part of *Separate Tables* directed by Nigel Patrick, with Trevor Howard, Celia Johnson, Wendy Hiller, Beatrix Lehmann and Richard Briers

*Lyric Theatre, London*   4 October, 1972. Edith Harnham in *The Day After the Fair* by Frank Harvey, based on Thomas Hardy's short story *On the Western Circuit* presented by Frith Banbury and Jimmy Wax, by arrangement with Arthur Cantor, directed by Frith Banbury, with Julia Foster, Duncan Lamont, Avice Landon and Paul Hastings

*Shubert Theatre, Los Angeles USA*   September 1973: toured in *The Day After the Fair* throughout the USA, and Toronto, Canada, closing in Washington, D.C., March 1974, with Vickery Turner, W. B. Bryden, Brenda Forbes and Michael Shannon

248

*Shubert Theatre, West 44th Street, New York USA*   26 January, 1975: Nancy in *Seascape* presented by Richard Barr, Charles Woodward and Clinton Wilder, written and directed by Edward Albee, with Barry Nelson, Frank Langella and Maureen Anderman

*Shubert Theatre, Los Angeles, USA*   28 October, 1975: Julie Stevens in *Souvenir* by George Axelrod and Peter Viertel, presented by Arthur Cantor and E. E. Fogelson, in association with Eric Friedheim, directed by Gerald Freedman, with Tony Musante, Laurence Hugo and Edmund Lyndeck

*Albery Theatre, London*   23 June, 1977: the title role in *Candida* by George Bernard Shaw, presented by Eddie Kulukundis, Bill Freedman and SRO Productions, directed by Michael Blakemore, with Denis Quilley, Leslie Sands and Patrick Ryecart

# AWARDS AND NOMINATIONS

| Year | Award | Film or Play |
|------|-------|--------------|
| 1947 | New York Film Critics' Award | *Black Narcissus/ The Adventuress* |
| 1949 | Academy Nomination (1) | *Edward, My Son* |
| 1953 | Academy Nomination (2) | *From Here to Eternity* |
| 1953/54 | Billboard Annual Donaldson Award, Best Début Actress | *Tea and Sympathy* |
| 1953/54 | Billboard Annual Donaldson Award, Best Actress | *Tea and Sympathy* |
| 1953/54 | Variety Drama Critics' Poll, Best Performance by an Actress in a straight play | *Tea and Sympathy* |
| 1954 | New York Publicists' Guild Star of the Year | |
| 1954/55 | Sarah Siddons Award, Outstanding Performance | *Tea and Sympathy* |
| 1956 | Photoplay Gold Medal Best Actress | *The King and I* |
| 1956 | Academy Nomination (3) | *The King and I* |

| 1956 | Hollywood Foreign Assoc. Best performance by an Actress in a musical | *The King and I* |
| 1957 | New York Film Critics' Award | *Heaven Knows, Mr Allison* |
| 1957 | Academy Nomination (4) | *Heaven Knows, Mr Allison* |
| 1957 | Photoplay Gold Medal Most Famous Actress | |
| 1958 | Academy Nomination (5) | *Separate Tables* |
| 1959 | Hollywood Foreign Press Assoc. World Film Favourite | |
| 1960 | New York Film Critics' Award | *The Sundowners* |
| 1960 | Academy Nomination (6) | *The Sundowners* |
| 1961 | Variety Club of Great Britain Best Film Actress of 1961 | *The Innocents* |
| 1964 | Prix Fermina Universal du Cinéma, Belgium, Best Actress | *The Chalk Garden* |
| 1964 | Film Daily. Filmdom's Famous Fives | |
| 1965 | Exhibition Laurel Awards Top 5, Dramatic Star | |
| 1967 | Sorrento Film Festival Best English Actress | |
| 1968 | Theatre Owners of America Star of the Year | |
| 1973 | Los Angeles Drama Critics' Circle Award | *The Day After the Fair* |
| 1973 | Press Club of San Francisco 'Black Cat' Award | *The Day After the Fair* |

# INDEX

253

257

of agent and image give added impetus to career, with sensational film role, New York stage début, 136–147; filming in England, the Virgin Isles, and highly successful entry into musicals, 147–156; comparisons with other female superstars, further movies for Metro and Twentieth Century-Fox, 156–161; films with Grant, Niven, Lancaster, Brynner, 162–168; divorce, filming in Austria, France, Hollywood, Australia, England, 168–178; marriage in Klosters to Peter Viertel, England again for Gary Cooper's last film, notable artistic achievement with Jack Clayton, first TV drama and fourth governess rôle, 179–191; Mexican location with Tennessee Williams, publication of Journal in Esquire, 191–194; book promotion with husband, filming for Sinatra, three movies in a row with Niven, 'a bad case of labyrinthitis', 195–204; attitude to critics and to nudity in filming for Frankenheimer and Kazan, 205–211; stardom in the cinema, then and now, 111–112, 205–211; return to British stage, TV, film offers, touring USA, 211–221; back to New York theatre for Albee, home in Switzerland, citation from Association of Suicidology, 222–229; building 'holiday home' in Los Monteros, 230–232; some of the animals in her life, 23–25, 96–97; Guapa, 230; first plays for Viertel and O'Neill in USA, Britain again for Jubilee production of Shaw, 232–235.

Kerr, John, 145–147, 156–158, 205–206
Kershner, Irvin, 219
Kid, The (film), 20
Kind Lady (play), 233
Kindness of Strangers, The (book), 226
Kinematograph Year Book, 20, 38
King, Dennis, 155
King, Henry, 172–173
King and I, The (musical play/film/LP); 35, 153–156, 162, 168, 177
King Solomon's Mines (book/film), 121–124, 152
Kingfishers Catch Fire (book), 229
Kitt, Eartha, 219
Klosters, 179–181, 186–187, 195, 198, 212, 222, 224–231
Knight, Esmond, 102
Korda, Sir Alexander, 44, 69, 74–76, 99, 114
Korda, Vincent, 46
Korda, Zoltan, 44
Kossoff, David, 170
Krasner, Milton, 132, 170
Krohn, Dr, 110
Kurnitz, Harry, 181

Ladd, Alan, 129–130
Lady Vanishes, The (film), 83
Laffan, Patricia, 125–126
Laird, Jenny, 100
Lamont, Duncan, 213, 215, 221
Lancaster, Burt, 141, 148, 166–167, 206–208, 210
Landon, Avice, 213, 221
Landstone, Charles, 40
Lang, Walter, 155
Langella, Frank, 224
Langford, Frances, 78
Langley, Noel, 118
Lansbury, Angela, 115
Lathrop, Philip, 208
Laughton, Charles, 132–133
Launder, Frank, 83, 88, 93–94, 100
Laurents, Arthur, 164
Lawford, Peter, 120
Lawrence, Gertrude, 147, 153–154
Lawson, Wilfrid, 183
Lazar, Irving, 181
Lean, David, 46, 52, 84–85
Lehman, Ernest, 155
Lehmann, Beatrix, 211
Leigh, Janet, 115
Leigh, Vivien, 42, 66, 75, 78, 131, 166
Leighton, Margaret, 166, 193, 219
Lejeune, C. A., 102
Lennart, Isobel, 174
LeRoy, Mervyn, 124
Leslie, Cole, 225
Lester, Olivia, 113
Letter, The (play), 141
Levien, Sonya, 125
Levin, Bernard, 235
Levitt, Alfred, 132
Lewis, David, 146
Lewis, Marjorie, 26
Lewton, Val, 120
Liebman, Marvin, 216
Lieven, Albert, 70
Life, 146
Life and Death of Colonel Blimp, The (film), 66–71, 76, 82, 86, 113
Life's Little Ironies—see Day After the Fair, The
Lillie, Beatrice, 78
Lindo, Olga, 98
Little Friend (film), 56
Litvak, Anatole, 168, 180, 201
Litvak, Sophie, 168, 180
Livesey, Roger, 66–67, 69–70, 189, 218
Livesey, Ursula—see Jeans
Lockwood, Margaret, 60, 79, 83
Loew-Lewin (American production team), 82
Lohr, Marie, 52

260

261

264